W9-CJC-924

CHOCOLATE DESSERTS BY

PIERRE HERMÉ

ALSO BY DORIE GREENSPAN

Desserts by Pierre Hermé

Baking with Julia

The Café Boulud Cookbook (with Daniel Boulud)

CHOCOLATE DESSERTS BY

PIERRE HERMÉ

written by DORIE GREENSPAN

photography by Jean-Louis Bloch-Lainé

LITTLE, BROWN AND COMPANY

Boston   New York   London

FIRST EDITION

Library of Congress Cataloging-in-Publication Data

Hermé, Pierre.
    Chocolate Desserts by Pierre Hermé / written by Dorie Greenspan ; photography
by Jean-Louis Bloch-Lainé. — 1st ed.
       p. cm.
    Includes index.
    ISBN 0-316-35741-3
     1. Desserts. 2. Cookery (Chocolate) I. Greenspan, Dorie. II. Title.
  TX773 .H4397 2001
  641.8'6 — dc21

                                             00-065555

10 9 8 7 6 5 4 3 2 1

PBI-IT

Designed by Cassandra J. Pappas

Printed in Italy

A ma femme Frédérick,
écrivain-cuisinière

P H

To my family

D G

CONTENTS

ACKNOWLEDGMENTS

We consider ourselves very fortunate because not only are we going into our sixth year as collaborators, but our partnership continues to enjoy the help of many good friends and colleagues. At Little, Brown, our project received its initial support from Jennifer Josephy, a friend and a colleague, and it was seen through to bookdom by Deborah Baker, editor, and Michael Pietsch, publisher. As was true with our first book, *Desserts by Pierre Hermé*, this book was made immeasurably better by Judith Sutton's intelligent copyediting.

It would be difficult to say enough — in either French or English — about the photographs of Jean-Louis Bloch-Lainé. It is an honor and a great pleasure to have his work in our book.

The recipes in this book were tested with the help of Rica Buxbaum Allanic, a gifted pastry cook, whose knowledge, patience, and sparkling good humor doubled the project's enjoyment quotient. And, as before, Nick Malgieri acted as the book's godfather, our best counsel on things culinary and Dorie's daily "Dear Diary."

In France, we thank Charles Znaty, friend and partner, for his wise business advice. Anne Roche-Noël must be thanked as much for her infectious good humor as for her admirable organizational skills. And Pierre is grateful to pastry chef Eric Rogard and Colette Petremant, the chef of the Pierre Hermé Paris shops, for their support of his work.

As always, our greatest thanks are reserved for our families. Thank you Frédérick Grasser-Hermé and Michael and Joshua Greenspan.

PIERRE HERMÉ AND DORIE GREENSPAN

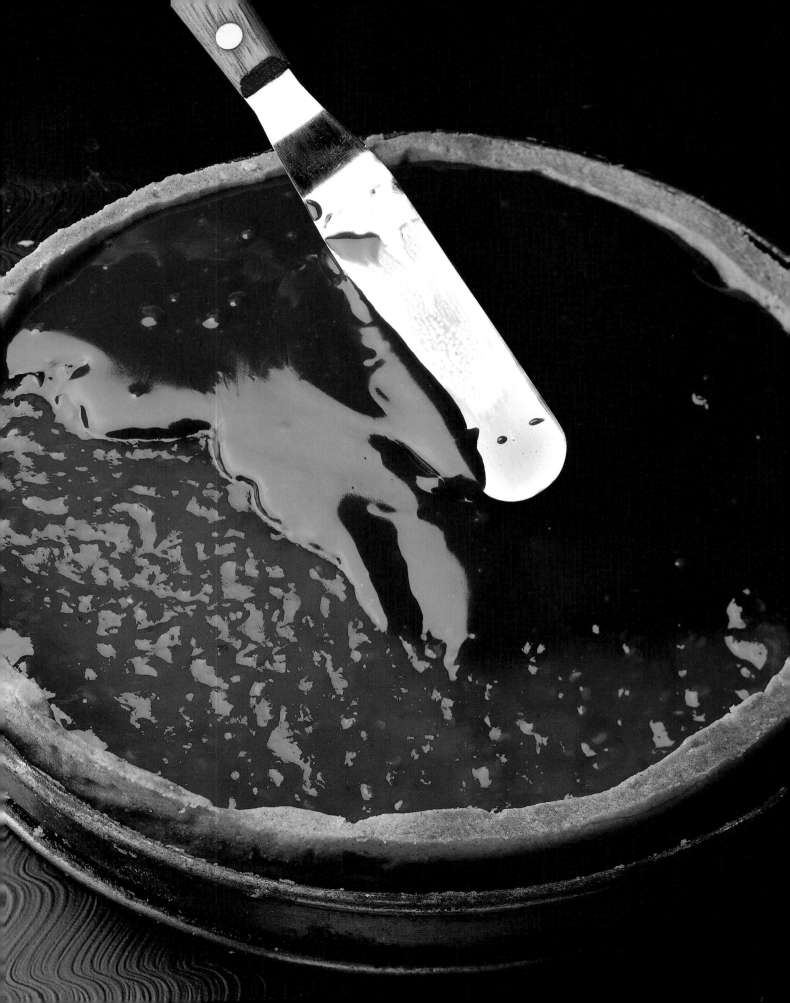

As soon as Pierre and I started work on our first book, we started talking about chocolate. For anyone who loves desserts, it's almost impossible not to talk about — indeed, dream about, obsess about, and crave — chocolate. It is an ingredient that borders on the mythical, and it has been that way for more than two thousand years.

Called the "fruit of the gods" — that's the translation of the ancient Greek word for the genus of cacao, *theobroma*, from which chocolate is derived — chocolate has been the coveted food of four legendary South American Indian tribes (the Olmecs, Mayans, Toltecs, and Aztecs); the exclusive treat of royalty, first in the court of Spain and later in the royal palaces of Italy, France, and England; and, from 1766, when ready-to-eat chocolate bars became available, to the present, an ingredient that has captured the imagination of everyone from chocolate makers, pastry chefs, and connoisseurs to sybarites, sophisticates, and generation after generation of kids wanting an after-school nibble.

And it is a mysterious ingredient. Just looking at a chocolate bar tells you nothing of its boundless possibilities. You can't hold a bar in your hand and know that it can be turned into a voluptuous mousse, that it will chill luxuriously to make ice cream and sorbet, or that it will melt into sauce, meld with cream to make ganache, or mix with butter to make a smooth and glossy glaze for a cake.

It is not an exaggeration to say that chocolate can be magical in the hands of a master. And Pierre Hermé is a master.

Now thirty-nine, Pierre has been a pastry chef for twenty-five years, although he claims he was born one. From earliest childhood, Pierre knew that he would be a pastry chef, as his father, his grandfather, and his great-grandfather were before him. That he became France's foremost pastry chef, its most respected and most innovative (as well as its most widely imitated), is a testament to his passion for the métier, its art and its craft, all of which you'll come to understand and relish as you make Pierre's chocolate desserts at home.

For this collection, Pierre has created more than one hundred recipes that offer countless variations of taste, texture, and temperature, the "Three Ts" Pierre so delicately balances. If there is a secret to the sensuality of Pierre's desserts, his intricate refinement of these elements may just be it. Surely it is what makes all of Pierre's desserts such a pleasure to eat.

Whether you make the simplest chocolate truffle, the Black-on-Black (page 159), a bite-sized ball of bittersweet ganache tossed in dark cocoa; the equally simple Apricot and Ginger Chocolate Loaf Cake (page 3), a dense chocolate cake that is both sweet and tangy; a chic little dessert such as the Triple Crème (page 140), individual ramekins layered with espresso crème brûlée, rich chocolate cream, and pure unsweetened whipped cream; a cup of French-style hot chocolate (page 203), or a *gâteau de résistance*, such as Plaisir Sucré (page 53), which is a variation in five parts on the *plaisir sucré*, or sweet pleasure, of milk chocolate, you will have the many pleasures of tasting chocolate in all its states — hot and cold, creamy and crunchy, smooth and custardy, thick and chewy, bittersweet and sweet, dark, milk, and white.

With these recipes, you will indulge in desserts that are totally and intensely chocolate, creations like Pierre's Grand Chocolate Tart (page 109), with its chocolate crust, chocolate ganache filling, and hidden layer of chocolate cake. And you will find sweets in which chocolate makes a cameo appearance, often coming in at the end to provide an accent and a little more excitement, as it does in tender profiteroles (page 135) topped with crystallized sugar and chopped almonds, filled with sparkling fresh-mint ice cream, and then drizzled with hot chocolate sauce.

Whether you are an expert in the dessert kitchen or a beginner with a passion for the delicious, this collection will introduce you to the myriad delights of Pierre's desserts, his unusual juxtapositions of ingredients, his conjurer's touch with textures, and his always perfect pitch when it comes to sweetness, tartness, and chocolatyness.

Even if your kitchen expertise extends only to brownies, you will find wonderfully original desserts you can make with ease and confidence, including Pierre's take on our American brownie (the moistest ever; page 61); his buttery Chocolate Sparklers (page 67), cookies that melt on your tongue; Suzy's Cake (page 5), a rich, velvety round whose texture falls somewhere between soufflé and pudding; truffles and caramels (the soft Chocolate and Lemon Caramels, page 169, are remarkable); rice pudding (page 125) of exquisite creaminess; loaf cakes; exceptional tarts (start with the Warm Chocolate and Raspberry Tart, page 97, and work your way through the chapter); and so many, many others that the range and quality of what you can turn out are bound to encourage you to try more. And if, as you're working, you need a little advice on an ingredient, further explanation of a technique, some information on a baking pan, or a definition of a term, you'll find everything you need to keep you going in the Dictionary, a chapter that is part glossary, part dessert primer.

Of course, if you have just a little more experience in the pastry kitchen, this collection will offer even more surprises. For those who treasure the classics, there are Pierre's signature versions of grand traditional desserts: his éclairs (page 9), filled with chocolate pastry cream and finished with a slick of chocolate glaze; his Black Forest Cake (page 11), embellished with both kirsch-flavored vanilla and chocolate whipped cream and studded with cherries that have been soaked in spiced port; and his mille-feuilles — one made with caramelized plain puff pastry (page 47), the other based on caramelized chocolate puff pastry (page 50) — which are above comparison.

Then there are the new desserts, the ones culled from the collections Pierre introduces twice a year the way couturiers show their season's fashions. To taste the desserts that prompted *Vogue* magazine to crown Pierre "the Picasso of pastry," make the whimsical Nutella Tart (page 119), whose silken chocolate filling rests on a thick layer of straight-from-the-supermarket-shelf Nutella, a spread of hazelnut butter and milk chocolate. It's a childhood favorite made extremely grown-up. Or consider the Chocolate, Coffee, and Whiskey Cappuccino (page 146), a brilliant mix of dark, slip-through-your-teeth chocolate pudding, frozen and scraped espresso-and-single-malt Scotch *granité*, and a dollop of whipped cream, a dessert that is a textbook lesson in how Pierre plays with the "Three Ts." And don't overlook his nougatines (page 82), crackly chocolate lace cookies that get extra crunch and even more flavor from tiny pieces of crushed coffee beans.

Best of all, your homemade desserts will rival Pierre's, because every recipe in this book, among them recipes Pierre created for his *pâtisseries* in Paris and Tokyo, for famous restaurants in Europe, for shops in the United States, and for grand celebrations here and abroad, has been translated, written, and tested for the American home kitchen. This means that each time you make one of these recipes, you can be certain it will deliver the full measure of Pierre's talent and the full promise of chocolate's magic.

None of these recipes is beyond the range of a committed amateur, although some are more complex and more time-consuming than others. But no matter which recipe you choose, we suggest you read it through at least once (twice is better) before setting to work, and that you do as the pros do and have all of the ingredients you need measured and at the ready. If you're working on a recipe with several elements, check to see if you can make one or two of them ahead — all of the recipes include do-ahead notes and information on keeping. And, if you have any questions, turn to the Dictionary or check the chapter of Base Recipes. Everything you need to be successful is in the recipe, the Dictionary, or the Base Recipes. All you need to do is follow the instructions, then savor your accomplishment.

It is *avec grand plaisir* that Pierre and I offer these recipes to you. We hope they will bring you and all those with whom you share them as much pleasure as they brought us in creating them for you.

DORIE GREENSPAN
New York City

CHOCOLATE CAKES

PLAIN AND GRAND

APRICOT AND GINGER CHOCOLATE LOAF CAKE

This is a dark-as-midnight chocolate cake that gets its strong chocolate flavor from cocoa and small chunks of premium-quality bittersweet chocolate (think the best chocolate chips imaginable). The cake's texture is soft and dense and, if you press a little against the roof of your mouth, melting. It would be a classic of its type were it not for the completely surprising addition of small cubes of dried apricots and intensely spicy stem ginger. Sweet and chewy, tangy and hot, it's the add-ins that make this cake remarkable.

Don't confuse soft stem ginger, sometimes called preserved ginger, with firm crystallized ginger, which is like a candy. Stem ginger, small knobs of ginger preserved and packed in heavy syrup, is a delicacy found in Chinese markets, specialty stores, and large supermarkets. The ginger is expensive, but, kept tightly sealed in the refrigerator, it will last for months.

■ I love the contrasting textures in this cake, the soft cake studded with fruits and melting drops of chocolate. To get the most from these textures, make sure to cut thick slices of the cake — this isn't a sweet to cut into slivers. ■ PH

- 1⅓ cups (180 grams) all-purpose flour
- ⅓ cup (40 grams) Dutch-processed cocoa powder, preferably Valrhona
- ½ teaspoon double-acting baking powder
- 4½ ounces (125 grams) moist, plump dried apricots, cut into small chunks
- ¾ cup (165 grams) sugar
- 5 ounces (140 grams) almond paste, broken into small pieces
- 4 large eggs, at room temperature
- ⅔ cup (150 grams) whole milk, at room temperature
- 2½ ounces (70 grams) bittersweet chocolate, preferably Valrhona Guanaja, cut into small chunks

- 1¾ ounces (55 grams) drained stem ginger, cut into small chunks
- 1½ sticks plus 1 tablespoon (6½ ounces; 180 grams) unsalted butter, melted and cooled

1. Center a rack in the oven and preheat the oven to 350°F (180°C). Butter a 9 x 5 x 3-inch (28-cm) loaf pan and place the pan on an insulated baking sheet or two regular baking sheets stacked one on top of the other; set aside.
2. Sift together the flour, cocoa, and baking powder, and set this mixture aside.
3. Bring about 1 cup (250 grams) water to the boil. Add the apricots, pull the pan from the heat, and soak the apricots for 1 minute, time enough for them to soften and plump. Drain and pat the apricots dry between paper towels; set aside.
4. Put the sugar and almond paste in a mixer fitted with the paddle attachment and beat on medium speed until the almond paste breaks up, blends with the sugar, and looks sandy. (If your almond paste is hard — a sign of age — and doesn't become sandy in the mixer, you can pulverize the paste and sugar in a food processor, then transfer the ingredients to the bowl of the mixer.) Add the eggs one at a time, beating for about 2 minutes after each addition. Replace the paddle with the whisk attachment, increase the mixer speed to high, and beat for 8 to 10 minutes, until the ingredients have formed an emulsion — the batter will look like mayonnaise and the whisk will leave tracks as it spins.
5. Reduce the mixer speed to low and add the milk, mixing until combined, and then the sifted dry ingredients. Continue beating on low speed until the batter is homogenous, then remove the bowl from the mixer. Working with a large rubber spatula, fold in the set-aside apricots, the chocolate chunks, and ginger, then gently fold in the melted butter.
6. Turn the batter into the prepared pan and smooth the top. Bake for 60 to 70 minutes, or until a slender knife inserted in the center of the cake comes out clean. (The cake will crack as it bakes. If you want to help it crack more evenly than it might by chance, wait until the cake just starts to develop a crust, then run a dough scraper dipped in melted butter lengthwise down the center of the cake.) If the cake appears to be baking too quickly — chocolate cakes have a tendency to darken around the edges — cover it loosely with an aluminum foil tent for the last 20 to 30 minutes.
7. Remove the cake from the oven and let it cool on a rack for 10 minutes before unmolding and turning it upright. Cool the cake to room temperature on the rack.

Makes 8 to 10 servings

KEEPING: Wrapped in plastic and stored at room temperature, the cake will remain moist for at least 5 days; wrapped airtight, it will keep in the freezer for a month.

P ierre and Frédérick Hermé's friend Suzy Palatin is a runway model, a cookbook author, and the inventor of this luxuriously soft, rich cake, the kind that in America might be given a name like Chocolate Decadence. The cake is spectacularly good and very easy to make. Indeed, the ingredients are so rudimentary (they're the baker's basics), and the method so simple (it's a cream-the-butter-and-sugar-together cake), that you have to wonder how it can be so good. Odds are it's the half pound or so of highest-quality chocolate (don't skimp on the quality) and the just-right baking — the center remains ever so slightly wet.

■ At home, my wife, Frédérick, and I serve this cake with ginger ice cream, lightly sweetened whipped cream, or Vanilla Crème Anglaise (page 217). Sometimes we make the cake with raspberries, putting a thin layer of batter over the bottom of the pan, tossing over fresh raspberries, then covering the berries with batter. ■ PH

- 8¾ ounces (250 grams) bittersweet chocolate, preferably Valrhona Guanaja, finely chopped
- 2¼ sticks (9 ounces; 250 grams) unsalted butter, at room temperature
- 1 cup (200 grams) sugar
- 4 large eggs, at room temperature
- ½ cup plus 1 tablespoon (70 grams) all-purpose flour

1. Center a rack in the oven and preheat the oven to 350°F (180°C). Butter a 9-inch (24-cm) round cake pan that is at least 2 inches (5 cm) high, line the bottom with parchment paper, butter the paper, and dust the inside of the pan with flour; tap out the excess and set the pan aside.

2. Place the chocolate in a heatproof bowl over — not touching — simmering water and heat until the chocolate is melted; or melt the chocolate in a microwave oven. Set the chocolate aside to cool; it should feel only just warm to the touch when you mix it with the rest of the ingredients.

3. Put the butter and sugar in the bowl of a mixer fitted with the paddle attachment and beat on medium speed for about 4 minutes, scraping down the

sides of the bowl frequently, until the butter is creamy and the sugar well blended into it. Add the eggs one at a time, beating for about 1 minute after each addition. Reduce the mixer speed to low, pour in the cooled chocolate, and mix just until it is incorporated. With the mixer still on low, add the flour and mix only until it disappears into the batter. Alternatively, you can fold in the last of the flour with a rubber spatula. You'll have a thick, smooth, satiny batter that looks like old-fashioned chocolate frosting.

4. Scrape the batter into the pan, smooth the top, and slide the pan into the oven. Bake for 26 to 29 minutes, or until the cake rises slightly and the top has lost its sheen. The top may crack a bit and the cake may not look entirely set in the center; when you test the cake by inserting a slender knife into the center, the knife will come out lightly streaked with batter, which is what you want. Transfer the cake to a rack to cool.

5. When the cake has cooled, chill it in the refrigerator for an hour or two to make it easy to unmold. Turn the cake out, remove the parchment, and invert the cake onto a serving platter so that it is right side up. Allow the cake to come to room temperature before slicing and serving.

Makes 8 to 10 servings

KEEPING: The cake can be wrapped in plastic and kept at room temperature or in the refrigerator for 3 to 4 days or frozen for up to a month.

CHOCOLATE
ÉCLAIRS

These are the same éclairs you see displayed in pastry shop cases all over France — they're classics. Made from tender cream puff dough, filled with chocolate pastry cream — which is not really *classic* classic (the original had vanilla cream) — and given a slick of chocolate glaze, they're as much a treat for school kids as for sophisticates.

■ For variety, fill the éclairs with Chocolate Whipped Cream (page 223) and add some chopped toasted nuts — almonds or macadamias — for crunch. You'll have very unclassic but very delicious éclairs. ■ PH

THE ÉCLAIRS

■ **Cream Puff Dough (page 233), just made and still warm**

1. Position the racks to divide the oven into thirds and preheat the oven to 375°F (190°C). Line two baking sheets with parchment paper and keep them close at hand.

2. Spoon the warm cream puff dough into a large pastry bag fitted with a ⅔-inch (2-cm) plain tip. Pipe out the dough onto the baking sheets in chubby fingers, 4 to 4½ inches (about 11 cm) long; make sure to leave about 2 inches (5 cm) of puff space between each strip of dough. You should have enough dough to pipe 20 to 24 éclairs.

3. Slide the baking sheets into the oven and bake for 7 minutes, then slip the handle of a wooden spoon into the door so that it remains slightly ajar. When the éclairs have baked for 12 minutes, rotate the sheets top to bottom and front to back and continue to bake for another 8 minutes or so, until the éclairs are puffed, golden, and firm. (The total baking time is about 20 minutes.) Transfer the éclairs to a rack to cool to room temperature. (*The éclairs can be kept in a cool dry room for several hours before filling.*)

TO ASSEMBLE

- **Chocolate Glaze (page 254)**
- **Chocolate Pastry Cream (page 221), cooled**

1. Using a serrated knife and a gentle sawing motion, slice the éclairs horizontally in half. Set the bottoms aside for the moment and put the tops on a rack placed over a sheet of parchment or waxed paper.

2. If the chocolate glaze has been chilled, place it in a bowl over — not touching — simmering water and reheat it, stirring it with a wooden spoon. (Go easy — you don't want to create bubbles.) Whether the glaze is just-made or reheated, you should use it when it is barely warm to the touch (from 95° to 104°F or 35° to 40°C, as measured on an instant-read thermometer). When the glaze is just right, spread it over the tops of the éclairs with a metal icing spatula. Allow the tops to set while you fill the bottoms.

3. You can pipe or spoon the pastry cream into the éclair bottoms. Either way, fill the bottoms with enough cream to mound above the pastry. Place the glazed tops over the filled bottoms, jiggling the tops to settle them, and serve the éclairs as soon as possible.

Makes 20 to 24 éclairs

KEEPING: The éclairs should be served as soon as they are filled.

What makes a chocolate cake a Black Forest Cake is whipped cream, cherries, and kirsch, a cherry-based eau-de-vie that is treasured in Germany and parts of France, particularly Alsace, Pierre's birthplace and the most German of France's regions. This Black Forest Cake has everything the classic has, but, as you'd expect from Pierre, the classic components have been reconsidered and some not-so-classic elements have been added. The three cake layers are made from a dark, soft-crumbed cocoa cake (the same one that forms the base of the Faubourg Pavé, page 17), soaked deeply with a kirsch syrup and piled high with two different kinds of whipped cream. The bottom layer is spread with a kirsch-flavored whipped cream that is fortified with a bit of gelatin so that it has enough body to support the top layers and to hold its shape when the cake is cut into wedges. Before the next layer is set into place, the whipped cream is amply studded with plump spice-and-port-soaked sour cherries. The next layer and the top of the cake get a swathing of thick chocolate whipped cream. The finish is simple: a covering of lightly sweetened whipped cream around the sides of the cake and a crown of dark chocolate curls on top. For reasons unfathomable, this rich and heady concoction is cloud-light.

A note on construction: This cake is taller than most and should be built in an 8¾-inch (22-cm) round cake ring that is about 2½ inches (6 cm) high. If you don't have such a cake ring, you can position one standard cake ring on top of another or use the sides of a springform pan.

■ Black Forest Cake was a bestseller in my father's pastry shop in Alsace. In fact, his, made as this one is, with two different whipped creams, was the inspiration for mine. My most striking addition to the cake is the port-and-spice soak for the cherries. ■ PH

THE CHERRIES

- ½ cup (125 grams) port
- 2 tablespoons freshly squeezed orange juice
- 4 black peppercorns, cracked

- 1 small piece cinnamon stick
- 1 strip lemon zest (removed with a vegetable peeler)
- 6 ounces (about 1 cup; 170 grams) bottled pitted griottes (imported small dark sour cherries) or sour cherries, drained and rinsed

Place all the ingredients except the cherries in a small nonreactive saucepan over medium heat. Bring the mixture to the boil, add the cherries, lower the heat to a simmer, and cook for 2 minutes. Pull the pan from the heat and allow the cherries to soak in the spiced liquid for 3 to 4 hours. (*If it's more convenient, you can cover and refrigerate the cherries in their liquid overnight.*) When you are ready to use the cherries, drain them well, discard the zest, spices, and liquid, and pat the cherries dry between paper towels.

THE CHOCOLATE WHIPPED CREAM

- 1½ cups (375 grams) heavy cream
- 1 tablespoon sugar
- 2¼ ounces (65 grams) bittersweet chocolate, preferably Valrhona Caraïbe, finely chopped

1. Bring the cream and sugar to a full boil in a heavy-bottomed medium saucepan. Pull the pan from the heat and stir in the chocolate, mixing energetically with a rubber spatula so that the chocolate is completely blended into the cream. Pour the mixture into a mixing bowl (choose one that is large enough for whipping the cream), cover, and chill for at least 5 hours, or overnight.

2. Just before you are ready to use the cream, place the bowl of cream in a larger bowl filled with ice cubes and cold water and, using a whisk, whip the cream until it is almost firm. Go easy — the cream will whip quickly. The consistency you're looking for is one that is firm enough to spread but soft enough to still feel light and creamy in your mouth.

THE SOAKING SYRUP

- Simple Syrup (page 252), cooled
- 2 tablespoons water
- 2 tablespoons kirsch, preferably imported

Stir all the ingredients together. You can use the syrup as soon as it is made or keep it aside until needed. (*The syrup can be made up to 3 days ahead and kept covered in the refrigerator.*)

THE KIRSCH-FLAVORED CREAM

- **1½ cups (375 grams) heavy cream**
- **Pulp from ¼ moist, plump vanilla bean (see page 279)**
- **2½ teaspoons powdered gelatin (or 3 grams sheet gelatin)**
- **1 tablespoon cold water**
- **1 tablespoon kirsch, preferably imported**

1. Make this cream just before you are ready to use it. Working in a microwave-safe bowl or a small saucepan, stir together ¼ cup (60 grams) of the heavy cream and the vanilla bean pulp. Bring this cream to a full boil in the microwave oven or over direct heat, then pull it from the heat and allow it to infuse for 10 minutes.

2. While the cream is infusing, sprinkle the gelatin over the cold water in a small cup and let it rest for a minute or so until it is softened and spongy. Dissolve the gelatin in the microwave oven for 15 seconds or in a saucepan over low heat. Transfer the dissolved gelatin to a bowl, stir in the vanilla-infused cream, and blend in the kirsch. Set the bowl aside until the mixture cools to room temperature. You can quicken the process by stirring the gelatin mixture over a bowl of ice cubes and cold water, just take care — you want to cool the mixture so you can fold it into the cream in the next step, but you don't want to chill it enough to set it.

3. Whip the remaining 1¼ cups (290 grams) heavy cream in a medium bowl until it holds medium peaks. Stir about one-quarter of the whipped cream into the bowl holding the gelatin mixture, then fold the gelatin mixture gently into the whipped cream. The filling is ready to be used and should, in fact, be used within 15 minutes.

TO ASSEMBLE

- **One 8¾-inch (22-cm) Cocoa Cake (page 228)**

1. Trim a cardboard cake round to match the diameter of the chocolate cake and fit the round into an 8¾-inch (22-cm) cake ring that is about 2½ inches (6 cm) high. (If you don't have a tall cake ring, stack two standard rings one on top of the other, or use the sides — minus the bottom — of a

9-inch [24-cm] springform pan.) Place the setup on a small baking sheet.

2. If necessary, trim the top of the cake so that it is level. Using a serrated knife and a gentle sawing motion, cut the cake into 3 layers. Slip the bottom layer, cut side up, into the cake ring. Brush or spoon enough of the soaking syrup over the layer to moisten it generously. Using a metal spatula, preferably offset, spread half of the kirsch-flavored whipped cream over the layer. Make certain that the cherries have been thoroughly drained and patted dry, then scatter them evenly over the whipped cream. Finish this layer by spreading the rest of the whipped cream over the cherries. This will be a very high layer of filling — that's just how it should be.

3. Fit the middle layer of cake into the ring, jiggling it very gently to settle it evenly into place. Soak this layer with some syrup, then spread it with about two-thirds of the chocolate whipped cream. Top with the last layer of cake, placing the flattest side up, and give it a soak as well. Finish the top of this layer with the remaining chocolate whipped cream, working to get as even a coating as possible. (If your cake ring is 2½ inches (6 cm) high, you will probably fill it just to the top, in which case you can use the rim of the ring as a guide to level the top of the cake.) Slide the cake, on the baking sheet, into the refrigerator and chill it for 2 to 3 hours. (*The cake can be made to this point and kept in the refrigerator — away from foods with strong odors — for up to 8 hours.*)

TO FINISH

- **½ cup (125 grams) chilled heavy cream**
- **2 teaspoons confectioners' sugar, sifted**
- **10 griottes or sour cherries (optional)**
- **Chocolate curls or shavings (see page 258)**

1. Using a hairdryer, warm the cake ring and lift it off the cake (see page 273). If you'd like, you can put the cake, still on its cardboard, on a decorating turntable.

2. Whip the heavy cream until it holds medium-firm peaks, then fold in the confectioners' sugar. Using a metal spatula, cover the sides of the cake with a coating of whipped cream. You've got a choice here — you can use all the cream to cover the sides and leave the cake with a dark top, or you can reserve some cream, then fit a pastry bag with a star tip and pipe 10 rosettes around the edge of the cake. If you do this, top each rosette with a cherry. Fill the center with chocolate curls or shavings. You can serve the cake now, or keep it refrigerated for up to 4 hours before serving.

Makes 10 servings

KEEPING: The components of the cake, including the cake, cherries, and syrup, can be made ahead. The chocolate whipped cream needs a few hours in the refrigerator, and the entire creation, filled, frosted, and topped, can be refrigerated for a few hours. However, this is not a keeper — it should be served the day it is made.

FAUBOURG PAVÉ

This was the first cake Pierre created when he took over the kitchens of the legendary Ladurée, Paris's oldest *pâtisserie* and tea salon. It is named for the Faubourg Saint-Honoré, the exclusive neighborhood surrounding the original Ladurée, and its shape is that of a pavé, or paving stone. Baked in a small loaf pan, the cake is a simple cocoa-based affair, but the layering of flavors and textures on this base earns the pavé its own place in legend. The Faubourg Pavé is an intriguing orchestration of chocolate and caramel. The chocolate cake is soaked in a caramel syrup, one that includes a touch of salted butter — you'll rarely find a Pierre caramel that doesn't have a soupçon of salt. Then the cake layers are spread with a caramel-chocolate ganache that is nothing short of brilliant. The caramel for the ganache is deglazed with salted butter, thinned with cream, and then poured over a mixture of chopped bittersweet and milk chocolate. Finally, it is made thick and silky with a generous amount of sweet butter. By using a combination of chocolates, Pierre gets just the right balance between the soft and sharp bitterness of the caramelized sugar and the sweetness of the chocolate, butter, and cream. To add an unexpected but, in the end, perfect note of tang, Pierre speckles the ganache with diced apricots that have been tossed in lemon juice and seasoned with black pepper. In typical Hermé style, this is a deceptively simple dessert.

This recipe makes two cakes — one for now and one that can be stored in the freezer for another time.

■ Once the cake is covered with ganache, it can be dusted with cocoa powder and served as is. However, you can give it a different finish by coating it with Chocolate Glaze (page 254) and topping it with an apricot reserved from the batch you made for the filling. ■ PH

THE SOAKING SYRUP

- ¼ cup (50 grams) sugar
- 2 teaspoons (10 grams) salted butter (or use unsalted butter plus a tiny pinch of salt)
- 6 tablespoons (100 grams) warm water

Put the sugar in a medium saucepan or a small skillet and place the pan over medium heat. As soon as the sugar starts to melt, stir it with a wooden spoon. Keep heating and stirring the sugar until it turns a rich brown color — you can test the color by putting a drop on a white plate. Standing away from the pan, drop the butter into the pan, then, as it melts, stir it into the caramelized sugar. Stand back again and add the water. When the mixture comes to the boil, pull the pan from the heat. Allow the syrup to cool to room temperature. (*The syrup can be made up to 3 days ahead and kept covered in the refrigerator.*)

THE APRICOTS

- **6 ounces (170 grams) moist, plump dried apricots**
- **1 cup (250 grams) water**
- **Juice of ½ lemon**
- **Pinch of freshly ground black pepper**

1. Put the apricots and water in a medium saucepan and bring to a gentle boil. Reduce the heat to its lowest setting and simmer for 3 to 4 minutes. Drain the apricots and let cool.
2. When they are cool, cut the apricots into small dice. (If you'd like, you can reserve 2 apricots and use them to decorate the tops of the cakes.) Toss the apricots with the lemon juice and black pepper and set them aside until needed. (*The apricots can be prepared a day ahead and kept at room temperature in a covered container.*)

THE GANACHE

- **6½ ounces (185 grams) bittersweet chocolate, preferably Valrhona Manjari, finely chopped**
- **4¼ ounces (120 grams) milk chocolate, preferably Valrhona Jivara, finely chopped**
- **⅔ cup (140 grams) sugar**
- **1½ tablespoons (¾ ounce; 20 grams) salted butter (or use unsalted butter plus a tiny pinch of salt)**
- **1 cup plus 2 tablespoons (275 grams) heavy cream**
- **3 sticks (12 ounces; 335 grams) unsalted butter, at room temperature**

1. Mix the bittersweet and milk chocolate together in a large heatproof bowl and set aside.

2. Set a heavy-bottomed medium saucepan over medium-high heat and sprinkle about one-third of the sugar over the bottom of the pan. As soon as the sugar starts to melt and color, stir it with a wooden spoon until it melts and caramelizes. Sprinkle over half of the remaining sugar and, as soon as it starts to melt, stir it into the caramelized sugar in the pan. Repeat with the last of the sugar and cook until the sugar is a deep brown color. (Test the color on a white plate.) Stand away from the pan and, still stirring, add the salted butter and then, when the butter is incorporated, the cream. Don't worry if the caramel seizes and clumps — stirring and heating will even it out. Bring the cream to the boil, then remove the pan from the heat.

3. Pour half of the hot caramel over the chopped chocolate and, using a rubber spatula, stir gently, starting in the center of the bowl and working your way out in concentric circles. When the chocolate is smooth, add the remaining caramel, stirring in the same manner. Set the ganache aside to cool for about 10 minutes, or until it feels only slightly warm to the touch.

4. While the ganache is cooling, beat the unsalted butter, using either the paddle attachment of a mixer or a spatula: You want to soften the butter until it is the consistency of mayonnaise, but you do not want to beat air into it. With this in mind, if you're working in a mixer, don't beat on high speed; or, if you are beating it by hand, don't use a whisk.

5. Working with a rubber spatula or a whisk, gently stir (don't beat) the butter into the ganache. (*The ganache can be used now, or you can store it in the refrigerator for up to 2 days, making sure to cover it tightly after it has cooled. When you are ready for it, allow it to come to room temperature, then stir gently to smooth it.*)

6. To work with the ganache, it must be the consistency of a very creamy frosting and must have enough body to mound — you're going to spread a thick layer of it between each of the cakes' layers. To get it to set to this consistency, you can either place the bowl of ganache in a larger bowl half-filled with ice cubes and water or refrigerate it, checking on it at 5-minute intervals. In either case, it's important to stir the ganache frequently (but gently), so that it doesn't become too firm around the edges.

TO ASSEMBLE

- **Two 7½ x 3½-inch (18-cm) Cocoa Cakes (page 228)**
- **Unsweetened cocoa powder for dusting**

1. Working with a long thin serrated knife, even the tops of the cakes by slicing off any portions that have domed. Then slice each cake horizontally into

3 even layers. Place the bottom layer of each cake on its own cardboard cake round and keep the remaining layers close at hand.

2. Using a pastry brush, dab the bottom layers with enough of the caramel syrup to moisten them thoroughly and give them a caramel boost. Switch to a metal spatula — you may find an offset spatula easiest to work with — and spread a layer of ganache over each moistened layer. Aim for a layer of ganache that is a scant ½ inch (1½ cm) thick, and work to get the layer as even as possible. There's always a tendency to have less ganache at the corners than in the center — try to avoid this. Dot the top of the ganache with half the apricots and very gently press the apricots into the ganache. Don't worry if some of the ganache oozes out over the sides of the cake — just spread it over the sides and carry on. Set the next layer into place on each cake, and moisten it with syrup. Smooth each layer with another layer of ganache and dot with the remaining apricots. Moisten the top layers of cake and settle them in place. Take a look at the cakes now, while the ganache is still soft, and, if they're leaning to one side or the other, use your spatula to gently right them. Spread a very thin layer of ganache over the sides and tops of the cakes — you'll put more on later — and transfer the cakes to the refrigerator to chill for 30 minutes. Keep the ganache at room temperature while the cakes are chilling.

3. Remove the cakes from the refrigerator and, again using a metal spatula, cover the cakes evenly with the remaining ganache. It's nice to get the tops as smooth as possible, but you don't have to fuss too much with the sides. Using a decorating comb or the tines of a fork, striate the sides of the cakes horizontally, making sure to wipe the comb or fork clean between passes. If you find that you're not getting clean lines, tuck the cakes into the refrigerator for about 5 to 10 minutes, just to firm the ganache slightly, then try again. (*At this point, the cakes can be frozen until firm, wrapped airtight, and kept frozen for up to 1 month.*)

4. If the ganache is not too soft, you can serve the cakes now, or you can keep them refrigerated for up to 12 hours. (If the cakes have been refrigerated for several hours, allow them to stand at room temperature for an hour before serving — if the cakes are too cold, the extraordinary texture of the ganache is diminished.) Just before serving, dust the tops lightly and evenly with cocoa powder — for best results, use a strainer or dredger — and, if desired, top each cake with a reserved whole apricot.

Makes 2 cakes, each serving about 8

KEEPING: The individual components of this cake can all be made ahead: The cakes can be wrapped airtight and kept at room temperature for 2 days or frozen for a month; the syrup can be made 3 days ahead; the apricots can be prepared a day ahead; and the ganache can be made 2 days ahead and refrigerated. In addition, the cakes can be assembled — minus the cocoa powder dusting — and frozen for up to 1 month, then defrosted in the refrigerator overnight and brought to room temperature before serving.

GÂTEAU
SAINT-HONORÉ

Gâteau Saint-Honoré is a Paris creation, first made in 1863 at Chiboust's pastry shop, which was then on the Rue Saint-Honoré. If the name Chiboust sounds familiar, it's because he created *crème Chiboust*, a mixture of vanilla pastry cream and meringue that was the traditional (if difficult to achieve) filling of Gâteau Saint-Honoré. While the cake was originally made on a base of brioche, today it is most often prepared with a base of tart dough or puff pastry (Pierre's choice) rimmed by caramelized cream puffs. In most versions, the current-day Gâteau Saint-Honoré is filled with whipped cream. Needless to say, Pierre has his own take on this classic.

Pierre's Saint-Honoré has the almost-traditional base of puff pastry and the cream puff tiara, but the puffs are filled with chocolate pastry cream and the entire center of the creation is piped with chocolate whipped cream. By using both pastry and whipped creams, Pierre gets a subtle play of chocolate flavors and a rich, much less subtle play of textures. The cake is then crowned — very untraditionally — with vanilla-scented pears and a riot of chocolate shavings.

■ For a nonpear, intensely chocolate version, fill the puff pastry base with Deep Chocolate Cream (page 224), then top the cake, as it is topped here, with swirls of chocolate whipped cream. ■ PH

THE PEARS

- One 29-ounce (825-gram) can pear halves packed in syrup
- 1 cup (250 grams) water
- ½ cup (100 grams) sugar
- 1 tablespoon freshly squeezed lemon juice
- Pulp from ½ moist, plump vanilla bean (see page 279)

1. Drain the pears and place them in a large bowl (a deep bowl is best); set them aside for the moment.

2. Bring the water, sugar, lemon juice, and vanilla bean pulp to a boil in a medium saucepan or in a bowl in the microwave oven. Remove the syrup from the heat and pour it over the pears. Press a piece of waxed paper against the pears, and if the paper alone isn't enough to submerge the pears in the syrup, place a plate on top of it. Cover the setup with plastic wrap and refrigerate overnight. (*The pears can be made up to 3 days ahead and kept covered in the refrigerator.*)

THE PUFF PASTRY DISK

- **6 ounces (170 grams) all-butter puff pastry dough, homemade (page 241) or store-bought, chilled and ready to roll**

Working on a floured surface, roll the puff pastry into a circle that is about ⅛ inch (4 mm) thick and at least 11 inches (28 cm) in diameter. Transfer the dough to a parchment-lined baking sheet and, using a 10¼-inch (26-cm) tart ring as a guide (or a ruler), trim the dough to a circle that size. Prick the dough all over, deeply — you should go right through to the parchment — with the point of a paring knife, then set the pastry aside for the moment. (*If it's more convenient, you can cover the pastry with plastic wrap and refrigerate it for an hour or two or wrap it airtight and freeze it for up to 1 month.*)

THE CREAM PUFFS

- **Cream Puff Dough (page 233), just made and still warm**
- **Chocolate Pastry Cream (page 221), cooled**

1. Position the racks to divide the oven into thirds and preheat the oven to 375°F (190°C). Line a baking sheet with parchment paper and keep it close at hand. Fit a large pastry bag with a ½-inch (1.5-cm) plain piping tip.
2. Spoon half of the warm cream puff dough into the pastry bag and pipe a ring of dough ¼ inch (7 mm) in from the edge of the puff pastry base. Move the bag to the center of the base and, working your way from the center out, pipe a spiral, leaving lots of space between the lines of dough. In fact, you don't want to make much of a spiral: A center squiggle and a circle and a half around it, rather like an @ symbol with a dot replacing the "a" in the center, should do it. Set the baking sheet aside for the moment.
3. Working with the cream puff dough that remains in the bag and then refilling the bag when necessary, pipe out as many small cream puffs as you can,

making each puff only slightly more than 1 inch (2.5 cm) across, first on the parchment-lined baking sheet and then using what space remains on the sheet with the puff pastry disk. Make sure to leave at least 2 inches (5 cm) of puff space between each mound of dough. You'll have many more puffs than you'll need for this cake, so you can either freeze the extras before baking them (you can use them to make profiteroles, page 135), or bake them and have a wonderful teatime treat on hand. (*Both the puff pastry base with its cream puff topping and the small cream puffs can be frozen unbaked. Frozen until firm and then wrapped airtight, they can be kept in the freezer for up to 1 month.*)

4. Slide the baking sheets into the oven and bake for 7 minutes, then slip the handle of a wooden spoon into the oven door so that it remains slightly ajar. When the sheets have been in the oven for 12 minutes, rotate them top to bottom and front to back and continue to bake until the base and the small puffs are, indeed, puffed, golden, and firm. The puffs will probably be baked after 17 to 20 minutes in all — just remove them from the oven when they're done; the base may need a total of 25 minutes, or even a few minutes more. Transfer the base and puffs to racks to cool to room temperature. (*The base and puffs can be kept in a cool, dry place for several hours before filling.*)

5. Fit a pastry bag with a ¼-inch (7-mm) plain piping tip and fill it with the pastry cream. If your cream puffs are perfectly round (a rarity), they should be filled through the bottom: Hold a cream puff upside down (in your nonpiping hand) and, taking care not to squish it, poke a small hole in the bottom of the puff with the piping tip, then fill the puff with pastry cream. If your cream puffs have an indentation in the side (as is often the case), fill them at that point: Just poke the hole in the side of a puff and pipe in pastry cream. Whichever method you use, put the filled puff on a baking sheet, and fill the remaining puffs in the same manner. Keep the puffs on the counter while you make the caramel.

THE CARAMEL

- **1 cup (200 grams) sugar**
- **5 tablespoons (100 grams) light corn syrup**
- **2 tablespoons water**
- **¼ teaspoon freshly squeezed lemon juice**

1. Set out a nonstick baking sheet, a baking sheet lined with a Silpat or other silicone baking mat, or a well-buttered regular baking sheet. Also prepare an ice-water bath. Find a bowl that's large enough to accommodate the bottom of a medium saucepan and fill it with ice cubes and water.

2. Put all the ingredients in a heavy-bottomed medium saucepan over medium heat and bring to the boil, swirling the pan from time to time until the sugar dissolves. If sugar crystals start to form on the sides of the pan, wash them down with a pastry brush dipped in cold water. Cook the mixture just until it is a light caramel color. When you've got the right color, pull the pan from the heat and cool the bottom of the pan by dipping it into the ice-water bath for 10 seconds.

3. One at a time, dip the tops of the cream puffs into the caramel and then place them caramel side down on the baking sheet. The best way to dip the puffs is to hold them very gently between your fingers, taking care not to squeeze them; be extra careful not to let the caramel touch your fingers — cooked sugar is exceedingly hot.

4. When all the puffs have been dipped and their caramel tops have hardened — they will harden almost immediately — put the baking sheet with the puff pastry/cream puff base on the counter. Check that the caramel in the pan is still liquid and smooth-flowing; if it's not, heat it briefly. Again, working with one puff at a time, dip the bottom of each puff in the caramel and quickly "glue" it atop the base's cream puff border. (If you've filled the puffs from the side, make sure that side faces in.) Keep working until you've encircled the base completely.

TO FINISH

- **Chocolate Whipped Cream (page 223)**
- **Chocolate curls (see page 258) (optional)**

1. Drain the pears, discarding the poaching liquid, and pat them dry between layers of paper towels. Keep close at hand.

2. Fit a large pastry bag with a ¾-inch (2-cm) star tip and fill the bag with the chocolate whipped cream. Piping in a spiral from the center out, cover the pastry base with whipped cream. Arrange the pear halves over the cream in a circle, pointing the narrow ends of the pears into the center of the cake. If there is a space in the center, fill it with a pear. Then, leaving about 2 inches (5 cm) of the pears bare as a border around the edge, pipe plump rosettes of whipped cream over the pears in concentric circles, finishing with a big rosette in the center. Top the cream with a few chocolate curls, if you've made them. The Gâteau Saint-Honoré can be served immediately or refrigerated for a few hours.

Makes 10 servings

KEEPING: The pears, pastry base, cream puffs, and chocolate pastry cream can be made ahead, but once the cake is assembled, it should be enjoyed soon thereafter. Although you can keep the cake in the refrigerator for a few hours — 6 hours, tops — it should be eaten the day it is made.

CINNAMON
SAVARIN
AU RHUM

Even though "savarin au rhum" sounds more like a sexy dance than a dessert, more South American than European, and more whimsical than worldly, it's a cake that's caused Frenchmen to throw restraint to the winds for more than two hundred years. The savarin and its next of kin, the baba, were created by the disgruntled King Stanislas of Poland. Exiled in Lorraine, France, the King was not amused by the regional sweet, the kugelhopf. A tall, yeast-raised cake studded with raisins and nuts, kugelhopf is doted on by those in Alsace-Lorraine and beyond, but his majesty found it much too dry. To satisfy his sweet tooth, he hit on the idea of drenching the kugelhopf to its saturation point in rum syrup — the "au rhum" in the name. The "savarin" part honors the gourmand and culinary philosopher Brillat-Savarin, while "baba" derives from the King's fondness for the *Thousand and One Tales of the Arabian Nights* — the cake is named for its hero, Ali Baba.

There's often confusion about the difference between a baba and a savarin: It's all in the shape of the baking pans. Baking pans shaped like timbales or small juice tumblers are called baba molds, and ring molds are called savarin molds. You can use this dough to make a savarin, as Pierre suggests, or you can use it to make small puff-topped babas. Or both: You can make a small savarin and a few babas — you'll just have to watch their baking times.

For this unusual recipe, the savarin is soaked — drenched is really more like it — in a traditional rum syrup piqued by orange zest and cinnamon sticks. Then it's served with chocolate whipped cream — lots of it.

■ So that the savarin will absorb as much syrup as possible — this is, quite literally, a sponge cake — I like to keep it out on the counter for a day or two. After this rest, the savarin is stale, thirsty, and just right for soaking. ■ PH

THE CAKE

- 1⅓ cups (180 grams) all-purpose flour
- ½ ounce (15 grams) fresh yeast, crumbled
- Pulp from 1 moist, plump vanilla bean (see page 279)
- Grated zest of ½ lemon
- Pinch of salt
- 6 large eggs, at room temperature
- 1 tablespoon honey
- 5 tablespoons (2½ ounces; 70 grams) unsalted butter, at room temperature

1. Put the flour, yeast, vanilla bean pulp, grated zest, and salt in the bowl of a mixer fitted with the paddle attachment and mix on low speed for half a minute, just to blend the ingredients. Break 3 of the eggs into the center of the mixture, pour in the honey, and beat on medium speed for about 3 to 4 minutes, until the mixture is elastic — you'll see strands of dough tugging at the band of dough that sticks to the sides of the bowl. Add 2 more eggs and beat until the mixture is smooth, another 3 to 4 minutes. Add the remaining egg and, still working on medium speed, beat the dough for a full 10 minutes — during which time you're not only mixing the dough, but also kneading it, encouraging the yeast to develop the gluten network that will give the savarin its distinctive structure. With the machine still running, drop the butter into the bowl in tablespoon-sized additions. The dough may be more liquid than a brioche dough, which it resembles, and that's fine. Continue to beat the dough until it is completely smooth and thoroughly homogenous — it will be beautifully satiny — then remove the bowl from the mixer and clean the sides of the bowl with a rubber spatula.

2. Cover the bowl with plastic wrap, place it in a draft-free spot, and allow the dough to rise for 30 minutes. It won't double in volume — it may not even rise dramatically — but that's all right.

3. While the dough is rising, generously butter a 10¼-inch (26-cm) ring mold (a low round mold with a center tube) that's at least 2½ inches (6 cm) high. (If your mold is smaller or shallower, you may have to use less of the dough and decrease the baking time, in which case you can make a small savarin and some babas too.)

4. At the end of its rest period, spoon the dough into the buttered mold — it should fill the mold to the halfway mark. Leave the mold at room temperature, covered with plastic wrap, until the dough fills three-quarters of the

mold, about 20 to 30 minutes (more or less, depending on the temperature of your room).

5. During the savarin's final rise, center a rack in the oven and preheat the oven to 400°F (200°C).

6. Put the savarin mold on a baking sheet and slide the sheet into the oven. Bake the savarin for 18 to 22 minutes, or until it is puffed and deeply golden. (If after 12 minutes or so it looks as though the savarin is coloring too quickly, cover it loosely with foil.) Immediately unmold the savarin onto a rack (you may have to run a blunt knife gently around the sides and center tube of the pan to loosen the cake) and cool to room temperature. (*The savarin can be left, uncovered, at room temperature for up to 2 days or wrapped airtight and frozen for 1 month. Defrost the cake in its wrapper before proceeding.*)

TO FINISH

- **1½ cups (375 grams) water**
- **¾ cup (150 grams) sugar**
- **1½ cinnamon sticks**
- **Zest of ¼ orange (removed with a vegetable peeler)**
- **¼ cup (65 grams) dark rum**
- **½ cup (175 grams) apricot jam**
- **Chocolate Whipped Cream (page 223)**
- **Fresh berries for decoration (optional)**

1. Bring the water, sugar, cinnamon, and orange zest to the boil in a medium saucepan. Pull the pan from the heat, pour in the rum, and allow the syrup to cool for about 10 minutes (it should still feel warm to the touch).

2. Transfer the savarin to a cake plate with a raised rim and, using a small paring knife, poke deep incisions all over the top of the savarin. Spoon or brush the syrup over the cake. Be wildly generous — and be patient. You want the cake to be completely saturated by the syrup, and this can take some time. When the cake is properly soaked, it will be exceedingly moist, just the way King Stanislas wanted it to be.

3. Bring the apricot jam and a few drops of water to the boil either in a small saucepan or in a bowl in the microwave oven. Push the jam through a sieve, then brush the strained jam over the top and sides of the cake.

4. To serve, fill the center of the savarin with the chocolate whipped cream and, if you're using them, decorate the cream with berries.

Makes 10 servings

KEEPING: The savarin can be frozen for up to a month before it is soaked. You could even freeze it for a month after it has been soaked. However, once it's glazed, it's time to serve it.

Named not for the supersonic plane but for the majestic Place de la Concorde in Paris, this cake is most closely associated with the celebrated Paris pastry chef Gaston Lenôtre, the chef under whom Pierre did his apprenticeship. This may be one of Lenôtre's earliest cakes; certainly it is one of his most beloved: It is still a best-seller after more than thirty-five years. And for good reason — it is chocolate, simple (there are just three elements), lively (each forkful is both crunchy and creamy), and, of course, delicious. The cake is built on three disks of chocolate meringue, each layered with chocolate mousse. When you pipe the meringue circles, you also pipe a raft of meringue cylinders that will form the cake's decoration. Pressed into the sides and top of the cake, the cocoa-colored rods, inevitably irregularly shaped and sized, create a craggy, appealingly bumpy, and obviously crunchy topography.

■ Chocolate meringue is naturally hard, so it's best (and convenient, also) to assemble the cake and freeze it, then defrost it. The freezing and unfreezing has a softening, tenderizing effect on the meringue. ■ PH

THE MERINGUE

- **1 cup (100 grams) confectioners' sugar**
- **3 tablespoons Dutch-processed cocoa powder, preferably Valrhona**
- **4 large egg whites, at room temperature (see step 3)**
- **½ cup (100 grams) sugar**

1. Position the racks to divide the oven into thirds and preheat the oven to 250°F (120°C). Line two large baking sheets with parchment paper. Pencil the outline of two 8½-inch (22-cm) circles on one piece of parchment and the outline of one 8½-inch (22-cm) circle on the other; turn the sheets of paper over. (If you can't see the outline of the circles clearly now that the paper is flipped over, darken the pencil lines.) Fit a large pastry bag with a plain ½-inch (1.5-cm) tip and a smaller bag with a ¼-inch (7-mm) tip. (If you only have one pastry bag, use it for the ½-inch [1.5-cm] tip and substi-

tute a zipper-lock plastic bag for the smaller pastry bag. After the plastic bag is filled with the meringue, you can seal it and then snip off a corner — it will work perfectly for this recipe.)

2. Sift the confectioners' sugar and cocoa powder together and keep close at hand.

3. For the egg whites to beat to their fullest volume, they need to be at room temperature. To get them to room temperature quickly, put them in a microwave-safe bowl and place them in a microwave oven set on the lowest power; heat the whites for about 10 seconds. Stir the whites and continue to heat in 5-second spurts until they are about 75°F (25°C). If they're a little warmer, that's okay too.

4. In a clean, dry mixer bowl with a clean, dry whisk attachment in place, whip the egg whites on high speed until they turn opaque and form soft peaks. Still whipping on high, add half the granulated sugar and continue to beat until the whites are glossy and hold firm peaks. Reduce the mixer speed to medium-low and gradually beat in the remaining granulated sugar.

5. Remove the bowl from the mixer and, working with a large rubber spatula, gently fold in the sifted confectioners' sugar and cocoa mixture. Work quickly and delicately, and don't be discouraged when your beautifully airy meringue deflates somewhat — it's inevitable.

6. Spoon two-thirds of the batter into the large pastry bag and begin piping the batter at the center of a traced circle. Work your way in a spiral to the penciled edge, trying to have each coil of batter touch the preceding coil. Pipe with light, consistent pressure and keep the disks thin — they shouldn't be more than ⅓ inch (1 cm) high. Pipe the remaining disks in the same manner. Fill the smaller pastry bag (or the plastic bag) with the remaining batter and pipe as many long strips of meringue as you can on the baking sheet with the single disk. (You'll use pieces of the meringue strips to decorate the sides and top of the cake.)

7. If there are any spaces or uneven sections in the disks, give them a once-over-lightly with a metal spatula. Place the baking sheets in the oven and insert the handle of a wooden spoon into the door to keep it slightly ajar. Bake the disks for 1½ to 2 hours, rotating the pans front to back and top to bottom two or three times during the baking period. The meringues should be firm but not colored. Turn off the oven and continue to dry the meringues for another 2 hours, or for as long as overnight, with the door closed.

8. Transfer the meringues, parchment and all, to racks to cool to room temperature. Run a thin metal spatula under the disks and strips to loosen them from the paper. (*The meringues can be made up to 1 week in advance and kept in a cool dry place, such as an airtight box.*)

THE MOUSSE

- 8¾ ounces (250 grams) bittersweet chocolate, preferably Valrhona Guanaja, finely chopped
- 2 sticks plus 1½ tablespoons (8¾ ounces; 250 grams) unsalted butter, at room temperature
- 6 large egg whites, at room temperature
- 1 tablespoon sugar
- 3 large egg yolks, at room temperature, lightly beaten with a fork

1. Melt the chocolate over — not touching — simmering water or in a microwave oven, then allow it to cool until it feels warm to the touch, 114°F (45°C), as measured on an instant-read thermometer. (It's important that the chocolate not be too hot when it's added to the butter — if it melts the butter, it will make the mousse heavy.)

2. Working in a mixer fitted with the whisk attachment (or using a hand-held mixer), beat the butter until it is very smooth. Add the cooled chocolate in three additions, beating until the mixture is well blended. Scrape the chocolate mixture into a large bowl and thoroughly wash and dry the mixer bowl and whisk.

3. In the clean, dry mixer bowl, with the whisk attachment in place, whip the egg whites on high speed until they hold soft peaks. With the mixer still on high, add the sugar and continue to whip until the whites hold firm, glossy peaks. Still beating, pour in the yolks and whip for another 30 seconds. The whites will be thinned by the yolks, and that's just fine.

4. Working with a large flexible rubber spatula, stir one-quarter of the egg mixture into the chocolate to lighten it. Then delicately fold in the remaining egg mixture. The mousse, which may remind you of a lightly whipped buttercream rather than a traditional mousse, is now ready to be used — and should be used quickly.

TO ASSEMBLE

1. Trim a cardboard cake round so that it is the same size as the meringue disks. Place a dollop of chocolate mousse in the center, and use the dollop of mousse to glue one meringue disk to the cardboard (save the disk with the smoothest underside for the top). Cover the disk with a little less than half of the mousse and smooth the surface with an offset spatula. Position another

disk over the mousse, jiggling the disk so that it settles evenly on the mousse. Cover this disk with a little more than half of the remaining mousse, again smoothing the top. Turn the last disk over, flat side up, and jiggle it onto the mousse. Cover the top and sides of the cake with a thin "masking" coat of the remaining mousse and slide the cake into the freezer. The cake should remain in the freezer for about 2 hours to set the mousse and prepare it for the blast of hot air it will get in the next step.

2. Using a serrated knife and a sawing motion, cut the meringue strips into pieces about ½ inch (1.5 cm) long. Don't worry if the strips break or the pieces are uneven — it's inevitable and unimportant. Even crumbs will be fine on this cake. Remove the cake from the freezer and, using a hairdryer, warm the sides and top of the cake to soften the mousse just a little — don't overdo it. Press the meringue pieces into the sides and top of the cake, either helter-skelter or in a pattern of your choice. You can serve the cake now, but the meringue will be more tender if you freeze it, wrap it well, and then keep it in the freezer for at least a day.

Makes 6 to 8 servings

KEEPING: The meringue disks and rods can be made up to 1 week ahead and kept in an airtight box at room temperature, but the mousse needs to be used as soon as it's made. Once the cake is assembled, it can be kept covered in the refrigerator, away from foods with strong odors, for up to 3 days, or frozen, then wrapped airtight, and kept in the freezer for up to 1 month. Defrost the cake, still wrapped, in the refrigerator overnight.

CRIOLLO

Anyone who knows a few words of Spanish will think of the word *criollo* as descriptive of Hispanic family cooking. And, indeed, when you look at the components that constitute this winning cake, there is a delightful South-of-the-Border theme. The main flavors of this creation are tropical — coconut, banana and chocolate — but they're given a French touch. The coconut layers are a dacquoise, a type of meringue disk. The filling is a chocolate mousse, but one that is unusual and piquant, since it has more than a hint of lemon zest and fresh ginger. And tucked inside the cake and decorating its top is the final tropical note: caramelized bananas.

But *criollo* has another meaning, one tied to Central and South America and close to the heart of any pastry chef: Criollo is the name of the rarest, most-difficult-to-cultivate cocoa bean. The criollo bean, found in Venezuela, Mexico, Nicaragua, Guatemala, Colombia, Trinidad, Grenada, and Jamaica, is the bean that is used to give complexity to finely blended chocolates.

■ Make sure to caramelize the bananas over high heat. Be timid with the heat, and you risk turning the bananas into mush. ■ PH

THE BANANAS

- **2 medium bananas**
- **1½ teaspoons freshly squeezed lemon juice**
- **1½ tablespoons (¾ ounce; 20 grams) unsalted butter**
- **2½ tablespoons light brown sugar**

1. Peel the bananas and cut them on a slight bias into ½-inch- (1.5-cm-) thick slices. Toss the bananas with the lemon juice and keep them close at hand.

2. Melt the butter in a medium skillet (preferably one that's nonstick) over high heat and, when the butter is bubbly, stir in the brown sugar. Toss in the bananas and cook them, stirring constantly and taking care not to let them get mushy, until they are golden and caramel-coated. Pull the pan from the heat,

transfer the bananas to a plate, and allow them to cool while you make the mousse.

THE MOUSSE

- 2 large eggs
- 1 large egg yolk
- ⅓ cup (70 grams) sugar
- 2 tablespoons water
- 1 cup (250 grams) chilled heavy cream
- 6 ounces (170 grams) bittersweet chocolate, preferably Valrhona Manjari, finely chopped
- Finely grated zest of 1 lemon
- ¼ teaspoon finely grated peeled ginger

1. Put the eggs and yolk into the bowl of a mixer fitted with the whisk attachment. With the mixer on the lowest speed, beat the eggs for a few seconds, just to blend them.

2. Put the sugar and water in a small heavy-bottomed saucepan and cook over medium heat, swirling the pan as needed to keep the sugar moistened, until the sugar melts. (If there's some sugar on the sides of the pan, wash it down with a pastry brush dipped in cold water.) When the sugar melts, stop swirling, turn up the heat, bring the mixture to a boil, and cook — without stirring — until it reaches 257°F (125°C), as measured on a candy or an instant-read thermometer (about 5 to 10 minutes). Immediately pull the pan from the heat.

3. Turn the mixer to its lowest speed and whisk the eggs again for a few seconds, then very slowly add the syrup in a thin, steady stream. To avoid splatters, try to pour the syrup down the side of the bowl, not into the spinning whisk. (Inevitably, some will splatter, but don't attempt to scrape the hardened syrup into the meringue — you'll get lumps.) Increase the mixer speed to high and beat the eggs for about 5 minutes, until they are at room temperature, pale, and more than double their original volume. While the eggs are beating, prepare the cream and the chocolate.

4. Beat the cream until it holds medium peaks. Keep it on the counter while you prepare the chocolate.

5. Melt the chocolate in a bowl over — not touching — simmering water or in a microwave oven. Remove the chocolate from the heat and, if necessary, pour it into a bowl large enough to hold all the ingredients for the mousse. Stir in

the zest and grated ginger, then cool the chocolate until it feels warm to the touch, 114°F (45°C), as measured on an instant-read thermometer.

6. Using a large rubber spatula, fold about one-quarter of the cream into the chocolate. Fold in the rest of the cream and then, very delicately, fold in the whipped egg mixture. (*It's really best to use the mousse now, but if it's necessary you can cover it well and keep it refrigerated for as long as overnight.*)

TO ASSEMBLE

- **Two 9-inch (24-cm) Coconut Dacquoise disks (page 231)**

1. Trim the two dacquoise disks so that they will slip into an 8¾-inch (22-cm) cake ring. The easiest way to do this is to place the ring (lightly) on top of each disk and, using a paring knife, carefully cut around the ring to remove the excess meringue. Alternatively, you can mark the meringues with the cake ring, then use a serrated knife and a gentle sawing motion to shave away the excess. And don't panic if the disks crack — you can fit the pieces into the ring and "glue" them together with mousse. It's not a tragedy.

2. Place the cake ring on a cardboard cake round and put one of the dacquoise disks into the ring. Cover the disk with about one-third of the mousse, smoothing the mousse with an offset spatula. Drain and pat dry the bananas, then cover the mousse with the bananas, spreading them out so that you can be pretty sure that every bite of the cake will include some fruit. Spread half of the remaining mousse over the bananas, again smoothing the top with an offset spatula; top with the second disk of dacquoise, smooth side up. Spread the remaining mousse evenly over the disk.

3. If you are going to serve the cake the same day, slide the cake (in its ring and on the cardboard) into the refrigerator and chill it until set, at least 3 hours. (*The cake can be kept in the refrigerator for about 12 hours; cover it well after it is set.*) If you are not serving the cake the day it is made, place it in the freezer and, when it is firm, wrap it airtight. (*The cake can be made to this point and frozen for up to 1 month. Defrost overnight in the refrigerator before serving.*)

TO FINISH

- **½ banana, peeled and cut on the bias into ¼-inch- (7-mm-) thick slices**
- **Squirt of freshly squeezed lemon juice**
- **1 tablespoon (½ ounce; 15 grams) unsalted butter**

- **1 tablespoon brown sugar**
- **Shredded unsweetened dried coconut (lightly toasted, if desired)**
- **Apple or quince jelly, warmed**

1. Toss the banana slices, which you will use to top the cake, with the lemon juice. Melt the butter in a skillet over high heat and add the sugar. When the mixture is bubbly, add the bananas and cook and stir until they are caramel-coated. Pull the pan from the heat, transfer the bananas to a plate, and allow the bananas to cool to room temperature. When they are cool, pat them dry.

2. Using a hairdryer, warm the cake ring and then lift it off the cake (see page 273). While you've got the hairdryer out, warm the sides of the cake a bit, to soften the mousse slightly. Press the shredded coconut onto the sides of the cake, then top the cake with a crescent of caramel bananas, overlapping the slices so that they form a semicircle. Brush the bananas with a light gloss of jelly. If you're not ready to serve the cake, put it back in the refrigerator until serving time; the cake should be served chilled.

Makes 8 to 10 servings

KEEPING: The decorated cake can be kept in the refrigerator, away from strong odors, for a day. Pre-banana topping, the cake can be frozen for up to a month; allow it to defrost overnight in the refrigerator.

A dacquoise — the name refers to both the dessert and the disks that sandwich the dessert's filling — is a delicacy that can be found in pastry shops all over France. Traditionally, it is made with almond-flavored disks — the disks are a cross between a nut-speckled meringue and a cake — and filled with hazelnut-flavored buttercream. Indeed, this original is still popular, and deservedly so. But the composition, the crunchy layers of dacquoise and the creamy filling, encourages innovations. It's not unusual now to find dacquoise featuring walnuts or pistachio nuts or, as Pierre has done for his semifreddo (page 186) and the Criollo, his tropical chocolate and banana cake (page 34), coconut. In this cake, Pierre stays close to traditional. The dacquoise disks are flavored with almond powder, but they've got an equal amount of hazelnut powder as well as a topping of coarsely cut, golden brown toasted hazelnuts. As for the filling — it is, as it should be, rich, satiny, and very smooth, but it's not buttercream. Instead, Pierre uses bittersweet chocolate ganache. In the end, Pierre's dacquoise seems less like an innovation than a new tradition.

■ The dacquoise layers can stand in for layers in other cakes. For example, they can be used instead of the chocolate meringue disks in the Concorde (page 29) — they'd be terrific with the Concorde's mousse — and they would be good, for a change, replacing the coconut disks in the semifreddo (page 186). ■ PH

THE DACQUOISE

- ⅓ cup (40 grams) finely ground almond powder (see page 265) or blanched almonds
- ½ cup (1½ ounces; 50 grams) finely ground hazelnut powder (see page 265) or toasted and skinned hazelnuts (see page 273)
- ¾ cup (150 grams) sugar

- **5 large egg whites, at room temperature**
- **⅔ cup (1¾ ounces; 80 grams) hazelnuts, toasted, skinned (see page 273), and cut in half**
- **Confectioners' sugar for dusting**

1. Line a baking sheet with parchment paper. Pencil the outline of two 9-inch (22-cm) circles on the parchment paper. Turn the paper over; if you can't see the outline of the circles clearly now that the paper is flipped over, darken the pencil lines. Set the baking sheet aside for the moment. Fit a medium-sized pastry bag with a plain ½-inch (1.5-cm) tip.

2. If you are not using almond and hazelnut powder, put the blanched almonds, skinned hazelnuts (*not* the halved nuts), and ¼ cup (50 grams) of the sugar in a food processor fitted with the metal blade and process until the mixture is as fine as flour, at least 3 minutes. Stop after every minute to check your progress and to scrape down the sides of the bowl. When the mixture is ground, using a wooden spoon, press it through a medium strainer. If you are using almond and hazelnut powder, mix these together with ¼ cup (50 grams) of the sugar; set aside.

3. Working in a clean, dry mixer fitted with the whisk attachment, whip the egg whites just until they turn opaque. Gradually add the remaining ½ cup (100 grams) sugar and continue to beat until the whites hold firm, glossy peaks. Remove the bowl from the mixer and, working with a flexible rubber spatula, gently fold the nut-and-sugar mixture into the beaten whites.

4. Spoon half the batter into the pastry bag and pipe a dollop of batter in each of the four corners of the baking sheet to "glue" down the parchment paper. Begin piping the batter at the center of one of the traced circles, working your way in a spiral to within about ½ inch (1.5 cm) of the penciled edge and trying to have each coil of batter touch the preceding coil; pipe with light, consistent pressure. Refill the bag and pipe the second disk. (Any leftover meringue can be piped into little buttons — they make great cookies.) If you see any spaces or uneven sections on the disks, give them a once-over-lightly with a metal spatula. Scatter the toasted hazelnut pieces evenly over the tops of the two disks, press them down gently, and lightly dust the tops with confectioners' sugar. Allow the disks to rest on the counter for 10 minutes, then dust them lightly a second time and again give them a 10-minute rest.

5. While the disks are resting, center a rack in the oven and preheat the oven to 325°F (165°C).

6. Slip the baking sheet into the oven and bake the disks for 25 to 30 minutes, or until they are golden brown and firm to the touch. Transfer the baking sheet to a rack and allow the disks to cool to room temperature. (*The disks*

can be wrapped airtight and kept at room temperature for up to 2 days or frozen for 1 month.)

TO FINISH

- **2½ to 3 cups (approximately 1½ recipes; 825 grams) Bittersweet Chocolate Cream Ganache (page 215), ready to pipe**
- **Confectioners' sugar for dusting**

1. Spoon the ganache into a large pastry bag fitted with a plain ½- to ¾-inch (1.5- to 2-cm) tip. Put one of the dacquoise disks nut side up on a cardboard cake round ("glue" the disk to the round with a little ganache) and pipe big balls of ganache (each about 2 inches in diameter) all around the edge of the disk. Fill in the center of the disk with the remaining ganache and cover the filling with the second disk, nut side up, jiggling the disk lightly to settle it into place. Put the dacquoise in the refrigerator, away from any foods with strong odors, and chill until the ganache sets, about 1 hour — although chilling it longer is a good idea since this is a cake that is meant to be served cold.

2. Dust the top of the dacquoise with confectioners' sugar just before you take it to the table.

Makes 8 servings

KEEPING: The finished dacquoise — minus its last dusting of confectioners' sugar — can be kept in the refrigerator overnight or wrapped airtight and frozen for 1 month. To defrost, leave the dacquoise in its wrapping and allow it to stand in the refrigerator overnight.

WHITE CHOCOLATE AND RHUBARB CHARLOTTE

Although it's called a charlotte, this cake doesn't fall neatly into any category. It's a mousse cake, but not really; and, indeed, a charlotte, but not really. In some ways it's reminiscent of an American shortcake (albeit a highly evolved shortcake) or that old-fashioned not-seen-too-much-nowadays dessert, Charlotte Russe, a ladyfinger-and-whipped-cream concoction that used to be served in cardboard cylinders you'd push up from the bottom to reveal more of the creamy dessert at the top. With these two sweets in mind, imagine a cake created from layers of lime-moistened ladyfinger disks, rhubarb compote, and white chocolate cream. Now — and here's where the cake takes on its most Charlotte-Russe-ish traits — imagine it finished with puffs of whipped cream, white chocolate curls, and a few red berries. It's an optional finish — the cake is luscious in its sleek, unadorned state — but take the extra step, and you'll have a truly captivating cake.

A word on white chocolate: It's a tricky ingredient. It is extremely sweet and, used without skill, its sweetness can be overpowering and capable of rendering an otherwise-well-made dessert uninteresting. But here the chocolate's sweetness becomes its star asset and the white chocolate cream becomes the perfect mild-mannered companion to the tangy, slightly acidic rhubarb. It's a combination that is revelatory — it's made die-hard dark chocolate fans reconsider white chocolate's worth.

■ In this cake, the white chocolate serves three important roles: It provides texture, adds flavor, and sweetens the cream that fills the charlotte. ■ PH

THE LADYFINGER DISKS

- **Ladyfinger Batter (page 226)**

For this dessert, you will need two 8¾-inch (22-cm) ladyfinger disks. Following the recipe's directions, pipe out the disks onto a parchment-lined baking sheet and bake and cool them. (*The disks can be made ahead, wrapped airtight, and kept at room temperature for 2 days or frozen for a month.*)

THE RHUBARB

- **1½ pounds (680 grams) rhubarb, trimmed, peeled, and cut into ¼-inch (7-mm) dice (you should have about 1 pound [450 grams] diced rhubarb)**
- **3 tablespoons freshly squeezed lemon juice**
- **¼ cup (50 grams) sugar**
- **3 tablespoons cold water**
- **2½ teaspoons powdered gelatin (or 3 grams sheet gelatin)**

1. Working in a heavy-bottomed medium saucepan set over medium heat, stir together the rhubarb, lemon juice, and sugar. Bring to the boil, then cook, stirring frequently, until the rhubarb softens and most of the liquid evaporates, 7 to 10 minutes; the mixture will look like a thin applesauce. Remove from the heat.
2. While the rhubarb is cooking, prepare the gelatin. Pour the cold water into a small microwave-safe bowl and sprinkle the gelatin over the water. When the gelatin is softened and spongy, heat it in the microwave oven for about 15 seconds, until it dissolves. Or soften the gelatin in a small saucepan, then dissolve it over low heat. Stir the gelatin into the rhubarb.
3. Line a baking sheet with parchment paper and put an 8¾-inch (22-cm) cake or tart ring on the sheet. Pour the rhubarb compote into the ring and slide the sheet into the freezer to set the compote, about 2 hours. (*Once the compote is frozen, you can remove the cake or tart ring. Wrap the compote airtight and keep it in the freezer for up to 2 weeks. When you're ready to assemble the charlotte, take the compote straight from the freezer — there's no need to defrost it.*)

THE WHITE CHOCOLATE CREAM

- **6½ ounces (185 grams) white chocolate, preferably Valrhona Ivoire, finely chopped**
- **2⅔ cups (665 grams) heavy cream**

1. Melt the chocolate in a medium bowl over — not touching — simmering water or in the microwave oven. Either way, don't leave the chocolate for a

second: Even more than dark chocolate, white chocolate shouldn't be overheated; it separates and burns quickly. While the chocolate is melting, bring ⅔ cup (165 grams) of the heavy cream to a boil.

2. When the chocolate is melted and the cream has boiled, stir the cream into the chocolate, using a whisk. Don't worry if the cream turns the chocolate yellow — that's natural. This mixture needs to cool to 75° to 80°F (23° to 27°C), so set it aside at room temperature or put it in a larger bowl of ice and water. In either case, stir the cream as it cools and stay close to it — white chocolate cools and hardens faster than dark chocolate.

3. Whip the remaining 2 cups (500 grams) cream until it holds medium-firm peaks. When the chocolate is cool, fold in the whipped cream. The filling is ready and, in fact, should be used immediately.

TO ASSEMBLE

- **1 lime, halved**

Place an 8¾-inch (22-cm) cake ring on a cardboard cake round and fit one of the ladyfinger disks into the ring. Moisten the disk with a little fresh lime juice, either by squeezing the lime directly onto the cake or by squeezing the juice into a bowl and using a pastry brush to dab the cake with juice. Remove the cake or tart ring from the rhubarb compote and place the rhubarb disk on top of the ladyfinger disk. Spoon on half of the white chocolate cream, smoothing the top with an offset spatula. Lay the second ladyfinger disk over the cream, lightly jiggling the disk so that it settles into place on its moussy cushion. Moisten this disk with a little lime juice, top it with the remainder of the chocolate cream, and smooth the top. The cream should come right to the top of the cake ring; if you've got extra, just spoon it into a cup and save it to enjoy on its own. Refrigerate the charlotte for at least 4 hours, or for as long as overnight, making certain it is kept away from foods with strong odors.

TO FINISH

- **2 cups (500 grams) heavy cream, lightly sweetened and whipped**
- **White chocolate shavings (see page 258)**
- **Raspberries or strawberries**

At serving time, or up to 2 hours ahead, remove the charlotte from the refrigerator. Using a hairdryer, remove the cake ring (see page 273). You can serve the dessert as is, with no further flourishes, or give it a thin finish of whipped cream

Makes 8 servings

KEEPING: Both the ladyfinger disks and the rhubarb compote can be made ahead and kept frozen until needed. Indeed, the rhubarb must be frozen to set and then, like the ladyfingers, can stay in the freezer for a few weeks. The white chocolate cream and the optional whipped cream finish are, however, best used as soon as they're made. Once assembled, the charlotte can be kept covered in the refrigerator overnight; once topped with whipped cream, it must be kept chilled and should be served within 2 hours.

all over its sides and top, or go all out and cover it with a mantle of whipped cream and a few fillips of chocolate and berries. If you decide to go all the way, pipe rosettes of lightly whipped cream over the top and sides of the cake, or spread the whipped cream on in swirls and swishes with a spatula or even a spoon. Then, in the same generous spirit, scatter white chocolate shavings over the top and sides of the charlotte and finish with a few red berries. None, any, or all of these additions would be fine. Serve immediately, or keep the cake in the refrigerator until serving time.

CHOCOLATE-FILLED
MILLE-FEUILLE

Mille-feuille means a thousand leaves or sheets in French, an allusion to the number of layers of featherweight dough composing a properly made piece of puff pastry. Mille-feuille is also the name of one of the most elegant desserts in the French pastry chef's repertoire, a voluptuous triple-decker sandwich of puff pastry and pastry cream. Sometimes (more often in this country than in France) the dessert is called a napoleon, sometimes it includes berries (see Pierre's suggestion below), sometimes it has a gloss of white icing, and sometimes the filling is little more than whipped cream, but rarely is it better than this very simple, and simply very, very delicious mille-feuille, in which both the puff pastry sandwich layers and the pastry cream filling are given small but significant twists: The pastry is caramelized so that it is even crispier, flakier, and more flavorful than the norm, while the pastry cream is enriched with bittersweet chocolate and then lightened with whipped cream.

■ When berries are in season, I like to add them to this mille-feuille. I make half a batch of the filling and delicately fold in, depending on what's available, an assortment of berries or only one kind, either strawberries (small wild strawberries — *fraises des bois* — are wonderful in this) or raspberries. And I change the construction: Instead of three layers of puff pastry and two of filling, I sandwich a single layer of the berry-studded pastry cream between two layers of the caramelized puff pastry. — PH

THE FILLING

- **Vanilla Pastry Cream (page 219)**
- **7 ounces (200 grams) bittersweet chocolate, preferably Valrhona Guanaja, finely chopped**
- **½ cup (125 grams) whole milk**
- **¾ cup (185 grams) heavy cream**

1. Prepare an ice-water bath for the filling by filling a large bowl with ice cubes and water. Set out a smaller bowl that can hold all the filling ingredients and fit inside the larger bowl.

2. Put the pastry cream in a heavy-bottomed medium saucepan over medium heat and, stirring constantly, bring it to the boil. Stir in the chocolate and milk and heat until the mixture boils again — this should take just a minute or so. Pull the pan from the heat and scrape the pastry cream into the small bowl. Place the bowl in the ice-water bath and cool the pastry cream, stirring frequently so that it chills quickly and evenly. When the pastry cream is cool, remove it from the water bath.

3. Whip the heavy cream until it holds medium peaks. Using a flexible rubber spatula and a light hand, gently fold the whipped cream into the chocolate pastry cream. The filling is now ready to use. (*The filling can be used right away or packed in an airtight container and refrigerated for up to 4 hours.*)

TO ASSEMBLE

- **Caramelized Plain Puff Pastry (page 248)**
- **Unsweetened cocoa powder for dusting**

1. Put the puff pastry shiny side up on a large cutting board covered with a cloth towel and, using a serrated knife and a sawing motion or — better yet — an electric knife, cut it crosswise into 3 pieces. Spread half of the filling smoothly over one of the pieces of puff pastry, then top with a second piece of pastry, shiny side up, jiggling the pastry gently to settle it against the filling. Spread the remainder of the filling smoothly over this second piece of pastry and top with the third piece of pastry, again shiny side up, and again jiggling it to set it into place.

2. At this point you have a choice: You can present the mille-feuille as a large cake or you can cut it into 6 portions. If you decide to present the mille-feuille intact, dust it with cocoa powder (see step 3 below) — then think about cutting it in the kitchen, since puff pastry shatters dramatically. Use an electric or a serrated knife and a sawing motion to get the cleanest cuts.

3. To finish each individual cake, dust two opposite corners of the pastry with cocoa powder, leaving a central block of pastry uncovered so its beautiful shiny finish is open to admiration.

Makes 6 servings

KEEPING: Although, if you must, you can keep the filling and the caramelized puff pastry for a few hours (the filling under refrigeration, the pastry at room temperature), you must not hold the mille-feuille. This dessert is meant to be assembled minutes before serving.

VANILLA-FILLED
CHOCOLATE
MILLE-FEUILLE

Think of this mille-feuille as the photographic negative of the Chocolate-Filled Mille-feuille (page 47). For that dessert, layers of caramelized plain puff pastry are spread with a velvety chocolate pastry cream. In this one, the puff pastry is also caramelized, but it's a chocolate puff pastry, and the filling is also a lightened pastry cream, but it is a vanilla cream flecked with grated orange zest. Here the chocolate is an accent and a surprise: Chocolate puff pastry is never expected.

THE FILLING

- 2½ cups (625 grams) whole milk
- 1 moist, plump vanilla bean, split lengthwise and scraped (see page 279)
- 8 large egg yolks
- ¾ cup (150 grams) sugar
- 6½ tablespoons (55 grams) cornstarch, sifted
- 4½ tablespoons (2½ ounces; 70 grams) unsalted butter, at room temperature, cut into 3 or 4 pieces
- ⅔ cup (165 grams) heavy cream
- Finely grated zest of ½ orange

1. In a small saucepan, bring the milk and vanilla bean (pulp and pod) to a boil over medium heat, or do this in the microwave oven. Cover the pan, remove from the heat, and allow the mixture to steep for 10 minutes.

2. Fill a large bowl with ice cubes and water and set aside a smaller bowl that will hold the finished pastry cream and can be placed in this ice bath. Set aside a fine-meshed strainer too.

3. Whisk the yolks, sugar, and cornstarch together in a heavy-bottomed medium saucepan. Whisking all the while, very slowly drizzle a quarter of the hot milk into the yolks. Still whisking, pour in the rest of the liquid in a steady stream. Remove and discard the vanilla pod (or save it for another use — see page 279).

4. Place the pan over medium heat, and, whisking vigorously and without stop, bring the mixture to the boil. Keep the mixture at the boil — whisking energetically — for 1 to 2 minutes, then remove the pan from the heat and scrape the pastry cream into the small bowl. Set the bowl in the ice-water bath and, stirring frequently so that the mixture remains smooth, cool the cream to 140°F (60°C), as measured on an instant-read thermometer. Stir in the butter in three or four additions. Keep the cream over ice, stirring occasionally, until it is completely cool. The pastry cream can be used now or packed for storage. (*The pastry cream can be made ahead and stored, tightly covered, in the refrigerator for up to 2 days.*)

5. Whip the heavy cream until it holds medium peaks. Sprinkle the grated orange zest over the cooled pastry cream, then top with the whipped cream. Using a flexible rubber spatula and a light hand, gently fold the whipped cream and zest into the pastry cream. The filling is now ready to use. (*The filling can be used right away or refrigerated in an airtight container for up to 4 hours.*)

TO ASSEMBLE

- **Caramelized Chocolate Puff Pastry (page 250)**
- **Confectioners' sugar for dusting**

1. Put the puff pastry caramelized side up on a large cutting board covered with a cloth towel and, using a serrated knife and a sawing motion or — better yet — an electric knife, cut it crosswise into 3 pieces. Spread half of the filling smoothly over one of the pieces of puff pastry, then top with a second piece of pastry, sugared side up, jiggling the pastry gently to settle it against the filling. Spread the remainder of the filling smoothly over this second piece of pastry and top with the third piece of pastry, again sugared side up, and again jiggling it to set it into place.

2. At this point you have a choice: You can present the mille-feuille as a large cake or you can cut it into 6 portions. If you decide to present the mille-feuille intact, dust it with confectioners' sugar (see step 3 below) — then think about cutting it in the kitchen, since puff pastry shatters dramatically. Use an electric or a serrated knife and a sawing motion to get the cleanest cuts.

3. To finish each individual cake, dust a strip of pastry at each end with confectioners' sugar, leaving a central block of pastry uncovered.

Makes 6 servings

KEEPING: Although, if you must, you can keep the filling and the caramelized puff pastry for a few hours (the filling under refrigeration, the pastry at room temperature), you must not hold the mille-feuille. This dessert is meant to be assembled minutes before serving.

I t's hard to believe that the structure of this cake, its five different components and the way in which they are combined, was created in 1993 — it is as exciting, daring, and demonically delicious today as it was then. In its first incarnation, the elements — hazelnut dacquoise, milk chocolate ganache, milk chocolate whipped cream, thin sheets of tempered milk chocolate, and a spread of milk chocolate, praline, and crushed crunchy wafers — were set inside a tall molded milk chocolate shell designed by the artist Yan Pennor's to resemble an oversized wedge of cake. It was called Cherry on the Cake and, indeed, the cake was topped with a large bright red cherry that looked more like a clown's nose than a piece of fruit. Pierre created this now-mythic cake for Paris's famous specialty food shop, Fauchon, and discovered that, in a country that gave short shrift to milk chocolate (if they gave it any shrift), the cake was revolutionary. More than that, it was newsworthy: The Cherry on the Cake was written about in tens of magazines as well as in the usually staid newspaper *Le Monde*.

This dessert (its name means Sweet Pleasure) is The Cherry on the Cake's baby sister, a plated version of the statuesque cake. It has all of the cake's components, all of its flavors, and all of its wonderful textural interplay — and, best of all, it's doable at home. (The Cherry on the Cake could never be made at home and would even have been difficult to replicate in another professional pastry kitchen.) Pierre has made a few changes to the ingredients list to make it possible to replicate this dessert without having to search out exotic products. Instead of mixing hazelnut paste with milk chocolate, as he did at Fauchon, he uses a product he uses in other desserts, Nutella (yes, Nutella from the supermarket), and, instead of crushed crispy wafers, he uses another of his favorite supermarket products: Rice Krispies.

■ The construction of Plaisir Sucré is exactly the same as the construction of The Cherry on the Cake, so you get the same sensations, the same play of textures, as with the original. Really, all I've changed is the size and shape, and I've added a bit more cream to this version. What's most important is that, as was true with the original, this dessert pleases all of your senses, even your sense of hearing — there's plenty of crackle and crunch. ■ PH

THE WHIPPED CREAM

- **10 ounces (285 grams) milk chocolate, preferably Valrhona Jivara, finely chopped**
- **1¾ cups (435 grams) heavy cream**

1. Put the chocolate in a mixing bowl that's large enough to be used for whipping the cream. Bring the cream to a full boil in a heavy-bottomed medium saucepan, pull the pan from the heat, and pour the cream over the chocolate. Mix the cream and chocolate together energetically with a rubber spatula so that the mixture is perfectly homogenous. Cover the cream with a sheet of plastic wrap, pressing the plastic against the surface of the cream to create an airtight seal, and chill the cream, keeping it away from foods with strong odors, for 5 to 6 hours, or, better yet, overnight.

2. Just before you are ready to use the cream, place the bowl of cream in a large bowl filled with ice cubes and cold water and, using a whisk, whip the cream until it is almost firm. Go easy — the cream will whip quickly. The consistency you're looking for is one that is firm enough to spread but soft enough to still feel light and creamy in your mouth. (*Once whipped, the cream is best used immediately, but it can be kept covered in the refrigerator for up to 4 hours.*)

THE DACQUOISE

- **⅔ cup (2½ ounces; 70 grams) finely ground hazelnut powder (see page 265) or toasted and skinned hazelnuts (see page 273)**
- **1 cup (100 grams) confectioners' sugar**
- **3 large egg whites, at room temperature**
- **2½ tablespoons sugar**
- **1 cup (4½ ounces; 140 grams) hazelnuts, toasted, skinned (see page 273), and cut in half**

1. Center a rack in the oven and preheat the oven to 325°F (165°C). Pencil the outline of a 10-inch (26-cm) square on a sheet of parchment paper. Turn the paper over; if you can't see the outline now that the paper is flipped over, darken the pencil lines. Place the parchment on a baking sheet and set aside for the moment.

2. If you are not using hazelnut powder, put the skinned hazelnuts (*not* the halved nuts) and the confectioners' sugar in a food processor fitted with the

metal blade and process until the mixture is as fine as flour. Using a wooden spoon, press the mixture through a medium strainer. If you are using hazelnut powder, just sift the powder with the confectioners' sugar and set aside.

3. Working in a clean, dry mixer fitted with the whisk attachment, whip the egg whites just until they turn opaque. Gradually add the granulated sugar and continue to beat until the whites hold firm, glossy peaks. Remove the bowl from the mixer and, working with a flexible rubber spatula, gently fold the nut-and-sugar mixture into the beaten whites.

4. Use a spoonful of batter to "glue" down the four corners of the parchment paper, then scrape the batter into the center of the square you traced on the parchment. Using an offset metal spatula, spread the batter into a rough 10-inch (26-cm) square that is about ½ inch (1.5 cm) thick. Don't fuss too much about the edges — you'll be trimming them away. If you see any spaces or uneven sections on the square, give them a once-over-lightly with the spatula. Scatter the hazelnut pieces evenly over the top of the dacquoise and lightly press them into the batter.

5. Slip the baking sheet into the oven and bake the dacquoise for 25 to 30 minutes, or until it is golden brown and firm to the touch. Transfer the baking sheet to a rack and allow the dacquoise to cool to room temperature. (*The dacquoise can be wrapped airtight and kept at room temperature for up to 2 days or frozen for 1 month.*)

THE PRALINE

-   **½ cup (200 grams) Nutella**
-   **1½ ounces (50 grams) milk chocolate, preferably Valrhona Jivara, melted and cooled until barely warm to the touch**
-   **1 cup (30 grams) Rice Krispies**
-   **1 tablespoon (½ ounce; 15 grams) unsalted butter, melted and cooled**

1. Put the Nutella in a medium bowl, then stir in the remaining ingredients in the order in which they are listed.

2. You will be spreading this praline mix over the dacquoise, but because you will be using only the central 8-inch (20-cm) square of the dacquoise for the individual desserts, you should concentrate on this area. Using an offset metal spatula, spread the praline evenly over the dacquoise, pressing down gently to get the praline between the nuts and working the praline into the central area before spreading it out as far as it will go to the edges. (These edges, which will be cut off later, make terrific snacks.) The layer should be

thin and even. Slide the dacquoise into the refrigerator and chill for at least 30 minutes. (*If it's more convenient, you can lightly cover the dacquoise when the praline is chilled and keep it in the refrigerator overnight.*)

THE SAUCE (*optional*)

- 3 ounces (85 grams) milk chocolate, preferably Valrhona Jivara, finely chopped
- ½ cup (125 grams) heavy cream
- ¼ cup (60 grams) whole milk

Put the chocolate in a bowl that is large enough to hold all the sauce ingredients. Fill a larger bowl with ice cubes and cold water. Bring the cream and milk to the boil, pull the pan from the heat, and pour over the chocolate. Stir the liquid into the chocolate until the sauce is smooth, then put the bowl in the ice-water bath. Stir now and then until the sauce is cold, then chill the sauce for at least 2 hours (overnight would be even better). The sauce, which is thin when hot, thickens when chilled. (*The sauce can be made up to 3 days ahead and kept in a tightly sealed jar in the refrigerator.*)

THE GANACHE

- 6½ ounces (190 grams) milk chocolate, preferably Valrhona Jivara, finely chopped
- ⅔ cup (165 grams) heavy cream

Place the chocolate in a bowl that's large enough to hold both it and the cream and keep it close at hand. Bring the cream to a full boil in a heavy-bottomed saucepan. Remove the pan from the heat and, working with a rubber spatula, gently stir the cream into the chocolate in two additions. Stir — without creating bubbles — until the chocolate is completely melted and the mixture is smooth. Allow the ganache to cool and thicken at room temperature to a pipeable consistency.

THE CHOCOLATE SHEETS

- 9 ounces (260 grams) milk chocolate, preferably Valrhona Jivara, tempered (see page 260)

1. Place three acetate sheets (see next page) on the counter near the tempered chocolate. Pour about one-third of the chocolate onto one acetate sheet, then immediately spread the chocolate smoothly over the sheet, using the edge of a long metal icing spatula (an offset spatula is good here). Don't worry about the edges, and don't worry about getting the size just right — if you will be able to cut an 8-inch (20-cm) square from the spread-out chocolate, you're in fine shape. Repeat with the remaining acetate sheets and chocolate.

2. The sheets of chocolate need to set just enough for you to score an 8-inch square in each with the point of a knife and then to score eight 2 x 4-inch (5 x 10-cm) rectangles within the square. You can either leave the chocolate on the counter until it sets just enough to hold the image of the knife's point — a condition that, depending on the temperature in your kitchen, could take from a couple of minutes to half an hour — or you can slide the acetate sheets onto baking sheets and refrigerate them until they reach the just-set point. If you opt for refrigeration, check the sheets after a minute or two. Once the sheets are scored, they should be stacked one on top of the other (still on acetate) and kept in the refrigerator until they are completely firm.

3. When the chocolate sheets are set, use a long slender knife to cut along the score lines; you will have 24 chocolate rectangles. If the rectangles are not perfectly shiny or if they have a slightly marbled look, don't be concerned. You can save the prettiest rectangles for the tops of the cakes — or you can just dust the top pieces of chocolate with cocoa powder. Whatever the look, the taste will be perfect. (*Once cut, the rectangles can be carefully layered between parchment, packed in an airtight tin, and kept refrigerated or at cool room temperature for up to 3 days.*)

TO ASSEMBLE

- **Unsweetened cocoa powder for dusting (optional)**

1. Working with a serrated knife, cut the praline-covered dacquoise into eight 2 x 4-inch (5 x 10-cm) rectangles. Place a piece of dacquoise in the center of each of eight dessert plates. Remove the milk chocolate rectangles from the refrigerator and, if necessary, turn them over so their shiny sides are up.

2. Fit a medium pastry bag with a plain ¼-inch (7-mm) tip and fill the bag with the ganache. Pipe a zigzag of ganache, leaving a little space between each zig and zag, over each of the 8 dacquoise rectangles. Pipe another

Makes 8 servings

zigzag of ganache over 8 of the milk chocolate rectangles, then top with another chocolate rectangle, shiny side up. Place the ganache sandwiches on top of the dacquoise pieces.

3. To finish, put a scoop or quenelle of the chocolate whipped cream on top of each cake and top with another chocolate rectangle, shiny side up. Dust with cocoa powder, if desired. If you've made the chocolate sauce, drizzle a little around each plate.

Note: You want the acetate sheets to be large enough to accommodate a 9- or 10-inch (24- or 26-cm) square of chocolate, but not so large that they'll be unwieldy. In the end, you'll only need 8-inch squares of chocolate, but it's better not to have to fuss about the size when you're working with the tempered chocolate.

CHOCOLATE COOKIES

SIMPLE AND SOPHISTICATED

These days, it's not unusual to find the all-American all-time favorite bar cookie, the brownie, on restaurant menus and pastry shop shelves in Paris. Along with pecan pie and carrot cake, the brownie — referred to as *"le brownie,"* to the horror of l'Académie Française — has found its way into the hearts of sweets-loving Parisians and, not surprisingly, into their kids' backpacks. And just as is true in the brownie's native land, in Paris, brownies can be insipid, indifferent, or sublime. Here is a prime example of brownies of the sublime variety. For starters, they are made with excellent bittersweet chocolate and an abundance of butter, a combination guaranteed to make them delectable. Then they're generously studded with nuts and baked only until they are just set; the center of each brownie remains moist — very moist.

■ So that the flavor of the nuts really stands out, I toast them and cut them into big pieces. And while I often use walnuts, the traditional nut for this bar cookie, I am just as likely to make brownies with pecans. I like the way the pecans' sweetness blends with the chocolate. ■ PH

- 5 ounces (145 grams) bittersweet chocolate, preferably Valrhona Caraïbe, finely chopped
- 2¼ sticks (9 ounces; 260 grams) unsalted butter, at room temperature
- 4 large eggs, at room temperature, lightly beaten
- 1¼ cups (250 grams) sugar
- 1 cup (140 grams) all-purpose flour
- 1¼ cups (5 ounces; 145 grams) pecans or walnuts, lightly toasted (see page 275) and very coarsely chopped (keep the pieces large)

1. Center a rack in the oven and preheat the oven to 350°F (180°C). Butter a 9 x 12-inch (24 x 30-cm) baking pan, fit the bottom with a piece of parchment paper, butter the paper, and then dust the inside of the pan with flour; tap out the excess and set the pan aside.

Makes 18 brownies

KEEPING: The brownies can be wrapped airtight and kept at room temperature for 2 days or frozen for up to 1 month.

2. Melt the chocolate in a bowl over — not touching — simmering water or in the microwave oven. Remove the chocolate from the heat and leave it on the counter to cool slightly. The chocolate should be warm to the touch (no more than 114°F [45°C], as measured on an instant-read thermometer) when you mix it with the other ingredients.

3. Working in a bowl with a flexible rubber spatula (or in a mixer fitted with the paddle attachment), beat the butter until it is smooth and creamy but not airy. Stir in the chocolate. Gradually add the eggs, then add the sugar, followed by the flour and nuts, stirring only until each ingredient is incorporated. (If the mixture separates when you add the eggs, use a whisk to blend the batter and continue with the whisk when you add the sugar; go back to the spatula or paddle for the flour and nuts.) This is not a batter to be beaten or aerated.

4. Scrape the batter into the pan and smooth the top with a spatula. Bake for 19 to 22 minutes; at this point, the top of the cake will be dry, but a knife inserted in the center will come out wet. Transfer the pan to a cooling rack and allow the brownies to cool for 20 to 30 minutes.

5. Run a blunt knife around the edges of the pan and unmold the brownies; remove the parchment paper and turn the brownies over to cool to room temperature right side up. When you are ready to serve, cut the brownies into 18 pieces.

VIENNESE
CHOCOLATE
SABLÉS

Soft and crumbly, buttery and chocolaty, these are the cookies of old-fashioned Austrian bakeries, the sweets you find tucked among the cherry-topped swirl and sandwich cookies when you buy an assortment. These are easy to make — the dough is mixed by hand and then piped out in the characteristic W shape — and easy to pair with coffee, tea, or ice cream desserts. The recipe makes a large batch, but the cookies are good keepers: Packed in a tin, they'll be fine for a week.

■ I learned to make these at the source — the famous Wittamer pastry shop in Vienna. But at Wittamer, these classic cookies were never made in chocolate, although they lend themselves so naturally to this flavor. The light chocolate taste that you get by using cocoa is ideal coupled with the melt-on-your-tongue texture that you get from lots of butter and confectioners' sugar. ■ PH

- 1¾ cups plus 1½ tablespoons (260 grams) all-purpose flour
- 5 tablespoons (30 grams) Dutch-processed cocoa powder, preferably Valrhona
- 2 sticks plus 1½ tablespoons (8¾ ounces; 250 grams) unsalted butter, at room temperature
- ¾ cup plus 2 tablespoons (100 grams) confectioners' sugar, sifted
- Pinch of salt
- 3 tablespoons lightly beaten egg whites (lightly beat 2 large egg whites, then measure out 3 tablespoons)
- Confectioners' sugar for dusting (optional)

1. Position the racks to divide the oven into thirds and preheat the oven to 350°F (180°C). Line two baking sheets with parchment paper and set aside. Fit a pastry bag with a medium-sized open star tip and keep it close at hand.

(The tip should be crenellated, but its piping hole should be open and somewhat straight, rather than curved and tightly rounded.)

2. Whisk together the flour and cocoa and keep close at hand. In a large bowl, beat the butter with a whisk until it is light and creamy — for the recipe to be successful, the butter must be very soft. Whisk in the sugar and salt, then stir in the egg whites. Don't be concerned when the mixture separates; it will come together when you add the dry ingredients. Gradually add the flour-cocoa and blend only until it is incorporated — you don't want to work the mixture too much once the flour is added, a light touch is what will give these cookies their characteristic crumbliness.

3. Because the dough is thick and somewhat heavy, it's best to work with it in batches. Spoon about one-third of the dough into the pastry bag. Pipe the dough into W-shaped cookies, each about 2 inches (5 cm) long and 1¼ inches (3 cm) wide, 1 inch apart onto the prepared baking sheets. (In reality, the W is closer to the letter's name than its look — it's best to pipe two attached Us, so that you have a kind of wave. But don't worry too much about this — the cookies will taste fine no matter the shape.)

4. Bake the cookies for 10 to 12 minutes — no more — or until they are set but neither browned nor hard. Using a wide metal spatula, transfer the cookies to a rack to cool to room temperature. Repeat with the remaining dough, making sure that you don't put the to-be-baked cookies on hot baking sheets. Before serving, you can dust the cookies with confectioners' sugar.

Makes about 65 cookies

KEEPING: The cookies will keep in a tightly covered tin at room temperature for almost a week. They can be wrapped airtight and frozen for up to a month; however, if you're going to freeze them, it's best not to dust them with confectioners' sugar.

Although these will taste rich and sophisticated and will be as delicate as fussily made petits fours, they're really just icebox cookies — the best ones ever. Because they're rolled in sugar before they're cut and baked, they have sparkly edges and a little crunch, a nice match to their crumbly texture. To get that just-right texture, take care not to mix the dough too much once you've added the flour.

■ Rolling the dough in sugar is not meant to add sweetness to the cookies, but rather to make the edges crisp. If you want to make the edges even crisper and to make their texture even more noticeable, try rolling the cookies in crystallized, or dazzle, sugar. ■ PH

- 2¾ cups (385 grams) all-purpose flour
- ⅓ cup (35 grams) Dutch-processed cocoa powder, preferably Valrhona
- Pinch of cinnamon
- Pinch of salt
- 2½ sticks (10 ounces; 285 grams) unsalted butter, at room temperature
- ½ cup plus 2 tablespoons (125 grams) sugar
- ¼ teaspoon pure vanilla extract
- 1 large egg yolk
- Sugar for coating

1. Sift the flour, cocoa powder, cinnamon, and salt together and keep close at hand. Place the butter in a mixer fitted with the paddle attachment and beat on medium speed to soften it. Gradually add the sugar and vanilla and continue to beat, scraping down the sides of the bowl as needed, until the mixture is smooth and creamy but not airy. Reduce the mixer speed to low and add the flour mixture, blending only until the ingredients are just combined — no more. Alternatively, you can remove the bowl from the mixer and stir the flour into the dough with a rubber spatula. The point is to mix the dough as gently and as little as possible — this light touch is what

will give the cookies their characteristic crumbly texture. As soon as the last of the flour is no longer visible, divide the dough in half, shape each half into a ball, wrap the balls in plastic, and chill for 30 minutes.

2. Working on a smooth surface, form each piece of dough into a log that's about 1½ inches (4 cm) thick and 7½ inches (19 cm) long. (Aim to get the thickness right, and the length will be fine.) To get a solid log, one without that commonly found hole in the center, use the heel of your hand to gently flatten the dough, then flatten the dough lightly each time you fold it over on itself to make the log. Assured that the log is solid, you can roll it gently under your palms to smooth it out. Wrap the logs in plastic and chill for 1 to 2 hours. (*The dough can be made ahead, wrapped airtight, and stored in the freezer for up to 1 month.*)

3. Position the racks to divide the oven into thirds and preheat the oven to 350°F (180°C). Line two baking sheets with parchment paper and set them aside.

4. In a small bowl, whisk the egg yolk until it is smooth and liquid enough to use as a glaze; keep it close at hand. Spread some sugar out on a piece of waxed paper.

5. Remove the logs of dough from the refrigerator, unwrap them, and brush them very lightly with a small amount of the egg yolk. Roll the logs in the sugar, pressing gently on the sugar to get it to stick if necessary. Then, using a sharp slender knife, slice each log into cookies ½ inch (1.5 cm) thick. Arrange the cookies on the baking sheets, leaving about an inch of space between each one, and bake for 15 to 18 minutes, rotating the pans front to back and top to bottom at the midway mark, until the cookies are just firm to the touch. Transfer the cookies to racks to cool to room temperature.

Makes about 30 cookies

KEEPING: The unbaked logs of dough can be frozen for up to 1 month, but once they're rolled in the sugar, they're unsuitable for freezing, because the sugar will melt. Once the cookies are baked, they can be kept in an airtight tin at room temperature for 3 to 5 days.

ablé means sandy in French and while the word doesn't always seem so attractive when it's used to describe food, it's a high compliment when applied to pastry dough (think of *pâte sablée*, meltingly tender French tart dough) and cookies. When a cookie is *sablé*, it's soft, tender, and crumbly, and, like rich shortbread, a close relative, it will melt delectably on your tongue. The dough for these slice-and-bake cookies is, indeed, *sablé*, but the cookie itself has some crunch — and ample depth of flavor — thanks to the addition of lots of very well toasted hazelnuts and a top and bottom layer of sweet tart dough. The sweet pastry crust gives the cookies another texture, another bit of butteryness, and an other-than-expected shape. Because the cookie and pastry doughs bake so differently (it's a function of the butter), you get cookies that are tubby around the middle. These sablés are slim and straight at the extremities, pot-bellied in the center, and appealing all around.

- 2 cups (300 grams) all-purpose flour
- ¼ cup (25 grams) Dutch-processed cocoa powder, preferably Valrhona
- 2 sticks plus 1½ tablespoons (8¾ ounces; 250 grams) unsalted butter, at room temperature
- 1 cup (100 grams) confectioners' sugar, sifted
- Pinch of salt
- 2 large eggs, at room temperature
- 1 cup (140 grams) hazelnuts, toasted, skinned (see page 273), and halved or quartered
- ½ recipe Sweet Tart Dough (page 235), chilled and ready to roll

1. Sift together the flour and cocoa powder and set aside for the moment. Working in a mixer fitted with the paddle attachment, beat the butter until it is soft and smooth. Add the sugar, followed by the salt, and continue to beat, scraping the bowl as needed, for about 3 minutes, or until the mixture is light, pale, and creamy. Add 1 of the eggs and beat to incorporate. At this

point, the mixture should be light and fluffy. Set the mixer speed to low, add the sifted dry ingredients, and mix just until they disappear into the dough — take care not to overwork the dough. Stir in the toasted hazelnuts.

2. Turn the dough out onto a smooth work surface — marble is ideal — and shape it into a 6 x 7-inch (15 x 18-cm) rectangle that's 1 inch (2.5 cm) high. Put the chocolate dough in the refrigerator while you work on the tart dough. (*The dough can be made ahead, wrapped airtight, and kept refrigerated for 2 days or frozen for a month.*)

3. Beat the remaining egg with 1 teaspoon cold water and keep this egg wash close at hand. Also have two sheets of parchment paper and a baking sheet nearby.

4. Working on a lightly floured work surface, roll each disk of tart dough into a rectangle that's a scant ¼ inch (7 mm) thick (the thickness is important here) and slightly larger than 6 x 7 inches (15 x 18 cm). Put one piece of the rolled-out dough on one sheet of parchment paper and brush the surface with egg wash, the glue that will keep these multilayer cookies together. Center the chocolate dough on the tart dough; then, using a sharp knife, cut away the excess tart dough. Brush the top of the chocolate dough with egg wash and place the second sheet of tart dough over the cookie dough. Top this setup with the second piece of parchment paper, flip everything over, and remove the top sheet of parchment. Trim the excess tart dough so that it's even with the other two layers. Slide the package (still sitting on the parchment paper) onto a baking sheet, cover it well, and chill for at least 4 hours. (*Wrapped airtight, the package can be frozen for a month; defrost in the refrigerator before baking.*)

5. Position the racks to divide the oven into thirds and preheat the oven to 325°F (165°C). Have another parchment-lined baking sheet at the ready.

6. Using a sharp thin-bladed knife and working from one 7-inch (18-cm) side of the dough package to the other, cut 6 even strips of dough, then cut each strip into ¼-inch- (7-mm-) wide cookies. Arrange the cookies on the two baking sheets, leaving a ½ inch (1.5 cm) or so of space between each cookie.

7. Slide the baking sheets into the oven and bake for 20 to 24 minutes, or until the cookies are firm and the tart dough is lightly browned; rotate the baking sheets front to back and top to bottom at the 10-minute mark. Gently transfer the cookies to racks to cool. Repeat with the remaining cookies, making sure to cool the baking sheets between batches.

Makes about 150 cookies

KEEPING: The dough can be made ahead, wrapped airtight, and kept refrigerated for 2 days or frozen for 1 month. The baked cookies can be packed in an airtight tin and kept for 3 to 4 days at room temperature.

More like small cakes than large cookies, these sweets were named for their rich ingredients — lots of butter and almonds — and the rich clients who ate them. The cookies were first made by a Parisian pastry chef whose shop was near the Bourse, France's stock exchange, and whose habitués were financiers. In fact, the originals were baked in small rectangular pans so that their shape would resemble gold ingots. Today, the ingredients remain rich, but financiers can be made in rectangular or boat-shaped molds and, as you'd expect, enjoyed by anyone, rich or not so rich, lucky enough to have them at arm's reach.

Financiers were traditionally made with *beurre noisette*, butter cooked until it turns brown and smells like hazelnuts, but this version hews to tradition only in its richness; its deep chocolate flavor breaks tradition and borders on rebellion. These are moist, dark, and fudgy and would be good with any chocolate-friendly ice cream.

■ I got this recipe from a Belgian friend who lives in Provence. We had had a long, wonderful Pentecost lunch at her house and because the meal had been so generous, I refused dessert — until I saw these chocolate financiers. It was the first time I'd encountered the cookie made with chocolate, and I gave in. Actually, I gave in several times over. ■ PH

- 3½ ounces (100 grams) bittersweet chocolate, preferably Valrhona Caraïbe, finely chopped
- 3 large eggs, at room temperature
- ½ cup plus 1 tablespoon (125 grams) sugar
- 1 cup (3½ ounces; 100 grams) finely ground almond powder (see page 265) or finely ground blanched almonds (see page 265)
- 1 stick plus 1 tablespoon (4½ ounces; 125 grams) unsalted butter, at room temperature
- ⅓ cup plus 2 tablespoons (100 grams) tepid water
- ⅓ cup plus 2 tablespoons (50 grams) all-purpose flour, sifted

1. Center a rack in the oven and preheat the oven to 350°F (180°C). Butter and flour about 20 rectangular or boat-shaped financier molds. (Financier molds come in many sizes; this recipe was tested with molds that hold about 3 tablespoons of water. If your molds are a different size, you'll have to make small adjustments in the baking time. If you don't have enough molds, make the financiers in batches; just be sure to cool the molds, then butter and flour them before you bake the second batch.) Set the molds aside on a jelly-roll pan.

2. Melt the chocolate in a bowl over — not touching — simmering water or in the microwave oven. Remove the chocolate from the heat and leave it on the counter to cool slightly. It should be just warm to the touch when you're ready to use it.

3. Working in a mixer fitted with the whisk attachment, whip the eggs, sugar, and almond powder together on medium-high speed until the mixture is pale. Scrape down the sides of the bowl as necessary while you're working. Reduce the speed to medium, add the butter in 4 or 5 chunks, and beat just until it is incorporated. The mixture may separate — don't be concerned. On low speed, add the chocolate and mix to blend. Then add the water, increase the mixer speed to medium, and beat until the mixture is homogenous. Remove the bowl from the mixer and, using a large rubber spatula, fold in the flour. (*The batter can be made ahead, covered airtight, and kept in the refrigerator for 2 to 3 days before baking.*)

4. Spoon enough batter into the molds to almost fill them and bake the financiers for 15 to 18 minutes, or until they feel springy to the touch and a knife inserted into the center of the cookies comes out clean. Transfer the pans to a rack and cool for about 3 minutes, then run a small blunt knife around the edges and unmold the cookies. Turn the cookies upright and cool them to room temperature.

Makes about 20 cookies

KEEPING: The batter can be kept covered in the refrigerator for up to 3 days. Once the cookies are baked, they can be wrapped airtight in plastic and kept at room temperature for 2 days or frozen for up to 1 month.

E ven if you come to this recipe already a committed florentine fan, this version will spoil you for all others — it is the gold standard for this cookie. What makes a florentine a florentine is its shiny, slightly chewy, honey-flavored candy topping, which always includes sliced almonds, almost always includes candied orange zest, and sometimes includes candied cherries. Then there are the options: a sugar cookie base and a dipped or spread chocolate coating.

In this florentine, the candy topping is made, following tradition, with butter and honey, cooked to a deep caramel color, and then mixed with an abundance of sliced almonds and a generous quantity of the finest candied orange zest you can find, preferably homemade. Some pastry chefs make their florentines using only this candy mixture, but here the almonds and zest are spread over a buttery layer of cookieish sweet tart pastry. The layer is thin, but it adds crunch to the topping. Once baked and cooled, the cookies are cut into squares and dipped diagonally to the midway mark in dark chocolate. Arranged on a plate, the cookies look oddly like polished mosaics or Byzantine jewels, but it's their taste and texture that are most notable: Because the honey and orange are tangy, the tart dough sweet, and the chocolate rich and fruity, these little cookies are delicate and bold, sweet and tart, crisp and tender. And they are fun to make — no matter how experienced you are in the kitchen, you're likely to be puffed with pride when you pull these from the oven.

A note on the almonds: The almonds are added to the candy topping mixture once the mixture has come up to temperature. In order not to lower the topping's temperature and make it difficult to spread, make sure the almonds are at room temperature. To be on the safe side, you can do what Pierre does: Put the almonds on a baking sheet and warm them for a couple minutes in the oven before stirring them into the topping.

■ If you like the flavor of honey and want to make that flavor stronger in these cookies, choose a full-bodied honey. My favorite is chestnut honey, but pine honey is also very good in this recipe. ■ PH

THE COOKIES

- ½ recipe Sweet Tart Dough (page 235), chilled and ready to roll
- ½ cup (125 grams) heavy cream
- Zest of 1 orange (removed with a peeler or zester), finely chopped
- 1 cup plus 1 tablespoon (220 grams) sugar
- ½ cup (125 grams) water
- 2 teaspoons light corn syrup
- 1 stick (4 ounces; 115 grams) unsalted butter, cut into 8 pieces
- ⅓ cup (100 grams) honey
- 10½ ounces (about 3 cups; 300 grams) sliced blanched almonds, at room temperature or warmed
- 3½ ounces (about ½ cup; 100 grams) candied orange peel, preferably homemade (page 257), drained and patted dry if necessary, cut into ¼-inch (7-mm) cubes

1. Have a nonstick 11½ x 16½-inch (29 x 41-cm) jelly-roll pan at the ready, or line a jelly-roll pan with a Silpat or other silicone baking mat. (For this recipe, there is no substitute for nonstick — parchment won't work — and you'll need the raised sides that a jelly-roll pan provides.) Working on a well-floured surface, roll the tart dough into a rectangle that's about ⅛ inch (4 mm) thick and the size of your jelly-roll pan. (This is a soft dough and you're rolling out a large piece of it, so you might find it easier to roll the dough between sheets of plastic wrap and, if the dough gets too soft, to chill it midroll.) Roll the dough up around your rolling pin, then unroll it into the pan. Fit the dough into the pan, taking care not to stretch it, then trim it if necessary so that it just covers the bottom of the pan. (If the dough tears, just patch the pieces together — the candy topping will cover everything.) Prick the dough all over with the tines of a fork, then slide the pan into the refrigerator and chill the dough for at least 30 minutes.

2. Center a rack in the oven and preheat the oven to 350°F (180°C).

3. Bake the chilled cookie base for 10 to 12 minutes, or until it is golden brown. Keep an eye on the dough and if, after 4 or 5 minutes, it looks as if it is browning unevenly, rotate the pan. As soon as the base is baked, transfer the jelly-roll pan to a cooling rack and increase the oven temperature to 425°F (220°C).

4. While the dough is in the oven (first choice), or as soon as it comes out, start making the candy topping. Put the cream and chopped orange zest (not the

candied peel) in a small saucepan and bring to the boil; turn off the heat as soon as it boils.

5. Meanwhile, working in a heavy-bottomed medium saucepan over medium heat, stir the sugar, water, and corn syrup together using a wooden spoon or spatula. Cook until the sugar melts and the mixture boils, then turns a deep caramel color. You don't want to burn the sugar, but you do want to cook it to a rich mahogany color — you can test the color of the caramel by putting a drop of it on a white plate. Standing away from the pan, stir in the butter in 2 to 3 additions, followed by the cream mixture and the honey. The mixture will sputter and bubble furiously — which is why you need to stand away — but it will calm down as the ingredients are incorporated. Stirring constantly, cook this mixture until it reaches 257°F (125°C), as measured on a candy or instant-read thermometer (a process that might, depending on the heat under the pan, take as long as 10 minutes). As soon as you hit the right temperature, pull the pan from the heat and stir in the sliced almonds and candied peel.

6. Working quickly, slide the jelly-roll pan with the cookie base into the hot oven to warm the base for just 1 minute if necessary. Transfer the pan to a cooling rack or counter and, working with an offset metal spatula or wooden spoon and alacrity, spread the hot candy mixture evenly over the warm cookie dough. Spread the candy as evenly as you can, but don't worry too much about getting it just so or making certain it reaches the sides and corners of the pan — it will even itself out somewhat in the oven. Slide the pan into the oven and bake for 4 to 6 minutes, or until the candy bubbles and browns — don't walk away from the kitchen during this step: You want the candy to turn molten and to spread across the cookie base, but you don't want it to burn, so keep an eye on it. It may need a minute more or less — you'll know by sight and smell: It should look appealingly brown and smell richly of cooked (but not burnt) caramel and nuts. Pull the pan from the oven and allow it to cool to room temperature on a cooling rack.

7. When you are ready to unmold the florentines, have two pieces of parchment paper and another jelly-roll pan, a baking sheet, or a large cutting board at hand. Carefully, so as not to mar the surface of your nonstick jelly-roll pan, run a blunt knife around the edges of the pan to loosen the candy's grip on the pan's rim. Lay a piece of parchment over the florentines, put the other pan (or cutting board) flat side down against the cookies, and flip the whole setup over so that the florentines drop out of the baking pan. (Remove the Silpat, if you used one.) Cover the cookie base with the second sheet of parchment, place the flat side of the jelly-roll pan (the one you used to bake

the cookies) over the paper, and flip the setup again so that the florentines are candy side up. Gently slide the florentines onto a cutting board. Using a long chef's knife, trim away any burnt edges if necessary, then cut the cookies into 1½-inch (4-cm) squares.

THE CHOCOLATE DIP

- **11 ounces (310 grams) bittersweet chocolate, preferably Valrhona Caraïbe, tempered (see page 260)**

Makes about 60 cookies

KEEPING: Packed in an airtight tin and kept away from heat and humidity, florentines will keep for up to 5 days.

Place a sheet of acetate (see page 265), parchment, or waxed paper on the counter. Dip one corner of each cookie into the chocolate so that the chocolate just reaches the cookie's midpoint and creates a chocolate triangle. Put the dipped cookie on the acetate or paper and dip the rest of the batch. (You can put the cookies in the refrigerator for a few minutes to set the chocolate.) When the chocolate is set, the cookies are ready to serve or pack for storage.

CHOCOLATE AND
LEMON MADELEINES

Not the madeleines that brought Proust's childhood back to him, but these are delicious enough to create memories on their own. These have a madeleine's characteristic light crust and tender crumb, but they're chocolate, much more deeply chocolate than you'd imagine possible given the tiny bit of cocoa powder that's creating the flavor. In fact, these are chocolaty enough to remind you of devil's food.

■ An overnight rest in the refrigerator is what gives these madeleines their characteristic bump in the center. If you're in a hurry, chill them for an hour — you won't get as pronounced a bump, but the cookies will bake better for the chill. ■ PH

- ½ cup plus 1 tablespoon (70 grams) all-purpose flour
- 3½ tablespoons Dutch-processed cocoa powder, preferably Valrhona
- ½ teaspoon double-acting baking powder
- ⅓ cup plus 2 tablespoons (90 grams) sugar
- Pinch of salt
- Grated zest of ¼ lemon
- 2 large eggs, at room temperature
- 6½ tablespoons (3¼ ounces; 100 grams) unsalted butter, at room temperature

1. Sift together the flour, cocoa, and baking powder and set aside. Put the sugar, salt, and lemon zest in a medium bowl and rub everything together with your fingertips until the sugar is moist, grainy, and very aromatic.

2. Using a whisk, beat the eggs into the lemon-sugar until the mixture is blended. Squish the butter through your fingers or smear it under the heel of your hand to create what is called a *pomade* and add it to the bowl. Still working with the whisk, beat in the butter just to get it evenly distributed. Gently whisk in the sifted flour mixture, stirring only until the flour is incor-

porated and the mixture is smooth. Press a piece of plastic wrap against the surface of the batter and chill it overnight before baking. The overnight rest helps the cookies develop the characteristic bump on their backs; if you don't have time for an overnight rest, try to give the batter at least an hour in the refrigerator.

3. When you are ready to bake the cookies, center a rack in the oven and preheat the oven to 425°F (220°C). Butter a 12-mold madeleine pan, then dust the molds with flour, tapping out the excess. (Even if you have a nonstick madeleine pan, it's a good idea to butter and flour the molds.)

4. Divide the batter evenly among the madeleine molds. Don't worry about flattening the batter — the heat will do that. Place the pan in the oven, insert a wooden spoon in the door to keep it slightly ajar, and immediately turn the oven temperature down to 350°F (180°C). Bake the cookies for 13 to 15 minutes, or until they are domed and spring back when pressed lightly. Unmold the cookies onto a work surface — you may have to rap the madeleine pan against the counter to release the cookies — then transfer them to a rack to cool to room temperature.

Makes 12 cookies

KEEPING: Madeleines can be kept at room temperature in an airtight tin for about 2 days or frozen for up to 2 weeks, but don't toss them away if they get a little stale — that's when they're best for Proustian dipping.

LACY COFFEE-COCOA NOUGATINE COOKIES

Nougatine is really more a nut candy than a cookie, more a component of a grand dessert than a dessert itself. That said, make cookie-sized nougatines, offer them with coffee (or hot chocolate or even milk), and rest assured no one will feel deprived of dessert. The dough is based on a caramel made with butter, sugar, and milk, but it's the addition of cocoa powder and small pieces of crushed coffee beans (regular or decaf) that turns the nougatine as dark as midnight. It's also what gives the crackly candy its extraordinary — and completely unexpected — flavor. With this mixture, you can make flat cookies or curved tuiles, the cookies named for their resemblance to French roof tiles. And you can use the cookies, flat, curved, or broken into shards, as a topping for the over-the-top Grand Chocolate Tart (page 109). You can even crush some perfectly good cookies and sprinkle them over ice cream — it's probably what Ben & Jerry would do if they were French.

A note on the coffee beans: They need to be crushed but not pulverized, so it's best either to put them in a food processor fitted with the metal blade and pulse on and off until you've got little pieces or, if you're feeling energetic or looking to blow off a little steam, to wrap the beans in a kitchen towel, place the packet on a cutting board, and bash the beans with the end of a French rolling pin (the kind without handles) or the bottom of a heavy pan. (If you use a food processor, consider chopping the almonds in the processor, then turning them onto a baking sheet to toast, and using the processor for the coffee beans — it will save you a little washup time.)

■ When I started making this kind of nougatine, I used small pieces of crushed cacao beans in the dough. Since cacao beans, the beans used to make chocolate, are only readily available to professionals, I had to search for a substitute that would bring the same intensity of flavor to the cookie and provide an equivalent crunch. Crushed coffee beans combined with cocoa powder are the perfect solution. Today, I don't think of the coffee-cocoa concoction as a substitute but rather as its own good creation. ■ PH

- ⅓ cup (70 grams) sugar
- 4½ tablespoons (2¼ ounces; 65 grams) unsalted butter, cut into 4 pieces
- 1½ tablespoons whole milk
- 1½ tablespoons light corn syrup
- 1½ tablespoons Dutch-processed cocoa powder, preferably Valrhona, sifted
- ½ cup (2¼ ounces; 70 grams) blanched almonds, finely chopped, lightly toasted (see page 275) and still warm
- 1 to 2 tablespoons (according to your taste) coffee beans, finely crushed (see headnote above)

1. Put the sugar, butter, milk, and corn syrup in a heavy-bottomed medium saucepan. Place the pan over medium heat and cook, stirring the ingredients gently with a wooden spatula or spoon, until the temperature reaches 223°F (106°C), as measured on a candy or instant-read thermometer. Stir in the sifted cocoa powder, the warm nuts, and the crushed coffee beans, and pull the pan from the heat.

2. Pour the nougatine into a heatproof bowl and allow it to cool. Press a piece of plastic wrap against the surface to make an airtight seal and chill the dough until it is completely cold. (*The dough can be covered tightly and kept in the refrigerator for up to 4 days or frozen for up to 1 month.*)

3. When you are ready to bake, center a rack in the oven and preheat the oven to 350°F (180°C). Have one or two nonstick baking sheets at the ready. (Only nonstick baking sheets will work for this recipe.)

4. Scoop out a slightly rounded half-teaspoonful of dough for each cookie, mold it into a ball between your palms and place on a baking sheet; make certain to leave about 3 inches (7.5 cm) of spread-space between the balls. Using the heel of your hand, press the balls into disks — there's no need to overdo it, as the dough will melt under the oven's heat, so the balls only need a little flattening at the start. Slide the baking sheet into the oven and bake the cookies for 5 to 7 minutes, or until the nougatine is bubbly and crinkly (but not burnt).

5. Pull the baking sheet from the oven and let the cookies rest on the sheet for a minute or so before removing them to a countertop or piece of parchment paper. Don't put the cookies on a cooling rack — they'll stick. (The hot cookies are really hot and they're delicate — the easiest way to get them from the baking sheet to their cooling place is to lift them off the sheet with a plastic dough scraper.) If you want to shape the cookies into curved tuiles, place them over a rolling pin or wine bottle. Repeat with the remaining dough, making sure to put the chilled dough on a cool baking sheet. Continue baking cookies one sheet at a time until you have as many cookies as you want. (*Remember, unused batter can be chilled or frozen.*)

Makes about 65 cookies

KEEPING: Although the dough for nougatines can be chilled for up to 4 days or frozen for as long as a month, the cookies themselves, no matter their shape or the use you put them to, should be eaten the day they're made — preferably shortly after they're made. This is especially true if you live in a humid environment — humidity will make the crispy nougatine go wobbly.

f you're like most of us, this is the first cookie you pick up from a petit four plate. It's a thin cookie that's rolled around itself to form a crunchy tube, or cigarette, and it's fun and elegant at the same time. This cigarette is chocolate flavored and can be served au naturel, solo, as part of a cookie assortment or as the finishing touch to a bowl of ice cream. If you want to dress the cookies up a bit, you can dip their ends in tempered chocolate. And if you want to go just a bit further, fill the cigarettes with ganache.

■ My favorite way to serve these cookies is to fill them with a mixture of Bittersweet Chocolate Cream Ganache (page 215) and Nutella. ■ PH

- ½ cup (70 grams) all-purpose flour
- 5 tablespoons (30 grams) Dutch-processed cocoa powder, preferably Valrhona
- 7 tablespoons (3½ ounces; 100 grams) unsalted butter, at room temperature
- ¾ cup plus 2 tablespoons (100 grams) confectioners' sugar, sifted
- 3 large egg whites, at room temperature, stirred just to break them up

1. The easiest way to bake and shape these cookies is to have all your tools out and ready. For starters, you'll need a very thin template. With a little handi-work you can construct one that's just right using two plastic tops from ice cream, yogurt, or cottage cheese containers. Cut out a 3¼-inch (8-cm) circle from the center of each top and remove the sides being sure to leave at least a ½-inch (1.5-cm) border all around the circle. Now tape the two tops together. Alternatively, you can cut a template from a piece of heavy card-board or a thick file folder. After you've made the template, assemble a non-stick baking sheet (only nonstick will do here), an offset icing spatula (to spread the batter out evenly), a plastic dough scraper (to lift the baked cook-ies off the baking sheet), and a wooden spoon — you'll wrap the cookies around the handle to turn them into cigarettes; set aside.

2. Center a rack in the oven and preheat the oven to 325°F (165°C).

3. Sift the flour and cocoa powder together and set the mixture aside for the moment.

4. Working in a medium bowl with a whisk or a sturdy rubber spatula, work the butter and confectioners' sugar together until the butter is smooth and creamy and the sugar is well blended into it. Stirring constantly, add the egg whites little by little. The mixture may separate as the whites go in, but it will smooth out as the dry ingredients are incorporated. When the whites are smoothed, add the flour and cocoa mixture, stirring only until the dry ingredients disappear. (*The batter can be made up to 3 days in advance and kept tightly covered in the refrigerator. If you want to make a small batch of cookies, just use as much batter as you need and keep the remainder in the refrigerator.*)

5. For each cookie, drop 1½ teaspoons of batter onto the baking sheet, leaving about 2 inches (5 cm) of space between each dollop. (You'll probably be able to put 9 cookies on a sheet.) To spread the batter, position the template flat against the baking sheet with a dollop of batter in the center of the circle and, using a small metal icing spatula (an offset spatula is best), spread the batter across the template, then lift off the template. Scrape whatever batter remains on the template back into the bowl and continue until you've shaped as many cookies as you can on the sheet. It's best to bake one sheet at a time, but you can fill additional sheets while one sheet bakes if you want.

6. Bake the cookies for 3 to 4 minutes, or until they are uniformly dull. If you touch the cookies lightly, the image of your fingerprint should remain. Pull the baking sheet from the oven and, working with one cookie at a time, lift a cookie off the baking sheet using the plastic dough scraper and turn the cookie upside down onto a countertop or sheet of parchment paper. Place the handle of the wooden spoon close to one edge of the cookie and roll the hot cookie up around the handle. As soon as you finish rolling the cookie into a cigarette, it should be firm enough for you to slide it off the handle and then shape the next cookie. If the last of the cookies cool too much to be shaped, slide the baking sheet back into the oven for a minute to soften the cookies. Cool the cookies on the counter or on a rack, and continue baking and shaping the rest of the batter. If you want to tip the cookies with chocolate or fill them with ganache, do so when they are completely cool. (The easiest way to fill the cookies is to put the ganache in a pastry bag and pipe the filling into the cigarettes.)

Makes about 40 cookies

KEEPING: The cookie batter can be made up to 3 days in advance and kept refrigerated. The baked cookies can be kept in an airtight tin at room temperature for 2 or 3 days, but they're really best the day they are made. This is especially true of filled cookies — ideally, you should fill the cookies shortly before you're going to serve them.

CHOCOLATE-COVERED CRUNCHY HAZELNUT COOKIES

These small but powerfully flavorful morsels pack a colossal triple crunch. The major crunch comes from an abundance of extra-large pieces of toasted hazelnuts, while the contrasting crunches come from the almost-meringue that constitutes the cookie part of the cookie and from the cookies' coating, a thin layer of slow-to-melt-in-your-mouth bittersweet chocolate. The batter for this cookie is nothing more than egg whites, sugar, and coffee flavoring, and you do nothing more to it than heat it and the nuts in a saucepan. After the batter cools, you cut it and bake it. It's remarkably simple and, in the end, just as remarkably alluring. Under heat, the batter bubbles around the nuts, forming a cocoon that keeps the nuts in a cluster, then sets and bakes to an airy crackle. Look at the cookies undipped, and you know immediately that they're light and delicate, but see them dipped, and it's anyone's guess what delights may be tucked within.

■ Dipping the cookies in chocolate increases their appeal. Not only does the chocolate coating add another flavor and texture, it emphasizes the cookies' original flavor and texture, intensifying both the coffee and hazelnut flavors and making the cookies' lightness and crunch even more apparent. ■ PH

- 1 tablespoon instant coffee granules
- 1 tablespoon boiling water
- 3 large egg whites, at room temperature
- 3⅔ cups (400 grams) confectioners' sugar, sifted
- 3⅓ cups (14 ounces; 400 grams) hazelnuts, toasted, skinned (see page 273), and coarsely chopped

1. Dissolve the instant coffee in the boiling water and set this "extract" aside to cool.

2. Set out a bowl that is large enough to hold all the ingredients; it should also fit over a large saucepan. Bring a few inches or so of water to a simmer in the saucepan (when the bowl is in place, the bottom of the bowl should not touch the water). Line half of a jelly-roll pan with aluminum foil — and keep the "tail" of the foil long so that it will be available for adjusting the size of the lining to match the amount of batter you have; keep this setup close at hand.

3. Put all of the ingredients in the bowl, stir them together with a heatproof spatula or a wooden spoon, and set the bowl over the pan of simmering water. Heat the batter, stirring regularly, until it reaches between 130° and 140°F (55° to 60°C), as measured on an instant-read thermometer. Pull the pan from the heat and pour the batter into the foil-lined pan. Crimp the foil, making a barrier with it, so that the batter is a scant 1 inch (2.5 cm) deep in the pan; you'll probably have a block of batter that is approximately 8 x 12 inches (20 x 30 cm). Allow the batter to cool to room temperature.

4. Position the racks to divide the oven into thirds and preheat the oven to 275°F (135°C). Line two baking sheets with parchment paper and set them aside.

5. Lift the block of batter out of the pan, peel away the foil, and put the block right side up on a cutting board. Cut the block into 1½-inch (4-cm) squares and arrange the pieces on the baking sheets, leaving about 2 inches (5 cm) between them. Slip the sheets into the oven and bake for 18 to 22 minutes, rotating the sheets top to bottom and front to back at the halfway point, until the cookies are golden, dry, and uniformly dull. In the oven, the squares of batter will bubble and spread irregularly — that's fine. Pull the sheets from the oven and transfer the cookies to a rack to cool to room temperature.

TO FINISH

Makes about 45 cookies

2 pounds (900 grams) chocolate, preferably Valrhona Caraïbe, tempered (see page 260)

KEEPING: Cookies that have not been chocolate-coated can be kept in an airtight container for up to 4 days; dipped cookies can be similarly kept, but they are really best eaten the day they are made.

Pour the chocolate into a container that will allow you to dip the cookies into the chocolate comfortably. Have a rack set over waxed paper close at hand, or place a Silpat or other silicone baking mat nearby. Working with one cookie at a time, balance each cookie on a fork, submerge the cookie in the chocolate, and then lift the cookie out, allowing the excess chocolate to drip back into the container; place the cookie on the rack or silicone mat. Put the cookies in the refrigerator and chill just until the chocolate is set, about 10 to 15 minutes.

I f, when you hear the word *macaroon,* you think of those heavy almond-paste macaroons found in groceries, or pyramidal macaroons based on coconut, you're not thinking of these. These are the classic French macaroons that are displayed like small jewels in the best *pâtisseries;* the macaroons whose merits connoisseurs argue with passion. Made with very finely ground almonds, the cookies are smooth and domed on top (defining characteristics), soft and chewy inside (another trait of perfection), and just a little ragged around the bottoms, where the cookies form a bumpy circlet that's referred to as "the foot" (the final giveaway that these are the real thing). To get that just-right soft and chewy texture, it's best to give the macaroons an overnight rest in the refrigerator, so plan ahead.

While there's no law that says you can't eat these plain, traditionally macaroons are sandwich cookies. Pierre's chocolate macaroons make remarkable sandwiches filled with Bittersweet Chocolate Cream Ganache and served as a petit four with coffee, or layered with aromatic Chocolate-Lavender Ice Cream and served as a frozen dessert. If you decide to fill the macaroons with the ice cream, you can play around with the size of the sandwiches — any size from pop-in-your-mouth to grab-with-two-hands is fun.

■ Egg whites are the key element in this recipe. Take care to beat them until they are only just firm and still shiny, and don't be concerned when, as you add the dry ingredients, they deflate — they're supposed to. Knocking some of the air out of the whites is what will give these macaroons their characteristic smooth top. Keep the whites too firm, and you'll end up with meringue. ■ PH

- 1⅓ cups (5 ounces; 140 grams) finely ground almond powder (see page 265) or blanched almonds
- 2 cups plus 2 tablespoons (250 grams) confectioners' sugar
- ¼ cup (25 grams) Dutch-processed cocoa powder, preferably Valrhona, plus more for dusting
- ½ cup (100 grams) egg whites (about 4 large egg whites; see step 3)

1. Line two large insulated baking sheets with parchment paper, or line two regular baking sheets and put each one on top of another baking sheet. Fit a large pastry bag with a plain ⅜-inch (1-cm) or ½-inch (1.5-cm) tip. Set these aside for the moment.

2. If you've got almond powder, just sift it with the confectioners' sugar and cocoa. If you're starting with almonds, place the almonds, sugar, and cocoa in the work bowl of a food processor fitted with the metal blade and process until the mixture is as fine as flour, at least 3 minutes. Stop after every minute to check your progress and to scrape down the sides of the bowl. This is not a quick on-and-off operation. Although the almonds may look as though they're pulverized after a minute or so, they won't be: The nuts really need 3 to 5 minutes to be ground to a powder or flour. When the almonds are ground, using a wooden spoon, press the mixture through a medium strainer.

3. For this recipe to succeed, you need ½ cup (100 grams) of egg whites, which means using 3 large egg whites plus part of a fourth white. The easiest way to get a portion of a white is to put the white into a cup, beat it lightly with a fork, and then measure out what you need. Once the eggs are measured, they need to be brought to room temperature so they can be beaten to their fullest volume. You can leave the whites on the counter until they reach room temperature, or you can put them into a microwave-safe bowl and place them in a microwave oven set on lowest power; heat the whites for about 10 seconds. Stir the whites and continue to heat them — still on lowest power — in 5-second spurts until they are about 75°F (23°C). If they're a little warmer, that's okay. To keep the eggs warm, run the mixer bowl under hot water. Dry the bowl well, pour the whites into the bowl, and fit the mixer with the whisk attachment.

4. Beat the egg whites at low to medium speed until they are white and foamy. Turn the speed up to high and whip them just until they are firm but still glossy and supple — when you lift the whisk, the whites should form a peak that droops just a little. Leave the whites in the mixer bowl or transfer them to a large bowl and, working with a rubber spatula, fold the dry ingredients gently into the whites in three or four additions. It will seem like a lot of dry ingredients to go into a relatively small amount of whites, but keep folding and you'll get everything in. Don't worry if the whites deflate and the batter looks a little runny — that's just what's supposed to happen. When all the dry ingredients are incorporated, the mixture will look like a cake batter; if you lift a little with your finger, it should form a gentle, quickly falling peak.

5. Spoon the batter into the pastry bag and pipe it out onto the prepared baking sheets (to keep each sheet of paper steady, "glue" it down by piping a bit of batter at each corner of the baking sheet): Pipe the batter into rounds about 1 inch (2.5 cm) in diameter, leaving about an inch (2.5 cm) between each round. (Because you're going to sandwich the baked cookies, try to keep the rounds the same size.) When you've piped out all the macaroons, lift each baking sheet with both hands and then bang it down on the counter. Don't be afraid — you need to get the air out of the batter. Set the baking sheets aside at room temperature for 15 minutes while you preheat the oven.

6. Center a rack in the oven and preheat the oven to 425°F (220°C).

7. You should bake these one pan at a time, so dust the tops of the macaroons on one pan with cocoa powder and slide one of the sheets into the oven. As soon as the baking sheet is in the oven, turn the temperature down to 350°F (180°C) and insert the handle of a wooden spoon into the oven to keep the door slightly ajar. Bake the macaroons for 10 to 12 minutes, or until they are smooth and just firm to the touch. Transfer the baking sheet to a cooling rack and turn the oven heat back up to 425°F (220°C).

   To remove the macaroons from the parchment — they should be removed as soon as they come from the oven — you will need to create moisture under the cookies. Carefully loosen the parchment at the four corners and, lifting the paper at one corner, pour a little hot water under the paper onto the baking sheet. The water may bubble and steam, so make sure your face and hands are out of the way. Move the parchment around or tilt the baking sheet so that the parchment is evenly dampened. Allow the macaroons to remain on the parchment, soaking up the moisture, for about 15 seconds, then peel the macaroons off the paper and place them on a cooling rack.

8. When the oven is at the right temperature, repeat with the second sheet of macaroons. Remove from the parchment as directed above and let cool.

TO FINISH

- **Bittersweet Chocolate Cream Ganache (page 215), cooled to a spreadable consistency, or Chocolate-Lavender Ice Cream (page 185)**

When the macaroons are cool, sandwich them with either ganache or ice cream.

For the ganache: For each sandwich, pipe a dollop of ganache about ½ inch (1.5 cm) across on the flat side of one cookie and top with another cookie, flat

Makes 24 to 30
sandwich cookies

KEEPING: Unsandwiched
macaroons can be kept in
an airtight tin at room
temperature for 3 days. Once
filled, macaroons with
ganache should be chilled and
served the next day; ice
cream–filled macaroons can
be frozen for up to 2 weeks.

side down, using it to spread the ganache so that it runs to the edge. Transfer the filled macaroons to a covered container and place them in the refrigerator to soften overnight before serving.

For the Chocolate-Lavender Ice Cream: Give the unfilled macaroons an overnight rest in the refrigerator to soften, then sandwich them with the ice cream the following morning. Ice cream–filled macaroons should, of course, be stored in the freezer. If they have been frozen solid, transfer them to the refrigerator to defrost for 15 minutes or so before serving.

CREAMY, CRUNCHY,

NUTTY, AND FRUIT-FILLED

CHOCOLATE TARTS

Beware this chocolate and raspberry tart — it's a gustatory seductress. It has a beckoning look, but it's the flavors and textures that get you. The ganache filling is warm, only just set, and almost like custard, soft and rich and silken and smooth. And it's studded with raspberries, a fruit that takes on a different character when heated. Baked, even just briefly as they are here, the berries have a gentle sweetness and an even more distinctive flavor, as though the warmth of the oven ripened them to perfection. The sweet almond crust that cradles the filling offers a little butteryness and a touch of crunch, a nice counterpoint to the creamy filling.

THE CRUST

- **1 fully baked 8¾-inch (22-cm) tart shell made from Sweet Tart Dough (page 235), cooled to room temperature**

Keep the cooled crust, with the tart ring still in place, on the parchment-lined baking sheet. (*The crust can be baked up to 8 hours ahead and kept at room temperature.*)

THE FILLING

- **½ cup (55 grams) red raspberries**
- **5 ounces (145 grams) bittersweet chocolate, preferably Valrhona Noir Gastronomie, finely chopped**
- **1 stick (4 ounces; 115 grams) unsalted butter, cut into 8 pieces**
- **1 large egg, at room temperature, stirred with a fork**
- **3 large egg yolks, at room temperature, stirred with a fork**
- **2 tablespoons sugar**

1. Center a rack in the oven and preheat the oven to 375°F (190°C).
2. Fill the tart crust with the raspberries.

Makes 6 to 8 servings

KEEPING: The crust can be made ahead, but the tart should be assembled as soon as the ganache is made. And while the tart is meant to be eaten soon after it comes from the oven, it can be kept overnight in the refrigerator and brought to room temperature before being eaten the next day. The filling will be firmer and denser, but still delicious.

3. Melt the chocolate and the butter in separate bowls either over — but not touching — simmering water or in the microwave. Allow them to cool until they feel only just warm to the touch (104°F [60°C], as measured on an instant-read thermometer, is perfect).

4. Using a small whisk or rubber spatula, stir the egg into the chocolate, stirring gently in ever-widening circles and taking care not to agitate the mixture — you don't want to beat air into the ganache. Little by little, stir in the egg yolks, then the sugar. Finally, still working gently, stir in the warm melted butter. Pour the ganache over the raspberries in the tart shell.

5. Bake the tart for 11 minutes — that should be just enough time to turn the top of the tart dull, like the top of a cake. The center of the tart will shimmy if jiggled — that's just what it's supposed to do. Remove the tart from the oven, slide it onto a rack, and allow it to cool for about 10 minutes before serving.

TO SERVE

- ¼ cup (25 grams) red raspberries
- Vanilla Crème Anglaise (page 217) (optional)

Scatter the fresh red berries over the top of the tart and, if you'd like, serve with some crème anglaise.

T his is a very simple tart — as simple and chic as a little black dress. It is nothing more than crust and ganache, but the not-so-sweet cocoa-and-salted-butter crust is remarkable, and the ganache, dark and bittersweet with a long elegant finish, is memorable. If you roll the crust out a little thicker than usual, you'll give the lissome filling a contrasting texture to play against, and you'll show off both elements to advantage.

■ The Nayla in the tart's name is my friend Nayla Audi. One summer she made a big country lunch at her house in Gordes and served a tart like this for dessert. The tart was a pleasure because it looked so ordinary, but its taste and texture were so special. ■ PH

THE CRUST

- 2 cups (280 grams) all-purpose flour
- ⅓ cup plus 1 tablespoon (40 grams) Dutch-processed cocoa powder, preferably Valrhona
- 1¾ sticks (7 ounces; 200 grams) salted butter, at room temperature (or use unsalted butter plus a pinch of salt)
- ½ cup (100 grams) sugar

1. Sift the flour and cocoa powder together and set aside for the moment. Place the butter in the bowl of a mixer fitted with the paddle attachment and beat at medium speed until it is smooth. Add the sugar and continue to beat until blended. Reduce the mixer speed to medium-low and add the sifted flour and cocoa, mixing only until the ingredients are incorporated: To get the characteristically crumbly texture this crust should have, it's best to mix the dough as little as possible once the flour is added. If the majority of the flour and cocoa is mixed in but some dry ingredients remain in the bottom of the bowl, turn the dough out onto a smooth work surface and blend the rest of the ingredients in by hand. The easiest way to get recalcitrant dry ingredi-

ents into the dough is to use the heel of your hand to smear a small portion of the dough at a time across the work surface. Gather the dough into a ball, flatten it into a disk, wrap it in plastic, and refrigerate it for at least 1 hour. (*Wrapped airtight, the dough can be refrigerated for 2 days or frozen for 1 month.*)

2. When you are ready to roll out and bake the dough, butter a 10¼-inch (26-cm) tart ring and place it on a parchment-lined baking sheet.

3. Working on a lightly floured work surface, roll the dough into a round that's a scant ¼ inch (7 mm) thick, lifting the dough often and making certain that the work surface and the dough are amply floured at all times. Fit the dough into the bottom and up the sides of the tart ring, then run your rolling pin across the top of the ring to cut off the excess. If the dough cracks or splits as you work (as it may), don't worry — patch the cracks with scraps (moisten the edges with water to "glue" them into place). Chill the dough for at least 30 minutes.

4. Center a rack in the oven and preheat the oven to 350°F (180°C).

5. Fit a circle of parchment or foil into the crust and fill it with dried beans or rice. Bake the crust for 30 to 40 minutes, or until it is firm, then transfer it to a rack, remove the paper and weights, and allow the crust to cool to room temperature.

THE FILLING

- **1 pound (454 grams) bittersweet chocolate, preferably Valrhona Guanaja, finely chopped**
- **2 cups (500 grams) heavy cream**
- **1 stick (4 ounces; 113 grams) unsalted butter, at room temperature, cut into 8 pieces**

1. Place the chocolate in a bowl that's large enough to hold the filling ingredients and keep it close at hand. Bring the cream to a full boil in a heavy-bottomed saucepan.

2. While the cream is coming to the boil, work the butter with a rubber spatula until it is very soft and creamy. Keep the butter aside for the moment.

3. When the cream is at the boil, remove the pan from the heat and, working with a whisk or rubber spatula, gently stir the cream into the chocolate. Stir — without creating bubbles — until the chocolate is completely melted and the mixture is smooth. Leave the bowl on the counter for a minute before adding the butter.

4. Add the butter to the chocolate bit by bit, stirring gently to blend the butter into the ganache. When the butter is fully incorporated, the ganache should be smooth and glossy. (*The ganache can be made ahead and kept covered in the refrigerator for 2 days or frozen for 1 month. It should be brought to room temperature and a spreadable consistency before you use it.*)

5. Pour the ganache into the crust and chill the tart for about 30 minutes to set the ganache.

TO SERVE (*optional*)

- **Vanilla Crème Anglaise (page 217) or lightly sweetened, lightly whipped cream**

Remove the tart from the refrigerator and allow it to come to room temperature before serving. If desired, serve with crème anglaise or whipped cream on the side.

Makes 8 to 10 servings

KEEPING: The crust and the ganache can both be made ahead, and the assembled tart can be kept covered in the refrigerator — away from any foods with strong odors — for up to 2 days or frozen for 1 month (defrost the frozen tart, still in its wrapping, overnight in the refrigerator). However, the tart is meant to be served at room temperature so you can enjoy the filling's supple texture.

I t's well known that chocolate and port are compatible — port is often recommended as a wine to be drunk with chocolate — but in this tart you come to realize that the two luxurious ingredients have an affinity for one another that goes beyond compatibility. The tart reveals how similar their flavors can be — how deeply rich, how lightly acidic, how spicy and fruity. All of chocolate and port's best and most engaging characteristics are heightened here and bound together by the addition of fresh purple figs — a fruit that shares so many of its partners' qualities. To intensify these qualities, the figs are poached in a spicy port blend and left to steep overnight before they are tucked into the chocolate crust and covered with velvety ganache. If you'd like, you can hold on to what remains of the poaching syrup: Boiled down and mixed with raspberry coulis, it makes the perfect finish for this polished tart.

■ Figs have more flavor cooked than fresh, and when they are cooked with port, zest, and spices, as they are here, the deepest and most characteristic of their flavors are emphasized and enhanced. ■ PH

THE FIGS

- 8 purple figs
- 2 cups (500 grams) ruby port
- 5 tablespoons (60 grams) sugar
- Zest from ½ lemon — removed in broad strips with a peeler
- Zest from ½ orange — removed in broad strips with a peeler
- 6 black peppercorns, cracked
- 1 cinnamon stick

1. Cut off the pointed top of each fig and, using a small sharp knife, cut an X about ½ inch (1.5 cm) deep in the center of the flat surface you just created — this will allow the wine to seep into the fruit.

2. Bring everything except the figs to the boil in a skillet or saucepan over medium heat. Add the figs, lower the heat so that the syrup simmers, and cook for 5 minutes. Pull the pan from the heat and allow the figs to cool in the syrup until the mixture reaches room temperature. Put the figs and their syrup in a bowl, cover, and chill overnight.

3. When you are ready to make the tart, lift the figs out of the syrup with a slotted spoon and dry them between layers of paper towels. Reserve the syrup if you want to make a sauce for the tart. Set 1 fig aside and cut the remaining figs into 8 wedges each, as you would an orange. The set-aside fig will be used to top the tart: Stand it up on its base and, using the small sharp knife, cut it into 8 to 10 sections, again as you would an orange, but this time taking care not to cut all the way through the fruit — leave the bottom ¼ inch (7 mm) or so intact. At serving time, gently pry apart the sections you've cut so that they form a flower.

THE CRUST

- **1 fully baked 9½-inch (24-cm) tart shell made from Chocolate-Almond Pâte Sablée (page 238), cooled to room temperature**

Keep the cooled crust, with the tart ring still in place, on the parchment-lined baking sheet. (*The crust can be made up to 8 hours ahead and kept at room temperature.*)

THE SAUCE (*optional*)

- **The reserved poaching syrup**
- **½ pint (110 grams) red raspberries**
- **2 tablespoons sugar**

1. Pour the poaching syrup into a small saucepan and bring it to the boil over medium heat. Cook the syrup until it is reduced to ¼ cup (60 grams), then strain it and set it aside for the moment.

2. Put the berries and sugar in a blender or food processor (or use an immersion blender) and puree. Strain the puree and stir it into the port syrup. The sauce is now ready to use. (*The sauce can be made up to 2 days ahead and*

kept tightly covered in the refrigerator. Allow the sauce to stand at room temperature a few minutes before serving — just to take the chill off it.)

TO FINISH

- **Bittersweet Chocolate Cream Ganache (page 215), warm and at a pourable consistency**

Makes 8 servings

1. Pour just enough of the ganache into the tart shell to cover the bottom of the crust. Scatter over the wedges of fig and cover with the remaining ganache. Put the tart in the refrigerator for about 30 minutes to set the ganache, then allow the tart to come to room temperature on the counter before serving. (*The tart can be made up to 2 days ahead and kept covered in the refrigerator, away from foods with strong odors.*)
2. Present the tart topped with the fig flower. Serve each wedge of the tart with a drizzle of the port-raspberry sauce, if you made it.

KEEPING: Both the tart and the sauce can be made up to 2 days ahead and kept covered in the refrigerator; however, the tart should be served at room temperature and the sauce should not be too cold.

LINZER TART

A classic Linzer Tart is simply a crust and some raspberry jam, but it has everything a dessert lover loves: The crust is cinnamony, sweet, and rich with almonds, at once meltingly buttery and pleasingly crunchy, and the jam is vibrant and only just sweet enough. Pierre's Linzer Tart has the perfect crust and a luscious homemade jam, but it's got something else to make it even more worthy of our affections — chocolate: Topping the raspberry jam is a layer of luxe dark chocolate ganache. As assertive as the ganache is, that's how companionable it is as well, emphasizing the wonderful spiciness of the crust and adding a mellow note to the sharpness of the jam. See page x.

■ The dough for this Linzer Tart is an Austrian specialty and, as is true with several Austrian preparations, it includes sieved hard-boiled eggs. The eggs give the dough its delicate crumbly texture, and they also make the dough forgiving: When you're putting the dough in the pan, you can handle it with less care than you would a regular pastry dough. On the other hand, once it is baked, it is more fragile than most doughs — and more special for it. ■ PH

THE CRUST

- 7 tablespoons (3½ ounces; 100 grams) unsalted butter, at room temperature
- 2½ tablespoons confectioners' sugar
- 2½ tablespoons finely ground almond powder (see page 265) or finely ground blanched almonds (see page 265)
- 1 hard-boiled large egg yolk, at room temperature, pressed through a fine strainer
- ¼ teaspoon cinnamon
- Pinch of salt
- 1 teaspoon dark rum
- Pinch of double-acting baking powder
- ¾ cup (105 grams) all-purpose flour

1. Place the butter in the work bowl of a food processor fitted with the metal blade and process until creamy, scraping down the sides of the bowl as needed.

Add the confectioners' sugar, almond powder, egg yolk, cinnamon, and salt; continue to process until smooth, scraping the bowl as necessary. Add the rum and pulse to blend. Whisk the baking powder into the flour and add the flour to the work bowl, pulsing until thoroughly blended. (Unlike tart dough, this dough can be worked past the clump-and-curd stage.) The dough will feel soft and look a little like the dough you'd use to make peanut butter cookies.

2. Scrape the dough out onto a piece of plastic wrap and, with the help of the plastic, gather it into a ball and gently press it into a disk. Wrap the disk and chill it for at least 4 hours before rolling and baking. (*The dough can be wrapped airtight and refrigerated for up to 2 days or frozen for up to a month.*)

3. Line a baking sheet with parchment paper and place an 8¾-inch (22-cm) tart ring on the sheet.

4. You can either roll the dough out to fit it into the tart ring — a job done most easily when both the dough and the work surface are kept well floured — or you can pat it into the ring. (If you're rolling, keep in mind that this dough is eminently breakable and just as eminently patchable — if it breaks, just patch it by pressing the dough together or putting a small piece of dough over the tear.) No matter whether you roll or pat, keep the dough thicker than usual; the crust should be a scant ¼ inch (7 mm) thick. When the dough has been fitted into the ring, trim the top even with the ring, cover the crust with a sheet of plastic wrap, and chill it for at least 30 minutes. You can gather the leftovers into a ball, flatten the dough into a disk, chill it, reroll it, and cut out cookies. Baked cookies are delicious sandwiched with raspberry jam.

5. Center a rack in the oven and preheat the oven to 350°F (180°C). Remove the plastic wrap and fit the crust with a circle of parchment, fill it with dried beans or rice. Bake the pastry for 18 to 20 minutes. Remove the parchment and beans and continue to bake the crust until it is honey brown, 3 to 5 minutes more. Transfer the baking sheet to a rack and cool the crust to room temperature.

THE JAM

- **1 pound (about 2 pints; 450 grams) red raspberries**
- **1⅓ cups (270 grams) sugar**
- **About 1 tablespoon freshly squeezed lemon juice**

1. Put the berries in the container of a food processor and process, turning the machine off briefly if it seems to be getting hot, for a total of about 5 minutes, in order to release the pectin in the seeds.

2. Scrape the berries into a large heavy-bottomed casserole and stir in the sugar. Bring the fruit to a rollicking boil, stirring occasionally and taking care that it doesn't stick to the bottom of the pot, and boil for 10 to 15 minutes, or until the jam thickens slightly and the bubbles look clear. (Since the jam will thicken as it cools, the best way to get a preview of its viscosity is to drop a small amount of it onto a cold plate.)

3. Stir in a teaspoon or so of the lemon juice and scrape the jam into a heat-proof jar or bowl; you'll have about 1½ cups (400 grams) jam. Allow the jam to cool to room temperature, then taste it and add a squirt more of lemon juice if you think it needs it. Once cool, the jam can be packed airtight and stored in the refrigerator. (*The jam can be kept in the refrigerator for about 1 month.*)

Makes 6 to 8 servings

KEEPING: The dough can be kept in the refrigerator for up to 2 days or wrapped airtight and frozen for a month. A frozen disk of dough will take about 30 minutes at average room temperature to reach a good rolling-out consistency. The jam can be made up to a month in advance, and the ganache can be made ahead and kept refrigerated for up to 2 days or frozen for up to a month. However, once the tart is assembled, it's best eaten the same day.

TO FINISH

- **About ¾ cup (240 grams) raspberry jam (from above)**
- **Bittersweet Chocolate Cream Ganache (page 215), warm and at a pourable consistency**

1. For this tart, the jam should be more spreadable than pourable. If your jam is too runny, you can either boil it for a few minutes in a saucepan over direct heat or pour it into a large microwave-safe container — a Pyrex measuring cup is good for this job — and boil it in the microwave oven until it thickens sufficiently. Let the jam cool for a few minutes if necessary, then spread an even layer of it over the bottom of the crust. Now pour the ganache into the crust, pouring it so that it comes just to the rim of the crust (you may have a little left over). Slide the tart into the refrigerator for about 30 minutes, or until the ganache is set.

2. Allow the tart to come to room temperature before serving.

GRAND
CHOCOLATE TART

As its name declares, this is a grand — indeed, a glorious — tart. It is composed of four parts, each simple but singular, so that when they are brought together they create a dessert of astonishing complexity and, most important, delight. The principal chocolate components are a dense chocolate ganache and an under-layer of soft flourless chocolate cake. The ganache and cake, both intensely chocolaty, are set in a slightly sweet almond tart shell, which offers just a little crunch and a spot of pale golden color. And the creation is finished, festooned really, with large shards of Lacy Coffee-Cocoa Nougatine cookies, featherlight, quintessentially crunchy, and fiercely flavorful. Even with pieces of translucent nougatine standing upright here and there like so many sails tossed in the wind, the tart has a sleek, supremely sophisticated, and very urbane look.

A word on the pan: Unlike most of Pierre's tarts, which are made in tart rings, this one is made in a fluted tart pan with a removable bottom — you need the extra little bit of depth the pan provides.

■ When I started to think about chocolate tarts, I knew that I wanted to create a tart with a pure chocolate taste, I wanted to balance the dry elements and the creamy, and I wanted to have a contrast in texture. In this tart, everything is chocolate, the dry cake is balanced with the creamy ganache, and the crunch of the crust on the bottom and the nougatine on top contrast with the smooth textured interior. ■ PH

THE CRUST

- **1 fully baked tart shell made from Sweet Tart Dough (page 235; made in a 10¼-inch [26-cm] fluted tart pan with a removable bottom), cooled to room temperature**

Keep the cooled crust, still in its pan, on the parchment-lined baking sheet. (*The crust can be made up to 8 hours ahead and kept at room temperature.*)

THE CAKE

- 1¼ ounces (40 grams) bittersweet chocolate, preferably Valrhona Guanaja, finely chopped
- ½ cup (100 grams) sugar
- 2 large eggs, separated, at room temperature

1. Center a rack in the oven and preheat the oven to 350°F (180°C). Using a pencil, draw a 9-inch (24-cm) circle on a piece of parchment paper. Flip the paper over and use it to line a baking sheet. (If, when you turn the paper over, you can't see the circle, darken the outline.) Alternatively, you can use a buttered 9-inch (24-cm) tart ring as the form for the cake — in which case you should just line the baking sheet with parchment and, when it's time, spoon (or pipe) the cake batter inside the ring. If you are going to pipe the batter, fit a pastry bag with a ½-inch (1.5-cm) plain tip and keep it close at hand.

2. Melt the chocolate over — not touching — simmering water or in a microwave oven, then let it cool briefly on the counter. When you are ready to use it, it should be just warm to the touch.

3. Working in a large mixing bowl, whisk ¼ cup (50 grams) of the sugar together with the egg yolks until thick and pale. Put this aside while you beat the egg whites in the clean, dry bowl of a mixer fitted with the whisk attachment. When the whites turn opaque and start to peak, steadily add the remaining ¼ cup (50 grams) sugar and continue to beat until the whites are stiff but still glossy. Using a flexible rubber spatula, gently fold one-third of the beaten egg whites into the yolks. (Don't worry about being too thorough at this point.) Next fold in the chocolate, then add the rest of the egg whites and continue to gently fold the ingredients together until you have a homogenous batter.

4. Spoon the batter into the pastry bag and, starting at the center of the traced circle, work your way in a spiral to the penciled edge. If you have any spaces between the spiral coils, just run the spatula gently across the circle to even out the batter. Or, if you are using a tart ring, spoon (or pipe) the batter into the ring.

5. Slide the baking sheet into the oven, then insert the handle of a wooden spoon into the door to keep it slightly ajar. Bake for 18 to 20 minutes, or until the top of the cake is crackly, dull, and light cocoa-colored and a knife inserted into the center of the cake comes out dry. Slide the cake, still on the

parchment, onto a rack and cool to room temperature. (*The cake can be made ahead, wrapped airtight, and kept at room temperature for 1 day or frozen for up to 1 month.*)

THE GANACHE

- **10 ounces (285 grams) bittersweet chocolate, preferably Valrhona Guanaja, finely chopped**
- **1¼ cups (310 grams) heavy cream**
- **5 tablespoons (2½ ounces; 70 grams) unsalted butter, at room temperature, cut into 6 pieces**

1. Place the chocolate in a bowl that's large enough to hold the ganache ingredients and keep it close at hand. Bring the cream to a full boil in a heavy-bottomed saucepan.

2. While the cream is coming to the boil, work the butter with a rubber spatula until it is very soft and creamy. Set the butter aside for the moment.

3. When the cream is at the boil, remove the pan from the heat and, working with a whisk or rubber spatula, gently stir the cream into the chocolate. Stir — without creating bubbles — until the chocolate is completely melted and the mixture is smooth. Leave the bowl on the counter for a minute before adding the butter.

4. Add the butter to the chocolate bit by bit, stirring gently to blend the butter into the ganache. When the butter is fully incorporated, the ganache should be smooth and glossy. (*The ganache can be made ahead and kept covered in the refrigerator for 2 days or frozen for 1 month. It should be brought to room temperature and a spreadable consistency before you use it.*)

5. Pour (or spread) a very thin layer of the warm ganache into the crust and use an offset spatula to smooth the ganache over the bottom. Remove the chocolate cake from the parchment and check to see whether or not it is an inch smaller in diameter than the tart shell. If it isn't, trim it to size. Place the cake in the center of the crust. If you made the cake in a tart ring, it may be higher than the edge of the crust — if so, just press it down with the palm of your hand. Pour the remaining ganache over the cake and use the offset spatula to smooth the top and to make certain that the ganache fills in the space between the cake and the crust. Chill the tart for about 30 minutes to set the ganache. (*The tart can be made ahead and kept covered in the refrigerator for 2 days or frozen, well wrapped, for 1 month.*)

KEEPING: The crust, the
cake, and the ganache can be
made ahead, and the
assembled tart — minus the
cookies, which must be
put on at the last minute —
can be kept covered in
the refrigerator, away from
foods with strong odors, for
up to 2 days or tightly
wrapped and frozen for
1 month. If the tart has been
frozen, defrost it, still in its
wrapping, overnight in the
refrigerator. Chilled or frozen,
the tart should be brought
to room temperature
before serving.

TO FINISH

■ **Lacy Coffee-Cocoa Nougatine Cookies (page 82)**

Because the nougatine cookies are fragile and susceptible to wilting if it's humid,
they should be put on the tart just before serving. Break the cookies into pieces
of varying sizes — leave some of them large, they're more dramatic that way —
and arrange the shards over the tart, poking a tip of each into the now-firm
ganache so that it stands up. The tart, which needed to be chilled to set the
ganache and give you a pokable foundation for the cookies, should be served at
room temperature.

See "grenobloise" on a dessert menu and you can be sure that what's in store will include a layer of nuts encased in soft caramel. The usual Tarte Grenobloise is a double-crusted affair, more a tourte than a tart, and it's filled with nuts, often an assortment. But in Pierre's rethinking of this classic, the nuts are pecan — a nut seen only recently in Paris with the widespread popularity of the candy-like all-American pecan pie — and they and the caramel form the topping of the tart. The layer beneath is a lovely bittersweet chocolate ganache. It could make you reconsider both the traditional Tarte Grenobloise and our pecan pie.

THE CRUST

- **1 fully baked 9½-inch (24-cm) tart shell made from Chocolate-Almond Pâte Sablée (page 238), cooled to room temperature**

Keep the cooled crust, with the tart ring still in place, on the parchment-lined baking sheet. (*The crust can be made up to 8 hours ahead and kept at room temperature.*)

THE CHOCOLATE LAYER

- **Bittersweet Chocolate Cream Ganache (page 215), warm and at a pourable consistency**

Pour the ganache into the cooled crust and put the tart in the refrigerator for about 30 minutes to set the ganache. (*The tart can be made up to 2 days ahead and kept covered in the refrigerator, away from foods with strong odors.*)

THE TOPPING

- **1 cup (250 grams) heavy cream**
- **⅔ cup plus 2 tablespoons (150 grams) sugar**
- **7 ounces (200 grams) pecan halves, lightly toasted (see page 275) and just warm**

Makes 8 servings

KEEPING: While the tart shell and the ganache can be made ahead and frozen for up to 1 month, the caramel must be used shortly after it's made. However, once assembled, the tart can remain at room temperature for up to 2 days.

1. Bring the cream to the boil in a small saucepan. Keep it in a warm spot and at the ready while you work with the sugar.

2. Set a heavy-bottomed medium saucepan or casserole over medium heat and sprinkle 2 to 3 tablespoons of the sugar over a small portion of the center of the pan. As soon as it starts to melt and take on color, stir the sugar with a wooden spoon or spatula until it caramelizes. Continue cooking and stirring the sugar, adding the remaining sugar a couple of tablespoons at a time, until it is a deep amber color. Standing back but still stirring, add the hot cream. Don't worry if it sputters, and don't be concerned if the caramel clumps — stirring and heat will even everything out. The caramel needs to be cooked to 226°F (108°C), which is what it probably will be just a few seconds after you stir in the liquid. Check the temperature with a candy or instant-read thermometer and, when it hits the mark, pull the pan from the heat.

3. Stir in the pecans, stirring only until the nuts are evenly coated with caramel. Transfer the caramel to a bowl and leave the bowl on the counter until the caramel is just warm to the touch (about 20 to 30 minutes, depending on the temperature of your kitchen).

4. Spoon the caramel over the tart, gently smoothing and leveling it with a spatula. As soon as the caramel cools to room temperature (about 30 to 60 minutes), the tart is ready to serve.

MILK CHOCOLATE
AND WALNUT TART

Milk chocolate is not an ingredient that turns up often in a French pastry chef's repertoire, mostly because of the almost nationwide preference of French pastry eaters for dark bittersweet chocolates. Can millions of Frenchmen be wrong? Not wrong, just a little narrowminded. As Pierre is quick to point out — and prove (just look at this recipe and the one for Plaisir Sucré, page 53) — milk chocolate can be completely satisfying if used properly and, for Pierre, "properly" includes pairing the chocolate with contrasting ingredients that enhance its best qualities: its unusual creaminess, its easygoing nature (milk chocolate doesn't have a bite), and, of course, its sweetness. For this tart, the milk chocolate is the star of a ganache filling, and the contrasts are provided by the cocoa-almond crust made from a coal-dark dough that's only barely sweetened and a handful of meaty, slightly bitter, toasted walnuts.

A word on the chocolate: As with all ganaches, it's important to choose a chocolate you enjoy eating out of hand, because the flavor doesn't change much when it's mixed with cream and butter. Here it's even more important because the chocolate is blended only with cream. If you can, use a milk chocolate imported from France or a premium-quality domestic milk chocolate.

■ This tart is equally delicious when the walnuts are replaced by peanuts — just make certain the peanuts are salted. ■ PH

THE CRUST

- **1 fully baked 8¾-inch (22-cm) tart shell made from Chocolate-Almond Pâte Sablée (page 238), cooled to room temperature**

Keep the cooled crust, with the tart ring still in place, on the parchment-lined baking sheet. (*The crust can be made up to 8 hours ahead and kept at room temperature.*)

THE FILLING

- **13¼ ounces (375 grams) milk chocolate, preferably Valrhona Jivara, finely chopped**
- **1⅓ cups (335 grams) heavy cream**
- **5 ounces (145 grams) walnuts, toasted (see page 275) and cooled**

1. Place the chocolate in a bowl that's large enough to hold the filling ingredients and keep it close at hand. Bring the cream to a full boil in a heavy-bottomed saucepan.
2. When the cream is at the boil, remove the pan from the heat and, working with a whisk or rubber spatula, gently stir the cream into the chocolate in two additions. Stir — without creating bubbles — until the chocolate is completely melted and the mixture is smooth.
3. Pour a very thin layer of the warm ganache into the crust, using an offset spatula to smooth the ganache over the bottom. Scatter the toasted walnuts evenly over the ganache and then pour in enough of the remaining ganache to come up to the rim of the crust. (You may have a little ganache left over — it can be kept covered in the refrigerator for a couple of days or frozen for a month.) Chill the tart for about 30 minutes to set the ganache.

TO FINISH

- **Milk chocolate shavings (see page 258) (optional)**

Shortly before you are ready to serve the tart, remove it from the refrigerator, top it generously with chocolate shavings, and allow it to come to room temperature.

Makes 8 servings

KEEPING: The tart — without the chocolate shavings — can be kept in the refrigerator, covered and far from foods with strong odors, for 2 days or frozen, tightly wrapped, for up to 1 month. (Defrost the frozen tart, still in its wrapping, in the refrigerator overnight.) Chilled or frozen, the tart should be allowed to come to room temperature before serving.

O riginally from Italy, but now manufactured around the world, Nutella is high-class snack food — Europe's answer to America's peanut butter. Nutella is, in fact, a type of nut butter, a creamy, swirl-it-around-with-your-knife spread made from hazelnuts, milk, and cocoa. In France, Nutella is commonly smoothed over breakfast breads and croissants, but here Pierre has made it the base of a bittersweet chocolate tart. A chocolate tart shell is spread with Nutella, filled with ganache, and then finished with large pieces of toasted hazelnuts. The tart is baked for only eleven minutes and served when it cools to room temperature — the perfect temperature to appreciate the contrast between the two chocolate fillings. Snack food never had it so good.

If you'd like, when the tart is cool you can fill a small paper piping cone with Nutella and pipe thin lines of the hazelnut spread over the top of the tart, just as we did in the photo.

■ I created this tart for my wife, Frédérick, when she was writing a book on "plaisirs cachés" — hidden pleasures. Nutella has been one of Frédérick's pleasures, hidden and not so hidden, since her childhood. ■ PH

THE CRUST

- **1 fully baked 8¾-inch (22-cm) tart shell made from Sweet Tart Dough (page 235), cooled to room temperature**

Keep the cooled crust, with the tart ring still in place, on the parchment-lined baking sheet. (*The crust can be made up to 8 hours ahead and kept at room temperature.*)

THE FILLING

- **⅔ cup (200 grams) Nutella**
- **4¾ ounces (140 grams) bittersweet chocolate, preferably Valrhona Noir Gastronomie, finely chopped**

- **7 tablespoons (3½ ounces; 200 grams) unsalted butter**
- **1 large egg, at room temperature, stirred with a fork**
- **3 large egg yolks, at room temperature, stirred with a fork**
- **2 tablespoons sugar**
- **1 cup (140 grams) hazelnuts (see page 273) toasted, skinned, and cut into large pieces**

1. Center a rack in the oven and preheat the oven to 375°F (190°C).
2. Spread the Nutella evenly over the bottom of the crust and set it aside while you make the ganache.
3. Melt the chocolate and the butter in separate bowls either over — not touching — simmering water or in a microwave oven. Allow them to cool until they feel only just warm to the touch (104°F [40°C], as measured on an instant-read thermometer, is perfect).
4. Using a small whisk or rubber spatula, stir the egg into the chocolate, stirring gently in ever-widening circles and taking care not to agitate the mixture — you don't want to beat air into the ganache. Little by little, stir in the egg yolks, then the sugar. Finally, still working gently, stir in the warm melted butter. Pour the ganache over the Nutella in the tart shell. Scatter the toasted hazelnuts over the top.
5. Bake the tart for 11 minutes — that should be just enough time to turn the top of the tart dull, like the top of a cake. The center of the tart will shimmy if jiggled — that's just what it's supposed to do. Remove the tart from the oven and slide it onto a rack. Allow the tart to cool for at least 20 minutes, or until it reaches room temperature — the best temperature at which to serve it.

Makes 6 to 8 servings

KEEPING: The crust can be made ahead, but the filling has to be baked the instant it is made. Although the tart is best served at room temperature, if you refrigerate any leftovers, you'll find happy takers the following day.

PUDDINGS, CREAMS,

CUSTARDS, MOUSSES,

AND MORE CHOCOLATE DESSERTS

SIMPLE CHOCOLATE MOUSSE

Mousse as it's meant to be: Whisper-light in texture, exclamatory in taste. The main ingredient is bittersweet chocolate, lightened by whipped egg whites, enriched by an egg yolk, and sweetened by just the tiniest bit of sugar. Milk is the unexpected but just-right ingredient in this recipe. Because it is lighter than cream, it brings smoothness to the mousse without adding richness or masking the flavor of the chocolate.

■ I think of this mousse as a base recipe, one I can play around with and change at whim. Often I'll add another flavor and texture just before serving, topping the mousse with chocolate shavings (see page 258); Caramelized Rice Krispies (page 256); thin slices of banana, raw or sautéed; whole raspberries or Raspberry Coulis (page 255); toasted nuts; or chopped fresh mint. Sometimes I'll add a different flavor to the mousse while I'm making it, infusing the milk with grated orange zest, a spoonful of instant coffee, a little ground cinnamon, or a pinch of cardamom. ■ PH

- **6 ounces (170 grams) bittersweet chocolate, preferably Valrhona Gastronomie, finely chopped**
- **⅓ cup (80 grams) whole milk**
- **1 large egg yolk**
- **4 large egg whites**
- **2 tablespoons sugar**

1. Melt the chocolate in a bowl over — not touching — simmering water or in the microwave oven. If necessary, transfer the chocolate to a bowl that is large enough to hold all of the ingredients. Keep the chocolate on the counter until needed. The chocolate should still feel warm to the touch when you're ready to use it.

Makes 6 servings

KEEPING: Although the texture of the mousse will be lighter if you serve it shortly after chilling it, it can be covered and kept in the refrigerator for up to 2 days – after which time it will be just as delicious, if a little denser.

2. Bring the milk to the boil, then pour it over the chocolate. Using a small whisk, gently blend the milk into the chocolate. Add the egg yolk and whisk it into the chocolate, again working gently; stop when the yolk is incorporated.

3. In a mixer fitted with the whisk attachment, beat the egg whites on medium speed just until they hold soft peaks. Increase the speed to medium-high and gradually add the sugar. Continue to beat the whites until they are firm but still glossy. Scoop one-third of the whites out of the bowl onto the chocolate mixture. Working with a whisk, beat the whites into the chocolate to lighten the mixture. Now, with either the whisk or a large flexible rubber spatula, delicately but thoroughly fold the rest of the beaten whites into the chocolate.

4. Turn the mousse into a large serving bowl — glass is very nice for this dessert — or into individual coupes or cups, and refrigerate for 1 hour to set.

Not your grandmother's rice pudding. Not even your mother's. This has all the cuddly, cozy warmth of a childhood dessert and all the sex appeal of a sweet for the *raffiné* crowd. Yes, it's creamy rice pudding as we know it, but it's made with Arborio rice — small, round risotto rice whose kernels stay firm at the core even when cooked through — plump golden raisins, and bittersweet chocolate, the ingredient that transforms this pudding, making its flavor deeper, its texture denser, and its character stronger.

■ The pudding, spooned into small coupes, stemmed glasses, or espresso cups, can be served without any topping or accompaniment, but it also can be paired easily with Caramelized Rice Krispies, Chocolate Sauce (page 253), Vanilla Crème Anglaise (page 217), Raspberry Coulis (page 255), or small cubes of fruit, such as pears or apples, sautéed quickly in butter and sugar. ■ PH

- 3¾ cups (935 grams) whole milk
- ½ cup (100 grams) Arborio rice
- 2½ tablespoons sugar
- Pinch of salt
- 2 tablespoons (1 ounce; 30 grams) unsalted butter, at room temperature
- 7 ounces (200 grams) bittersweet chocolate, preferably Valrhona Guanaja, melted
- ½ cup (60 grams) moist, plump golden raisins

1. Pour the milk into a heavy-bottomed medium saucepan and add the rice, sugar, and salt. Bring to the boil, stirring frequently — don't walk away, because milk boils over quickly — then lower the temperature so that the milk is at a slow, steady simmer. Stirring now and then, allow the milk to simmer for about 12 to 15 minutes, or until the rice is cooked through. (The timing depends on your rice and the strength of your simmer. Because you're using Arborio rice, the rice, when properly cooked, will remain ever so slightly al

dente, meaning it will be firm at its center.) About one-quarter of the milk will have boiled away, and that's fine.

2. Remove the pan from the heat and, using a heatproof spatula, stir in the butter. When the butter is melted and incorporated, pour a little of this hot mixture into the melted chocolate and stir gently. Now scrape the chocolate into the pot and stir it into the rice mixture, stirring in ever-widening concentric circles and stirring only enough to combine the ingredients. Stir in the raisins and then spoon the rice pudding into a serving bowl or individual cups. Press a piece of plastic wrap against the surface of the pudding to create an airtight seal and, once the pudding reaches room temperature, put it in the refrigerator to chill.

TO FINISH (*optional*)

- **Caramelized Rice Krispies (page 256)**

Remove the pudding from the refrigerator about 10 minutes before serving. Top with a sprinkling of the caramelized Rice Krispies, if desired.

Makes 6 servings

KEEPING: Packed in an airtight container, the pudding can be kept in the refrigerator for up to 2 days. If you're finishing the pudding with Caramelized Rice Krispies, add them at serving time.

CHOCOLATE CRÊPES

The American pancake and the French crêpe may be related, but they'd never be mistaken for twins. Whereas our pancake is thick and hearty, the French crêpe is dainty and thin; our pancake is a rustic, theirs, particularly in this rendition, a city slicker; and, finally, our pancake is a breakfast special, while theirs is either a dessert or a snack bought on the street and eaten out of hand, the way we might grab a donut.

French crêpes can be either sweet or savory, and, at a *crêperie* (a crêpe restaurant), you can have an entire meal of crêpes, from starter to dessert. But even at a *crêperie* with a large repertoire, it would be unlikely that you'd find a chocolate crêpe; certainly you wouldn't find one like this chocolate crêpe, which is without-a-doubt chocolate, but only a touch sweet. Since it is classically thin, moderately rich, and deliciously chocolaty, it is also, as crêpes should be, as versatile as pound cake.

A word on equipment: Not surprisingly, crêpes are most easily made in a crêpe pan, a small frying pan with very low, slightly flaring sides. The traditional crêpe pan is made of iron and must be seasoned before use. Today there are nonstick crêpe pans on the market that do a fine job and require very little in the way of special care. However, whether you use an iron crêpe pan, a nonstick pan, or even a skillet, you must be sure that its cooking surface is smooth — nicks and dings will grab the batter and may cause the crêpes to tear.

■ This is a very simple recipe for a very simple dessert. It can be served with nothing more than a little whipped cream or whatever kind of ice cream you like best with chocolate. ■ PH

- ⅔ cup (95 grams) all-purpose flour
- 3½ tablespoons Dutch-processed cocoa powder, preferably Valrhona
- 1½ tablespoons sugar
- 2 large eggs, preferably at room temperature
- 1 cup (250 grams) whole milk, preferably at room temperature
- 3 tablespoons beer, preferably at room temperature
- 2 tablespoons (1 ounce; 30 grams) unsalted butter, melted

1. Sift the flour and cocoa powder together into a bowl that can hold all the ingredients, then whisk in the sugar. In another bowl, or a measuring cup with a spout, whisk the eggs and milk together just to blend, then whisk in the beer and, finally, the melted butter.

2. Pour the liquid ingredients into the bowl with the dry ingredients and whisk to blend well — you'll have a very thin batter. (Alternatively, you can make the batter in a blender or food processor by first blending the eggs, sugar, milk, and beer together. Add the butter and process until the mixture is homogenous. Finally, add the flour-cocoa mixture and process just until it is incorporated — don't overmix.) Pour the batter into a pitcher or a container with a pouring spout (a Pyrex measuring cup is ideal), rap the pitcher on the counter to burst any air bubbles, cover, and refrigerate overnight. (*The crêpe batter can be kept covered in the refrigerator for up to 3 days.*)

3. When you are ready to cook the crêpes, whisk the batter gently just to blend the ingredients. If the batter is too thick — it should pour easily and have the consistency of heavy cream — add a little milk, a drop at a time. Rub a seasoned or nonstick 7½-inch (19-cm) crêpe pan or a similar-sized skillet with a thin film of oil (apply the oil with a crumpled paper towel), then place the pan over medium-high heat. As soon as the pan is hot, lift it from the heat, pour in about 3 tablespoons of batter, and swirl the pan so that the batter spreads across it in an even, thin-as-possible layer. To get the most even layer, you'll probably find it easiest to pour in more batter than you need — that's fine. After swirling the pan, pour the excess batter back into the pitcher. (If you're new to crêpe making, it can take some practice to hit a rhythm and master the techniques — keep at it even if you end up, as most people do, having to toss out your first few attempts.) When the batter has set, a matter of seconds, cut off the little tail that formed when you poured the excess back into the pitcher, and continue to cook until the crêpe is set on top.

4. Run a blunt knife or small icing spatula around the edges of the crêpe to release it, then take a peek at the underside — it should be the "cocoa equivalent" of golden. If the underside is uniformly cooked, flip the crêpe over (fingers are fine for this — just be careful) and cook until the other side is lightly browned. The second side will cook faster than the first, but it will never be — and shouldn't be — as dark. Transfer the crêpe to a plate and sprinkle it very lightly with sugar. Continue with the rest of the batch (you'll have enough batter for 10 to 12 crêpes), oiling the pan as needed, and stacking the crêpes on top of one another in stacks of 5 or 6. Serve now, or pack the crêpes for keeping.

Makes 10 to 12 crêpes

KEEPING: The crêpes can be used as soon as they're made, or they can be wrapped airtight and refrigerated for a day or frozen for a month. To keep the crêpes from sticking to one another, and to make it easy to peel off one crêpe at a time, insert a piece of waxed paper between each crêpe.

SAUCER-SIZED SPICY CHOCOLATE SABLÉS WITH ALLSPICE ICE CREAM

Sablés are melt-in-your-mouth cookies prized for their simplicity and, often, their soothingness. These, like all sablés, melt in your mouth, but when they do, they sing the "Hallelujah Chorus." Spicy Chocolate Sablés get their energy from a touch of white pepper and a pinch of finely chopped habanero chile, zesty complements to chocolate and ground almonds, and they look great rolled out and cut into large rounds. Best served warm or freshly baked, the cookies are offered on large dinner plates, circled with warm chocolate sauce and topped with scoops of almost-Christmasy allspice ice cream.

Allspice, so named because it was thought to combine the flavors of cloves, black pepper, nutmeg, and cinnamon, is an odd but brilliant choice for an ice cream. Blended into the ice cream's custard base and chilled, allspice seems to taste even more like a combination of all spices, and even spicier. In fact, there's something gingerbready about this ice cream's lingering flavor. Whatever it is, the ice cream is lovely solo, lovelier with cookies, and loveliest with a swirl of chocolate sauce; and in each of its renditions, it is revelatory — once you've had this ice cream, you'll never think of allspice as the also-spice in a holiday apple or pumpkin pie.

A note on the cookie dough: To roll a thin layer of this dough, you'll need to keep your work surface and the dough very well floured. Or, if you'd like, you can roll the dough out between sheets of plastic wrap. If, when you're rolling, the dough cracks — it can happen — just fold the dough up and start all over again. And, if it gets too soft, just give it a brief chill, then set back to work. It's the hard-boiled egg yolks in the dough that give it the body to withstand more handling than other pastry doughs. However, while the dough is not fragile in the rolling stage, it can be a tad touchy once it's baked — the same quick-to-crumble quality that makes these cookies so delectable makes them ticklish when you're transferring them from cookie sheet to cake plate. Work with a broad, fairly long offset spatula, and you'll be fine.

■ You can serve this dessert in another, more casual form: Make ice cream sand-wiches, using the cookies to sandwich a generous serving of the allspice ice cream. Freeze the sandwiches on a baking sheet, then, when they're firm, wrap them well in plastic wrap. You can serve them as a snack or as a plated dessert, offering two sandwiches for each serving, along with some chocolate sauce. ■ PH

THE ICE CREAM

- 2 cups (500 grams) whole milk
- ½ cup (125 grams) heavy cream
- 1 tablespoon whole allspice berries, bruised, broken, or crushed
- 5 large egg yolks
- ½ cup (100 grams) sugar

1. Bring the milk, cream, and crushed allspice berries to the boil in a medium saucepan. Remove the pan from the heat, cover, and allow the mixture to rest for 15 minutes, time enough for the liquid to be thoroughly infused with the flavor and perfume of the allspice. Strain and discard the allspice.

2. While the mixture is infusing, set up an ice-water bath: Fill a large bowl with ice cubes and cold water. Set aside a smaller bowl that can hold the finished cream and be placed in the ice-water bath. Set aside a fine-meshed strainer too.

3. Working in the smaller bowl, whisk the egg yolks and sugar together until the mixture is lightly thickened and the sugar is dissolved. Still whisking, drizzle in about one-quarter of the hot liquid. When the liquid is incorporated, whisk in another cup or so more, then whisk the egg mixture into the saucepan with the remaining liquid. Set the pan over medium heat and, stirring constantly with a wooden spatula or spoon, cook the custard until it thickens slightly, lightens in color, and, most important, reaches 180°F (80°C), as measured on an instant-read thermometer — all of which will take less than 5 minutes. (Alternatively, you can stir the custard, and then draw your finger down the spatula or the bowl of the wooden spoon — if the custard doesn't run into the track you've created, it's done.) Immediately pull the pan from the heat. Rinse and dry the smaller bowl, strain the custard into it, and set the bowl in the ice-water bath to cool. Stir the custard occasionally as it cools.

4. When the custard is cool, pour it into an ice-cream maker and churn according to the manufacturer's directions. Spoon the ice cream into a freezer container and freeze for at least 2 hours before using. (*The ice cream can be packed airtight and kept in the freezer for up to 1 week, but its flavor is at its peak the day it is made.*)

THE COOKIES

- 5¼ ounces (150 grams) bittersweet chocolate, preferably Valrhona Caraïbe, finely chopped
- 1⅓ cups plus 2 tablespoons (200 grams) all-purpose flour
- Pinch of double-acting baking powder
- Pinch of salt
- Pinch of freshly ground white pepper
- 1¾ sticks (7 ounces; 200 grams) unsalted butter, at room temperature
- 1 (scant) cup (100 grams) confectioners' sugar, sifted
- 5½ tablespoons (1 ounce; 35 grams) finely ground almond powder (see page 265) or finely ground blanched almonds (see page 265)
- 2 hard-boiled large egg yolks, at room temperature, pressed through a fine strainer
- 1 large egg yolk, at room temperature
- 1/10 habanero pepper, seeded and finely chopped
- 1 tablespoon dark rum

1. Melt the chocolate over — not touching — simmering water or in a microwave oven; set the chocolate aside for the moment.
2. Sift the flour, baking powder, salt, and pepper together and set aside.
3. Place the butter in the bowl of a mixer fitted with the paddle attachment and beat until creamy. With the mixer on medium-low speed, blend in the confectioners' sugar, almond powder, egg yolks (both cooked and uncooked), and habanero. Continue to mix until smooth, scraping down the sides of the bowl as necessary. Mix in the rum, then the chocolate. Gradually add the flour mixture to the bowl, mixing only until the flour is incorporated. This is a delicate dough and you don't want to overmix it, so stop as soon as the last speck of flour disappears. You'll have a very soft dough.
4. Form the dough into 2 disks, wrap the disks in plastic, and refrigerate them for at least 3 hours. (*The dough can be refrigerated for up to 2 days or wrapped airtight and frozen for up to 1 month.*)
5. Line two baking sheets with parchment paper and keep them close at hand.

6. Working with one piece of dough at a time (keep the remaining piece refrigerated) and keeping the work surface and the dough well floured, roll the dough to a thickness of between ⅛ and ¼ inch (5 and 7 mm). If the dough softens and sticks as you work, give it a 15-minute chill and then carry on. Brush off any excess flour from the surface of the dough and, using a round cutter that's 3 to 3½ inches (about 8 cm) in diameter, cut the dough into as many cookies as you can, pressing the cutter firmly against the dough, then lifting the cutter straight up. (You should get about 8 cookies from each disk of dough). When you've made all the cuts, pull away the excess dough by lifting it off the work surface with an offset spatula. Lift the rounds of dough onto a parchment-lined baking sheet with the aid of a lightly floured metal spatula. When all the cutouts are on the baking sheet, prick them all over with the tines of a fork. Cover the cookies with plastic wrap and slide the baking sheet into the refrigerator to chill for at least 30 minutes. Repeat with the remaining dough. If you'd like, you can gather the leftover dough into a ball, flatten the dough into a disk, chill it, reroll it, and cut out more cookies.

7. While the cookies are in the refrigerator, position the racks to divide the oven into thirds and preheat the oven to 350°F (180°C).

8. Remove the plastic wrap from the baking sheets and bake the cookies for 14 to 16 minutes, rotating the pans from top to bottom and front to back halfway through the baking period. When the cookies are baked, their tops will be dull and they'll feel firm to the touch. Transfer the cookies, paper and all, to racks to cool for 5 minutes before serving.

TO FINISH

- **Chocolate Sauce (page 253), warmed**

For each serving, place one or two cookies (your choice) in the center of a large plate. Surround the cookie(s) with plenty of chocolate sauce, top with a generous scoop of allspice ice cream, and serve immediately.

Makes at least 8 servings

KEEPING: The ice cream can be made up to a week ahead, and the chocolate sauce up to 2 weeks in advance. But while the cookie dough can be made ahead and refrigerated for 2 days or frozen for up to a month, once the cookies are baked, they should be served that day.

MINT PROFITEROLES
WITH HOT CHOCOLATE SAUCE

Profiteroles would be a hard dessert for France to claim as its own. Hard too for Italy, where the dessert goes by the same name and includes the same three essential elements: bite-sized cream puffs; ice cream, usually vanilla but sometimes coffee, to spoon into the puffs; and warm chocolate sauce to pour over them. These profiteroles have the essentials — and then some. The puffs are made from an unusually rich dough that produces sweets that are soft and custardy on the inside and lightly crispy on the out, a nice contrast made more evident by a sprinkling of crunchy chopped almonds and crystal sugar. The sauce is classic — warm, dark, and glossy — but it's more bitter than sweet and more voluptuous than most because it is made with premium chocolate. However, it's the fresh mint ice cream that's the startler. Because it's made with handfuls of fresh mint leaves — some steeped in the milk and then blended into the custard base, and some finely chopped and added when the ice cream has just a moment more to churn — the flavor is invigorating, like a zephyr whistling through your mouth.

A note on the ice cream: Although you can churn the mint custard as soon as it is cool, the ice cream will be very much better — smoother and more flavorful — if you allow the custard to cool overnight. Also, this recipe makes a quart of ice cream, more than you'll need to fill the profiteroles. If you'd like, you can cut the recipe in half. Or make the full quantity and keep what's left over in the freezer.

■ I love the flavor of mint — but only of certain mint. I don't like spearmint, but I do like peppermint that's more pepper than mint, and I prefer mint with large thin leaves to mint whose leaves are small and curly. For this ice cream, and for all other mint desserts, I'd suggest you taste a selection of mints and choose the one that pleases you most. ■ PH

THE ICE CREAM

- **1 big bunch fresh mint (about 2 ounces; 55 grams)**
- **2 cups (500 grams) whole milk**
- **½ cup (125 grams) heavy cream**
- **6 large egg yolks**
- **½ cup (100 grams) sugar**
- **Freshly ground black pepper (about 3 to 4 turns of the pepper mill)**

1. Remove the leaves from three-quarters of the mint sprigs; discard the stems and wash and dry the leaves. Roughly chop the leaves and keep them close at hand. Keep the remaining one-quarter of the mint in the refrigerator — wrap the base of the stems in a piece of damp paper towel and put the sprigs in a plastic bag.

2. Bring the milk and cream to the boil in a medium saucepan. Remove the pan from the heat, stir in the chopped mint leaves, cover, and allow the mixture to rest for 15 minutes, time enough for the liquid to be thoroughly infused with the flavor and perfume of the mint. Strain the mixture, keeping both the liquid and the leaves.

3. While the mixture is infusing, set up an ice-water bath: Fill a large bowl with ice cubes and cold water. Set aside a smaller bowl that can hold the finished cream and be placed in the ice-water bath. Set aside a fine-meshed strainer too.

4. Working in the smaller bowl, whisk the egg yolks and sugar together until the mixture is lightly thickened and the sugar is dissolved. Still whisking, drizzle in about one-quarter of the hot milk and cream. When the liquid is incorporated, whisk in another cup or so more, then whisk the egg mixture into the saucepan with the remaining liquid. Set the pan over medium heat and, stirring constantly with a wooden spatula or spoon, cook the custard until it thickens slightly, lightens in color, and, most important, reaches 180°F (80°C), as measured on an instant-read thermometer — all of which will take less than 5 minutes. (Alternatively, you can stir the custard and then draw your finger down the spatula or the bowl of the wooden spoon — if the custard doesn't run into the track you've created, it's done.) Immediately pull the pan from the heat. Rinse and dry the smaller bowl, strain the custard into it, and stir in the black pepper. Set the bowl in the ice-water bath to cool. Stir the custard occasionally as it cools.

5. When the custard is cool, pour it into the jar of a blender, add the chopped mint leaves you used to infuse the liquids, and blend just until the leaves are

pureed and the custard is smooth. (Don't puree so long that the mint leaves turn brown.) Pour the custard into a refrigerator container, cover, and chill, preferably overnight.

6. The following day, pull the reserved mint leaves from their stems. Discard the stems, then wash, dry, and very finely chop the leaves. Pour the chilled custard into an ice-cream maker and churn according to the manufacturer's directions; just before the ice cream is churned to the proper consistency, add the chopped fresh mint. Spoon the ice cream into a freezer container and freeze for at least 2 hours before using. (*The ice cream can be packed airtight and kept in the freezer for up to 1 week, but its flavor is at its peak the day it is made.*)

THE CREAM PUFFS

- **Cream Puff Dough (page 233), just made and still warm**
- **Coarsely chopped blanched almonds**
- **Crystal sugar**

1. Position the racks to divide the oven into thirds and preheat the oven to 375°F (190°C). Line two baking sheets with parchment paper and keep them close at hand.

2. Spoon the warm cream puff dough into a large pastry bag fitted with a ⅔-inch (2-cm) plain tip. Pipe out about 30 small mounds of dough, each about 1½ inches (4 cm) across, onto the prepared baking sheets. Alternatively, you can shape the cream puffs by dropping the dough onto the baking sheet using a tablespoon. In either case, make sure to leave about 2 inches (5 cm) of puff-space between each dollop of dough.

3. Sprinkle the tops of the puffs with almonds and sugar and slide the baking sheet into the oven. Bake for 7 minutes, then slip the handle of a wooden spoon into the oven door so that it remains slightly ajar and continue to bake the cream puffs for another 13 minutes or so, until they are golden and firm (the total baking time is about 20 minutes). You'll get the most even bake if you rotate the sheets top to bottom and front to back at the 12-minute mark. Transfer the puffs to a rack to cool to room temperature. (*The cream puffs can be kept in a cool, dry spot for several hours before filling.*)

TO SERVE

- **Chocolate Sauce (page 253)**

1. If the chocolate sauce is not hot, warm it over gentle heat or in a microwave oven set to medium power.
2. Slice each cream puff on the diagonal with a serrated knife, cutting from one-third of the way down one side of the puff to the bottom of the opposite side, stopping just before the puff is cut in two. Gently open each cream puff, keeping it intact if possible, and fill with a scoop of mint ice cream.
3. For each serving, place 3 to 4 cream puffs in the center of a dinner plate, and pour over the hot chocolate sauce. Serve immediately.

Makes 8 to 10 servings

KEEPING: The ice cream can be kept in the freezer for a week, and the chocolate sauce can be refrigerated for a week or frozen for a month. However, when it's time to serve the dessert, you need to construct it quickly and serve it immediately.

TRIPLE CRÈME

Three creams, smoothed over one another, make this dessert nothing short of extravagant. The first layer is an espresso-flavored crème brûlée minus the brûlée, or burnt sugar topping. The second layer is Deep Chocolate Cream, dark and very much like chocolate pudding. And the third layer is cool, clean-tasting unsweetened whipped cream, surprising for its spareness. The differences in textures between the layers is subtle and the harmony among the flavors perfect.

■ This is not so much a mix of creams but a superimposition. Each layer keeps its own flavor and texture and only combines with the others after a second or two in your mouth. The espresso crème brûlée is light and refreshing; the chocolate cream is a little heavier and its flavor a little more likely to linger; and the whipped cream, the lightest layer, is almost neutral, providing a kind of middle ground between the other two very distinctive flavors. ■ PH

THE CRÈME BRÛLÉE

- **1⅓ cups (300 grams) whole milk**
- **3 tablespoons very finely ground espresso**
- **1 cup (250 grams) heavy cream, preferably at room temperature**
- **5 large egg yolks**
- **½ cup (100 grams) sugar**

1. Center a rack in the oven and preheat the oven to 200°F (95°C). (Actually, the perfect temperature is 210°F [100°C]. If your oven can be set to this temperature, so much the better.) Place eight shallow ovenproof gratin dishes, ramekins, or soup plates on a rimmed baking sheet. Ideally, the gratin dishes should be 4 inches (10 cm) in diameter and only 1 inch (2.5 cm) high. (Ovenproof glass and porcelain gratin dishes and ramekins are available in kitchenware shops.)

2. Bring the milk to the boil in a medium saucepan or in a microwave oven, remove from the heat, and stir in the espresso. Allow the milk to infuse for 1 minute, then pour it through a cheesecloth-lined strainer; discard the cof-

fee grounds. Meanwhile, bring the cream to the boil, then remove it from the heat.

3. Whisk the yolks and sugar together in a medium bowl, beating until they are well blended but not airy. Whisking constantly, drizzle in about one-quarter of the cream. When the yolks are acclimatized to the heat, add the rest of the cream and the espresso-infused milk to the bowl. Rap the bowl against the counter to burst any bubbles, then pour the custard through a strainer into a pitcher. Divide the custard among the gratin dishes; it should come about three-quarters of the way up the sides of the dishes — remember, you'll need room for the chocolate cream.

4. Bake the custards for about 45 minutes, or until the centers are set; if you tap the dishes gently, the centers of the custards shouldn't shimmy. Cool the custards on a rack, then, when they have come to room temperature, transfer them to the refrigerator to chill for at least 2 hours. (*The crème brûlée can be made up to 2 days ahead and kept tightly covered in the refrigerator.*)

THE CHOCOLATE LAYER

- **Deep Chocolate Cream (page 224), cooled but still pourable**

Pour an even layer of the cooled chocolate cream over each of the chilled custards. (You'll have some cream left over to eat as a treat.) Return the dishes to the refrigerator and chill the custards for at least 1 hour more. (*Once cooled, the custards can be covered and kept in the refrigerator for several hours, or, if the crème brûlée wasn't refrigerated for very long, for up to 2 days.*)

TO FINISH

- **⅓ cup (80 grams) heavy cream**
- **2 tablespoons toasted sesame seeds**

Whip the cream until it holds medium peaks. Spoon an even amount over each dessert, sprinkle with toasted sesame seeds, and serve immediately, or refrigerate for up to 1 hour.

Makes 8 servings

KEEPING: The dessert can be made — without the whipped cream topping — up to 2 days ahead and kept tightly covered in the refrigerator. You can top the dessert with the whipped cream either at serving time or up to 1 hour ahead — just put the dishes back in the refrigerator. Whatever you do, make sure the dessert is cold at serving time.

PISTACHIO WAFFLES WITH CHOCOLATE CREAM

Forget all-American breakfast waffles, and don't even think about maple syrup. These waffles are French and, in the French style, are meant for dessert. The waffles themselves are luscious — lightly crusted on the outside and soft, sweet, cakey, and studded with pistachio nuts within — but they are not intended to be served by themselves. They are one part of a tripartite dessert that includes a scoop of Deep Chocolate Cream and a spoonful of syrupy saffron-scented raisins. Not only does this dessert play with textures — there's the crunch of the waffle, the silky smoothness of the cream, and the chewiness of the raisins — but it offers a subtle and delightful play of temperature: The contrast between the hot waffles and the cool chocolate cream has the effect of making the cream seem even colder, as cold, in fact, as ice cream. The heightened differences make the dessert that much more appealing.

The recipe for the waffles was tested in a Belgian waffle iron — Belgian wafflers are the ones whose grids have the deepest pockets — and produced six 4½-inch (11.5-cm) square waffles; if you use a different size waffle iron, the waffles will still be fine but your yield may be different from ours.

■ You can make the waffles ahead of time. When you're ready to serve them, just dust their tops with confectioners' sugar and run them under the broiler for a couple of minutes until the sugar is lightly browned. You'll have reheated the waffles and caramelized their tops at the same time. ■ PH

THE RAISINS

- ½ cup (60 grams) golden raisins
- 1⅓ cups (330 grams) water
- 1½ tablespoons honey
- 3 thin slices peeled fresh ginger

- **Pinch each of salt and freshly ground black pepper**
- **4 to 6 saffron threads (no more), according to your taste**
- **1 teaspoon cornstarch, dissolved in 1 tablespoon cold water**

1. Put the raisins in a strainer and rinse them under running water for a minute. Toss the raisins into a medium saucepan along with the water, honey, ginger, and salt and pepper and bring to the boil. As soon as the water bubbles, turn the heat to its lowest setting and simmer gently for 15 minutes, until the raisins are puffed.

2. Using a slotted spoon, scoop out the raisins and ginger; discard the ginger, save the syrup, and put the raisins in a small bowl. Whisk the saffron and cornstarch into the syrup and bring to the boil. Strain the syrup over the raisins. Let the mixture cool to room temperature, then cover and chill for at least 2 hours before serving. (*The raisins can be made a day ahead and kept covered in the refrigerator.*)

THE WAFFLES

- **1 large egg white, at room temperature**
- **⅔ cup (165 grams) chilled heavy cream**
- **½ cup plus 2½ tablespoons (100 grams) all-purpose flour**
- **1 teaspoon double-acting baking powder**
- **3 large egg yolks, at room temperature**
- **2 tablespoons whole milk**
- **⅓ cup (70 grams) sugar**
- **Pinch of salt**
- **5 tablespoons (2½ ounces; 70 grams) unsalted butter, melted and cooled**
- **2¾ ounces (about ⅔ cup; 80 grams) skinned pistachio nuts, coarsely chopped**

1. Beat the egg white until it is stiff but still glossy; keep it aside. Now, whip the heavy cream until it holds medium peaks; keep this aside as well.

2. Whisk together the flour and baking powder and set them aside for the moment. Working in a large bowl, whisk together the egg yolks, milk, sugar, and salt. When the ingredients are blended, use a rubber spatula to fold in the beaten egg white, followed by the whipped cream. Don't worry about being thorough at this point. Slowly and gently fold in the flour mixture with the spatula. Still working gingerly, fold in the melted butter and then, when it is fully incorporated, the pistachio nuts. You'll have a thick mixture, one

that will look more like a cake batter than a traditional waffle batter. Cover the bowl with plastic wrap and put it in the refrigerator to settle and chill for 1 hour.

3. About 10 minutes before you are ready to prepare the waffles, preheat your waffle iron. If you want to hold the finished waffles for up to 15 minutes, preheat the oven to 200°F (95°C). Lightly butter or spray the grids of your iron if necessary; brush or spray the grids again only if subsequent waffles stick.

4. Spoon the batter onto the hot iron — the amount of batter you need will depend on your waffler (in most cases, one waffle will need ½ to ¾ cup [about 100 grams] of batter). Using a metal spatula or wooden spoon, smooth the batter evenly across the grids. Close the lid and bake until the waffle is browned and crisp. If you're going to serve the waffles now, transfer them to a cutting board; if you're going to keep them until you finish the batch, place them in a single layer on a rack in the preheated oven. Continue making waffles until you finish the batter. (*The waffles can be made ahead, cooled, and kept covered at room temperature for up to 6 hours or wrapped airtight and frozen for up to 1 month. Before serving, dust the waffles with confectioners' sugar and run them under the broiler to reheat them and caramelize the sugar.*)

TO SERVE

- **Deep Chocolate Cream (page 224), chilled**

For each serving, cut a waffle in half on the diagonal and place one half of the waffle in the center of a warm dinner plate. Put a scoop of chocolate cream in the center of the waffle, lean the other half of the waffle against the cream, and spoon some of the raisins and their saffron syrup around the waffles. Serve immediately, while the waffles are hot and the cream and raisins are cold.

Makes 6 servings

KEEPING: The raisins can be made a day ahead and the chocolate cream 2 days ahead; the waffle batter needs an hour's rest before it's used. Once the waffles are made, they can be served immediately, kept at room temperature for about 6 hours, or frozen for up to 1 month.

CHOCOLATE, COFFEE, AND WHISKEY CAPPUCCINO

I f you were to serve this dessert to a French person, he or she would surely exclaim, "*Épatant!*" Indeed, this dessert is "amazing." It's not that any of its four elements are so amazing, though, it's that together they are a surprising mix of flavors, textures, and temperatures. At the base of this dessert is Pierre's Deep Chocolate Cream, actually a dense chocolate pudding of exceptional quality. On top of this is a layer of espresso and malt whiskey *granité*. *Granité*, the French version of Italian granita, is a scraped ice that always seems colder than anything else in the freezer, but this *granité* is not just icy, it is also a little prickly and very boozy, a delightful contrast to the smooth chocolate cream and the next layer, a puff of airy unsweetened whipped cream — it's what gives this dessert its cappuccino look. The dessert is finished with a sprinkling of Rice Krispies, a slightly loony and completely lovely addition. Once softened a little by the cream, the Rice Krispies' texture falls somewhere between the smoothness of the pudding and the sharpness of the *granité*'s crystals. Pierre serves this dessert in martini glasses, where its layers are immediately visible, but wine goblets or even coffee cups would be fine.

■ The subtle alliances among and differences between this dessert's elements transform it from a recipe of great simplicity to one that offers a constantly changing play of flavors and sensations. Because each spoonful has a different proportion of the different preparations, each provides a different sense of pleasure — and I like that in a dessert. ■ PH

THE *GRANITÉ*

- 1 cup (250 grams) strong espresso, hot
- ⅓ cup (70 grams) sugar
- ¼ cup (60 grams) Scotch whiskey, preferably single malt
- Finely grated zest of ¼ orange

1. Stir the espresso, sugar, Scotch, and grated orange zest together, then pour the mixture into a shallow metal baking pan — an 8-inch (20-cm) square pan is fine. Slide the pan into the freezer and allow the mixture to set just until it is slushy — don't let it freeze into a solid block — 1 to 2 hours.

2. When the mixture is set, stir it around with a whisk for a minute or so, making sure to get into the corners, until it is liquid again, then return the pan to the freezer for another 3 to 4 hours, until the *granité* is solid. (*Once the granité has been stirred, it can be covered and kept in the freezer for a day or two.*)

THE CHOCOLATE CREAM

- **Deep Chocolate Cream (page 224), just made and still warm**

Pour enough of the chocolate cream to come one-third to halfway up the sides of the martini glasses, wine goblets, or coffee cups you've chosen for serving the dessert. (You'll have some cream left over to enjoy.) Press a piece of plastic wrap against the surface of the cream in each glass — creating an airtight seal will keep the cream from forming a skin — and chill the glasses for at least 2 hours. (*The cream can be made up to 2 days in advance and kept covered in the refrigerator.*)

THE WHIPPED CREAM

- **1 cup (250 grams) chilled heavy cream**

At the last minute, or up to 30 minutes ahead of time, beat the cream until it thickens and holds very soft peaks. You want the cream to be more billowy than firm. Cover the cream and store it in the refrigerator until needed.

TO ASSEMBLE

- **½ cup (7 grams) Rice Krispies**

When you are ready to serve the dessert, remove the glasses of chocolate cream from the refrigerator. Pull the *granité* from the freezer and, working quickly, scrape the tip of a metal spoon against the surface of the *granité* to create shards and crystals — think snow cones. As soon as you've "grated" the *granité*, divide it among the dessert glasses. Top each dessert with a spoonful of lightly whipped cream, sprinkle over a smattering of Rice Krispies, and immediately take the dessert to the table.

Makes 6 servings

KEEPING: Once assembled, there's not a minute to lose in serving this dessert. However, the chocolate cream and *granité* are do-aheadable — they must be made a few hours ahead, and they can be kept a day or two — the whipped cream can be made up to 30 minutes ahead, and the Rice Krispies need no preparation.

PEAR AND FRESH MINT TEMPURA WITH CHOCOLATE RICE PUDDING

If you've already tasted Pierre's Chocolate Rice Pudding, you may think that adding anything to it is a mistake. But you haven't tasted the pudding served with slices of fragrant warm batter-fried pears and fresh mint leaves. The combination — cool and warm, creamy and firm, crackly and juicy — is splendid, especially when capped by a drizzle of hot chocolate sauce.

The pear and mint tempura should be eaten as soon as it is fried or when still a little warm, so have the rice pudding prepared and chilled ahead of time. You can also make the chocolate sauce ahead and, at serving time, warm it over a pan of simmering water or in the microwave.

■ If you have a favorite recipe for tempura batter, by all means use it. But the dessert is delicious made with the boxed tempura mix found in the Asian foods section of most supermarkets — it's what I use. ■ PH

- ¾ cup (100 grams) tempura batter mix, such as Kame
- ¾ cup (185 grams) water
- ¼ teaspoon salt
- About 4 cups (1 liter) vegetable oil, for deep-frying
- 3 large ripe pears, preferably Comice or Anjou
- Freshly squeezed juice of 2 lemons
- 1 bunch fresh mint
- Sugar for sprinkling

1. Working in a small mixing bowl, whisk together the tempura batter mix, water, and salt. Set the batter aside until needed. (*You can mix the batter a*

few hours ahead of time and keep it covered in the refrigerator. If it seems a little thick after it's chilled, just thin it with a few drops of cold water.)

2. Pour the oil into a deep pot and heat it to 325° to 350°F (165° to 180°C), no hotter, as measured on a deep-fat or instant-read thermometer. Put a plate covered with a triple thickness of paper towels next to the stove.

3. Meanwhile, one by one, peel the pears, cut them in half from stem to bottom, and, using a melon baller, scoop out the cores. Cut each half lengthwise into 3 to 4 slices — the number of slices will depend on the size of the pears. Toss the slices in some lemon juice as you work to keep them from darkening. Remove the mint leaves from their main stems by pulling off tender sprigs of 3 or 4 leaves each.

4. Working with a few slices of pear at a time, dip the fruit into the tempura batter, then drop the batter-dipped pieces into the hot oil; don't crowd the pot. Fry the pears just until they are lightly golden on all sides — about 1½ minutes — then lift them out of the oil with a slotted spoon or wire spider and transfer them to the paper towel–lined plate to drain. Continue until all the pears are fried and then dip and fry the mint sprigs, which will need less than a minute in the oil; drain the mint as well. Sprinkle each piece of tempura lightly with sugar and give each a drizzle of fresh lemon juice.

TO FINISH

- **Chocolate Rice Pudding (page 125)**
- **Chocolate Sauce (page 253), warmed**

For each serving, scoop a mini-mountain of chocolate pudding into the center of a wide shallow soup plate. Lean 3 or 4 tempura-fried pear slices against the pudding and top with a few sprigs of fried mint. Finish the dessert by pouring a rivulet of hot chocolate sauce over the pears. Serve immediately.

Makes 6 servings

KEEPING: You can make both the chocolate pudding and the chocolate sauce ahead. You can even prepare the tempura batter a few hours in advance. But the tempura pears and mint sprigs should be served shortly after they're made so that they're hot — or at least still warm.

WARM CHOCOLATE CROQUETTES IN COLD COCONUT-MILK TAPIOCA SOUP

Contrast is the key word in this dessert, starting with the croquettes, their own small study in textural differences. Really coconut-coated chocolate truffles, the croquettes are frozen, then deep-fried until their outsides are firm and golden and their insides soft and seductively oozy. When the dessert is assembled, you get the crunch of the croquettes and then the fluidity of the tapioca soup in which they float. The soup is a lovely blend of large pearl tapicoa, coconut milk, and heavy cream, gently cooked like a luxurious bisque. Of course, there's the play of hot and cold between the croquettes and the soup, and, finally, the contrast in flavors: Speckling the soup are spicy strands of candied ginger and a few spoonfuls of tart and tangy passion fruit, both of which act like sparklers against the rich chocolate and tapioca. The look of the dessert is simple — it borders on plain — but its pleasures are sophisticated and swell.

THE CROQUETTES

- 5 ounces (145 grams) bittersweet chocolate, preferably Valrhona Guanaja, finely chopped
- 1 stick (4 ounces; 115 grams) unsalted butter
- 1 sliver habanero pepper (optional)
- 3 large eggs, 1 at room temperature
- 3 large egg yolks
- 1½ tablespoons sugar
- About 1½ cups (125 grams) very finely grated unsweetened dried coconut

1. Melt the chocolate in a bowl over — not touching — simmering water or in the microwave oven. Keep the chocolate on the counter until needed; it should still feel warm to the touch when you are ready to use it.
2. Melt the butter, with the pepper, if you're using it, in a small saucepan; discard the pepper and keep the butter aside for the moment. Gently whisk together the room-temperature egg, the yolks, and sugar in a medium bowl.

(Don't be too energetic — you don't want to beat in air.) Just as gently, stir in the chocolate, then the butter. Pour the ganache into a baking pan and refrigerate for at least 2 hours, until it is cold and firm. (*Once the ganache is cool, it can be covered and kept in the refrigerator overnight.*)

3. Line a baking sheet with parchment paper and keep it close at hand. Beat the remaining 2 eggs in a small bowl; turn the coconut into another small bowl. Remove the ganache from the refrigerator and, with a small spoon, scoop out enough ganache to form a ball that's about 1 inch (2.5 cm) in diameter, no larger. (You can roll the ganache between your palms to make a ball, but it's not necessary — bumpy rounds are fine.) Dunk the dollop of ganache into the beaten egg, then roll it around in the coconut to coat it well; put the croquette on the lined baking sheet. Continue until you've made croquettes from all the ganache — you'll have 24 or more — then slide the baking sheet into the freezer to chill the croquettes for at least 30 minutes. Set the beaten egg and coconut aside.

4. When the croquettes are set, give them another coating of egg and coconut. (It's important to have a good double layer of coconut since this is what will insulate the chocolate when the croquettes are deep-fried.) Return the croquettes to the freezer, again for at least 30 minutes, preferably longer. (*Once frozen, the croquettes can be wrapped airtight and kept frozen for up to 1 month.*)

THE GINGER CONFIT

- **1 Ping Pong–ball-sized knob of ginger, peeled**
- **⅔ cup (165 grams) water**
- **¼ cup (50 grams) sugar**

Using a lemon zester or a sharp knife, cut the ginger into very thin strands. (If you're using a knife, cut the ginger crosswise into very thin slices, then into slivers.) Bring the water and sugar to the boil in a small saucepan, add the strands of ginger, and reduce the heat to the lowest setting so that the syrup simmers very gently. Cook the ginger for about 20 minutes, or until it is soft and each strand is coated with syrup. Cool, then pack in a covered jar. (*The ginger confit can be made up to 1 month in advance and kept tightly covered in the refrigerator.*)

THE TAPIOCA SOUP

- **2 cups (500 grams) whole milk**
- **2 tablespoons sugar**
- **3 strips orange zest**

- **2 quarter-sized coins ginger, peeled**
- **5½ tablespoons (65 grams) large pearl tapioca (not granulated or instant)**
- **1 cup (250 grams) heavy cream**
- **One 13½-ounce (400-gram) can unsweetened coconut milk**

1. Bring the milk, sugar, orange zest, and ginger to a boil in a heavy-bottomed medium saucepan. Stirring constantly, add the tapioca in a slow, steady stream. Reduce the heat to its lowest setting and cook, stirring frequently, for about 10 minutes, or until the tapioca is soft.

2. While the tapioca is cooking, bring the heavy cream to the boil. Remove from heat and keep close at hand.

3. Add the coconut milk and heavy cream to the tapioca and, stirring constantly, cook over low heat for 3 minutes. Pour the tapioca soup into a container (a measuring cup with a spout is ideal), and cool to room temperature.

4. When the soup is cool, remove and discard the orange zest and ginger, cover, and refrigerate until it is thoroughly chilled, about 2 hours. (*The soup can be made ahead and kept covered in the refrigerator for 2 days.*)

TO FINISH

- **About 4 cups (1 liter) cooking oil, for deep-frying**
- **3 ripe passion fruits, halved**

1. Pour the oil into a deep pot and heat it to about 350°F (180°C), as measured on a deep-fat or instant-read thermometer. Meanwhile, prepare the dessert plates: Spoon a little passion fruit into the center of each of eight shallow soup plates or coupes. Have the chilled tapioca and ginger confit on the counter. Place a triple-thick layer of paper towels on a plate close to the stove.

2. When the oil is hot, drop a few croquettes into the pot and fry for no more than 3 minutes. If your croquettes were frozen for 6 or more hours, they will probably need about 3 minutes to crisp on the outside and melt within; however, if they were only quick-frozen, they may need only a minute or less. To be on the safe side, fry one or two as a test. Lift the croquettes from the oil with a skimmer or slotted spoon and drain them on the paper towels. Working quickly, fry the rest of the croquettes.

3. For each serving, put 3 to 4 croquettes (the number depends on how many croquettes you've made) over the passion fruit in each plate. Pour the tapioca soup around the croquettes and scatter a few strands of ginger confit over the soup. Serve immediately.

Makes 8 servings

KEEPING: All the components can — indeed, must — be made ahead, but once the croquettes are fried and the dessert is assembled, it needs to be served immediately.

CHOCOLATE AND
BANANA BROCHETTES

For anyone who loves the classic combination of chocolate and banana, this dessert will become the ne plus ultra of the genre. It is nothing more than squares of chocolate ganache threaded onto a brochette with rounds of banana, but it is splendid. Indeed, this dessert is as simple as it sounds and as delicious as it looks (see page vi).

A note on the assembly: The brochettes are best made on long hors d'oeuvre picks or short barbecue skewers. If you can't find either, you can arrange the ganache and the banana rounds on plates and serve the dessert with a knife and fork.

- **Double recipe Bittersweet Chocolate Cream Ganache (page 215), still warm and at a pourable consistency**
- **Freshly squeezed juice of 1 lemon**
- **3 large ripe but firm bananas**
- **Dutch-processed cocoa powder, preferably Valrhona, for dusting**

1. Pour the ganache into an 8-inch (20-cm) square pan; you will have a layer of chocolate that is about 1 inch (2.5 cm) thick. Slide the pan into the refrigerator and chill for at least 1 hour, or until the ganache is firm. (*If it's more convenient for you, you can cover the ganache and keep it in the refrigerator overnight.*)

2. When the ganache is firm, cut it into 1-inch (2.5-cm) cubes. Return the ganache to the refrigerator for the moment.

3. Put the lemon juice in a large bowl and keep it close at hand. Peel the bananas and cut them into rounds about ¼ inch (7 mm) thick; drop the rounds into the lemon juice as soon as they are cut to keep them from turning dark.

4. When you are ready to serve the dessert, put the cocoa powder in a large bowl. Remove the ganache cubes from the refrigerator and turn them into the cocoa powder. Toss the cubes so that each one is dusted with cocoa, then very gingerly toss the cubes between your hands to shake off the excess. Thread the ganache and bananas onto picks or skewers, alternating cubes of ganache and rounds of banana: Each brochette should have 2 cubes of ganache and 2 rounds of banana. Serve as quickly as you can.

Makes 24 brochettes or
8 to 12 servings

KEEPING: This dessert is meant to be eaten as soon as it is made. You can keep it in the refrigerator for a few minutes, but it's best not to keep it waiting.

TRUFFLES AND OTHER LUXURIOUS
CHOCOLATE CANDIES

Dark, velvety, lumpy, bumpy chocolate truffles are as prized as the fungi for which they were named, and after which they were modeled. These luxurious candies are the simplest of the truffle family, made of nothing more than cream, butter, and bittersweet chocolate. In French, dark chocolate is called *chocolat noir* or black chocolate, so you can understand why Pierre dubbed these "black truffles." Once the black truffles are shaped between your palms, they're plunged into cocoa powder, giving truth to the name "black on black."

■ I usually eat these straight from the refrigerator, in part because chilled truffles are firm, and I like them that way, and in part because the cocoa powder, once chilled, is not as powdery and dry as it can be when it's warmer. ■ PH

- **9 ounces (260 grams) bittersweet chocolate, preferably Valrhona Caraïbe, finely chopped**
- **1 cup (250 grams) heavy cream**
- **3½ tablespoons (1¾ ounces; 50 grams) unsalted butter, at room temperature, cut into 4 pieces**
- **Dutch-processed cocoa powder, preferably Valrhona, for dusting**

1. Put the chocolate in a heatproof bowl that can hold all of the ingredients. Bring the cream to a full boil in a saucepan or microwave oven, then pour the hot cream into the center of the chocolate. Working with a spatula, gently stir the cream into the chocolate in ever-widening concentric circles until the ganache is homogenous and smooth. Allow the ganache to rest on the counter for about a minute before adding the butter.

2. Add the butter 2 pieces at a time, stirring gently to blend. When all the butter is blended into the mixture, pour the ganache into a baking pan or bowl. Put the pan in the refrigerator and, when the ganache is cool, cover it with plastic wrap and chill for at least 3 hours. (*The ganache can stay in the refrigerator overnight, if that's more convenient for you.*)

Makes about 40 truffles

KEEPING: The truffles can be served as soon as they are coated or they can be stored in the refrigerator for a day or two, covered and away from foods with strong odors.

3. When you are ready to shape the truffles, spoon a generous amount of cocoa powder into a bowl, and set out a baking sheet lined with parchment or waxed paper. Remove the truffle mixture from the refrigerator and scoop up a scant tablespoonful of ganache for each truffle; put the dollops of ganache on the paper-lined pan. Dust the palms of your hands with cocoa powder and, one by one, roll the mounds of ganache between your palms to form rounds. Don't worry about making them even — they're supposed to be gnarly and misshapen. As you shape each truffle, drop it into the bowl of cocoa powder, toss it in the cocoa so that it is well coated, and then very gingerly toss it between your palms to shake off the excess cocoa. Alternatively, you can roll the truffles around in a sieve to encourage them to shake off their extra cocoa. As each truffle is finished, return it to the parchment-lined pan.

SICHUAN-PEPPER
CHOCOLATE TRUFFLES

Because Sichuan pepper has more flavor than burn, more sweetness than heat, it is a delectable — and surprisingly mild-mannered — addition to a chocolate truffle. One caveat: Do not use the round white Sichuan peppercorns that are commonly sold in supermarkets. What you need for this recipe are the rose-colored, flaky, husk-like pieces of Sichuan pepper that can be found in specialty shops and spice markets (see Source Guide).

■ You can enhance the pepper flavor by toasting the peppercorns lightly in a dry skillet over medium heat. ■ PH

- 9 ounces (260 grams) bittersweet chocolate, preferably Valrhona Caraïbe, finely chopped
- 1 cup (250 grams) heavy cream
- 2 tablespoons Sichuan pepper, crushed
- 3½ tablespoons (1¾ ounces; 50 grams) unsalted butter, at room temperature, cut into 4 pieces
- Dutch-processed cocoa powder, preferably Valrhona, for dusting

1. Put the chocolate in a heatproof bowl that can hold all of the ingredients.
2. Bring the cream and pepper to a full boil in a saucepan. Remove the pan from the heat, cover tightly with plastic wrap, and let the cream rest for 10 minutes so that it will become flavored by the pepper.
3. Pour the cream through a strainer lined with a piece of dampened cheesecloth, return the cream to the saucepan, and spoon in about one-third of the pepper that's in the strainer; discard the remaining pepper. Bring the cream to the boil again, then remove the pan from the heat and strain the hot cream into the center of the chocolate. Working with a spatula, gently stir the cream into the chocolate in ever-widening concentric circles until the ganache is homogenous and smooth. Allow the ganache to rest on the counter about a minute before adding the butter.

4. Add the butter 2 pieces at a time, stirring gently to blend. When all the butter is blended into the mixture, pour the ganache into a baking pan or bowl. Put the pan in the refrigerator and, when the ganache is cool, cover it with plastic wrap and chill for at least 3 hours. (*The ganache can stay in the refrigerator overnight, if that's more convenient for you.*)

5. When you are ready to shape the truffles, spoon a generous amount of cocoa powder into a bowl, and set out a baking sheet lined with parchment or waxed paper. Remove the truffle mixture from the refrigerator and scoop up a scant tablespoonful of ganache for each truffle; put the dollops of ganache on the paper-lined pan. Dust the palms of your hands with cocoa powder and, one by one, roll the mounds of ganache between your palms to form rounds. Don't worry about making them even — they're supposed to be gnarly and misshapen. As you shape each truffle, drop it into the bowl of cocoa powder, toss it in the cocoa so that it is well coated, and then very gingerly toss it between your palms to shake off the excess cocoa. Alternatively, you can roll the truffles around in a sieve to encourage them to shake off their extra cocoa. As each truffle is finished, return it to the parchment-lined pan.

Makes about 40 truffles

KEEPING: The truffles can be served as soon as they are coated, or they can be stored in the refrigerator for a day or two, covered and away from foods with strong odors.

For anyone who loves caramel, this is the defin-
itive truffle. The caramel flavor is front
and center, but as you allow the truffle
to slowly melt in your mouth, its sub-
tlety is revealed. What you taste is just a touch of salt, which enlivens the
caramel, and a mellow blend of chocolates, a mix of milk and not-too-bitter bittersweet, which provides the chocolate base, of course, but which also intensifies
the caramel taste. Like all traditional truffles, these are dusted with cocoa powder, a nice counterpoint.

■ The decisive step in this recipe is the caramelization of the sugar. If the sugar
turns too dark, the flavor will be bitter; too light, and the flavor won't be strong
enough. To get the right color, test the sugar as you work by putting a few drops
on a white plate. ■ PH

- **1 cup (250 grams) heavy cream**
- **10 ounces (285 grams) bittersweet chocolate, preferably Valrhona Caraïbe,
  finely chopped**
- **6 ounces (170 grams) milk chocolate, preferably Valrhona Jivara, finely chopped**
- **1 cup (200 grams) sugar**
- **2½ tablespoons (1¼ ounces; 40 grams) salted butter, at room temperature,
  cut into small pieces (or use unsalted butter plus a tiny pinch of salt)**
- **Dutch-processed cocoa powder, preferably Valrhona, for dusting**

1. Bring the cream to a boil in a saucepan or the microwave and keep it hot.
   (Alternatively, you can bring the cream to the boil, then reheat it quickly in
   the microwave when you need it.) Mix the chocolate together in a heatproof
   bowl that's large enough to hold all of the ingredients; set aside.

2. Working in a heavy-bottomed medium saucepan over medium heat, melt
   about 3 tablespoons of the sugar. When the sugar starts to take on color, stir
   it with a wooden spoon or heatproof spatula and add another 3 tablespoons
   of sugar. Stirring constantly, caramelize this new batch of sugar, then add

another 3 tablespoons. Continue until all of the sugar has been added and it turns a rich amber color. To check the color, dab a few drops on a white plate. Lower the heat and, still stirring, add the butter. The caramel will bubble and froth — just stir in the butter, then, still stirring, stand away from the pan and add the hot cream in a slow, steady stream. The caramel will froth even more furiously — just keep stirring until it is smooth. (If the caramel seizes, don't be concerned — it will smooth out as you stir it over heat.) When the caramel settles down and is smooth, remove the pan from the heat.

3. Pour about one-third of the caramel into the center of the chocolate and, working with the wooden spoon or spatula, gently stir the creamy caramel into the chocolate in ever-widening concentric circles. When the ganache is smooth, add half of the remaining caramel, blending it into the chocolate in circles, then finish with the rest of the caramel in the same manner. Pour the ganache into a baking pan or bowl. Put the pan in the refrigerator and, when the ganache is cool, cover it with plastic wrap and chill for at least 4 hours. (*The ganache can stay in the refrigerator overnight, if that's more convenient for you.*)

4. When you are ready to shape the truffles, spoon a generous amount of cocoa powder into a bowl, and set out a baking sheet lined with parchment or waxed paper. Remove the truffle mixture from the refrigerator and scoop up a scant tablespoonful of ganache for each truffle; put the dollops of ganache on the paper-lined pan. Dust the palms of your hands with cocoa powder and, one by one, roll the mounds of ganache between your palms to form rounds. Don't worry about making them even — they're supposed to be gnarly and misshapen. As you shape each truffle, drop it into the bowl of cocoa powder, toss it in the cocoa so that it is well coated, and then very gingerly toss it between your palms to shake off the excess cocoa. Alternatively, you can roll the truffles around in a sieve to encourage them to shake off their extra cocoa. As each truffle is finished, return it to the parchment-lined pan.

Makes about 55 truffles

KEEPING: If the truffles are not too soft (because of the caramel, these truffles have a tendency to soften quickly), they can be served as soon as they are coated, or they can be stored in the refrigerator for a day or two, covered and away from foods with strong odors.

MILK CHOCOLATE AND PASSION FRUIT TRUFFLES

Everything about these truffles is unusual, starting with the passion fruit. Passion fruit is an exotic fruit with a tang that's only slightly soft around the edges. It has a startlingly bright and fresh flavor, not one you'd readily think to pair with chocolate. But Pierre makes the passion fruit–chocolate match easily and perfectly by bringing in another unusual ingredient, milk chocolate. Beloved in America, milk chocolate is not frequently found in French recipes. Yet here it is the ideal chocolate because it is mild, slightly sweet, and amenable — it will soften the passion fruit and, in turn, allow the passion fruit puree to give it a little pucker. To make both the contrasts and complements more notable, the truffles are smoothed with a touch of honey, studded with tiny pieces of sweet-tart dried apricots, and rolled in confectioners' sugar.

- 14¾ ounces (420 grams) milk chocolate, preferably Valrhona Jivara, finely chopped
- 1¾ ounces (50 grams) moist, plump dried apricots (about 8), cut into tiny dice
- 2 tablespoons water
- Scant ⅔ cup (160 grams) passion fruit puree (see Source Guide)
- ⅓ cup plus 2 tablespoons (90 grams) heavy cream
- 1 tablespoon honey
- 4 tablespoons (2 ounces; 60 grams) unsalted butter, at room temperature, cut into 4 pieces
- Confectioners' sugar for dusting

1. Put the chocolate in a heatproof bowl that is large enough to hold all of the ingredients; set aside.
2. Stir the apricots and water together in a small saucepan and place the pan over gentle heat for a few minutes, until the apricots are moist. Pull the pan from the heat, drain the apricots if necessary, and pat them dry between a double thickness of paper towels.

3. Bring the passion fruit puree, cream, and honey to a full boil in a saucepan or microwave oven, then pour it into the center of the chocolate. Working with a spatula, gently stir the cream into the chocolate in ever-widening concentric circles until the ganache is homogenous and smooth. Allow the ganache to rest on the counter about a minute before adding the butter.

4. Add the butter 2 pieces at a time, stirring gently to blend. When all the butter is blended into the mixture, fold in the apricot pieces and pour the ganache into a baking pan or bowl. Put the pan in the refrigerator and, when the ganache is cool, cover it with plastic wrap and chill for at least 4 hours. (*The ganache can stay in the refrigerator overnight, if that's more convenient for you.*)

5. When you are ready to shape the truffles, have a parchment-lined baking sheet close at hand. Remove the truffle mixture from the refrigerator and scoop up a scant tablespoonful of ganache for each truffle; put the mounds of ganache on the paper-lined pan. One by one, roll the mounds between the palms of your hands to form a ball. Don't worry about making them even — they're supposed to be lumpy. As you shape each truffle, drop it into the bowl of confectioners' sugar, toss it in the sugar so that it is well coated, and then very gingerly toss it between your palms to shake off the excess. Alternatively, you can roll the truffles around in a sieve to encourage them to shake off their extra sugar. As each truffle is finished, return it to the parchment-lined pan.

Makes about 50 truffles

KEEPING: The truffles can be served as soon as they are coated, or they can be stored in the refrigerator for a day or two, covered and away from foods with strong odors.

Like the sugar that is its base, caramel is a chameleon, capable of changing the intensity of its flavor, the depth of its color, and the firmness of its texture according to how long it is cooked, over how much heat, and to what temperature or stage. For this confection, the sugars (there's granulated sugar and corn syrup, which is a natural sugar) are heated and stirred to a rich mahogany color before anything else is added; it is this depth of color that contributes so much to the depth of flavor. Then — skipping ahead for the moment — the mixture is cooked just past the soft ball stage, so that when it cools, it is firm enough to be cut into neat cubes but tender enough to melt languorously on your tongue. These caramels are, as the French would say, *mou*, or soft. They are also chocolate, lusciously and unmistakably, and lemony, surprisingly and subtly. The addition of bittersweet chocolate is the middle part, the step that comes between coloring the sugar and cooking the mixture to 243°F (117°C). The chocolate is added along with the butter and cream and then cooked well past the point that most experts tell you is advisable for an ingredient as delicate as fine chocolate. Fear not: The chocolate emerges unscathed and blends beautifully with the slight bitterness of the caramelized sugar and the touch of sharpness that the lemon zest contributes.

■ Caramel always needs some salt, a counterpoint to the cooked sugar's sweetness. Here, the salt comes from salted butter. If you don't have salted butter, remember to add a pinch of salt to the pot. ■ PH

- 1¾ cups (435 grams) heavy cream
- 1⅔ cups (340 grams) sugar
- ¾ cup plus 2 tablespoons (280 grams) light corn syrup
- Finely chopped or grated zest of ½ lemon

- **3 tablespoons (1½ ounces; 45 grams) salted butter, cut into 3 pieces (or use unsalted butter plus a pinch of salt)**
- **4 ounces (115 grams) bittersweet chocolate, preferably Valrhona Guanaja, finely chopped**

1. Line an 8-inch (20-cm) square pan with aluminum foil. (Alternatively, you can use a 9-inch (24-cm) pan — you'll just have shorter candies.) Spray the foil with a vegetable spray such as Pam, or butter it, then set the pan aside. Have a candy or instant-read thermometer close at hand.

2. Bring the heavy cream to the boil in a saucepan or a microwave, then set it aside.

3. Put the sugar, corn syrup, and lemon zest in a large heavy-bottomed pot — a 4-quart (4-liter) Dutch oven or casserole is perfect. (You must use a large deep pot, because the sugar will boil furiously when the other ingredients are added.) Place the pot over medium heat, stir the ingredients with a wooden spatula or spoon to blend, and then cook until the sugar melts and the mixture comes to the boil. Continue to cook, stirring regularly, until the sugar caramelizes deeply; the color should be rusty mahogany. Still stirring — but taking care to stand away from the pot — add, one by one, the pieces of butter, the warm cream, and the chocolate. Now, stirring without stop, cook the caramel until it reaches 243°F (117°C), as measured on a candy or instant-read thermometer. As soon as the caramel reaches the right temperature, pull the pot from the heat and pour the caramel into the foil-lined pan.

4. Put the pan on a cooling rack or counter and allow the caramel to stand undisturbed until it cools to room temperature and firms. The caramel will need at least 5 hours to firm enough to be cut and wrapped, and, if you have the time, it is best to leave it overnight. (If the kitchen is warm — particularly if it is humid — the caramel may not firm properly, so let it cool to room temperature, then put the pan in the refrigerator for a few hours if necessary.)

5. When you are ready to cut the caramel, turn it out onto a cutting board, peel away the foil, and invert the caramel so it is right side up. Using a long thin knife, cut the caramel into 1-inch (2.5-cm) squares. (It's best to cut only as much caramel as you need and to keep the remainder wrapped in waxed paper or plastic wrap.) If you'd like, you can cut the caramel into larger or smaller squares, or even into long thin rectangles. Serve the caramel immediately, or wrap the pieces individually in cellophane, waxed paper, or plastic wrap.

Makes about 60 candies

KEEPING: Wrapped well or stored in an airtight tin, the caramels will keep for at least 4 days at room temperature.

The name tells you everything you need to know about these candies except how good they are — and they are *very* good. Indeed, they are very good on their own, savored as you would any chocolate candy, and they are just as good served with a cup of full-strength espresso. What makes these candies so special are their three flavors and textures. Whole, meaty almonds, toasted to a golden brown, are at the heart of the candy. Next, encasing the almonds, comes a thin layer of sweet, crackly caramel. Finally, the candied almonds are given a dip in tempered chocolate, a sleek and luscious finish.

■ The technique for caramelizing and chocolate-coating the almonds is one that you can use with other nuts. This recipe will work equally well with macadamia nuts or even walnuts. And if you use salted peanuts, you'll have a sophisticated version of an American childhood treat — Goobers. ■ PH

- ⅓ cup (70 grams) sugar
- 3 tablespoons water
- 7 ounces (200 grams) blanched whole almonds, toasted (see page 275) and still warm or at room temperature
- 5 ounces (145 grams) bittersweet chocolate, preferably Valrhona Caraïbe, tempered (see page 260)

1. Line a baking sheet with a Silpat or other silicone baking mat, or use parchment paper, and keep it on the counter near the range. Bring the sugar and water to a boil in a heavy-bottomed medium saucepan set over medium heat. Swirl the ingredients around to dissolve the sugar, then allow the mixture to boil, without stirring, until it reaches 248°F (119°C), as measured on a candy or an instant-read thermometer. (If any sugar sticks to the sides of

the pan, as might happen at the start of the cooking, wash it down with a pastry brush dipped in cold water.)

2. Add the almonds all at once and, working with a wooden spoon or spatula, stir the nuts into the sugar, then continue to cook and stir over medium heat. As you stir the almonds, which will clump together at the start, they will separate and their sugar coating will turn white and sandy. Continue to cook and, above all, stir and the coating will start to caramelize. (The caramel coating will be bumpy — and that's just the way it should be.) When the sugar is a pale caramel color, turn the almonds out onto the lined baking sheet. After a minute or so, use the spoon or spatula to separate the almonds as best you can. Don't worry if you have a few two- and three-nut clusters. Allow the almonds to cool to room temperature on the baking sheet. (*The cooled caramelized almonds can be packed in an airtight container and kept at cool room temperature for up to 4 days.*)

3. Have the tempered chocolate on the counter and have a Silpat- or parchment-lined baking sheet close at hand.

4. Turn the almonds into the chocolate and, using a fork, gently stir them two or three times just to be certain that all the nuts are covered with chocolate. Pour the chocolate-coated nuts onto the lined baking sheet and use the fork to spread the almonds apart. Put the baking sheet in the refrigerator and chill just until the chocolate is set, about 15 minutes. When the chocolate is dry, the nuts are ready to eat.

Makes about ½ pound (225 grams) candy

KEEPING: The candies can be made up to 4 days ahead and kept in an airtight container at cool room temperature.

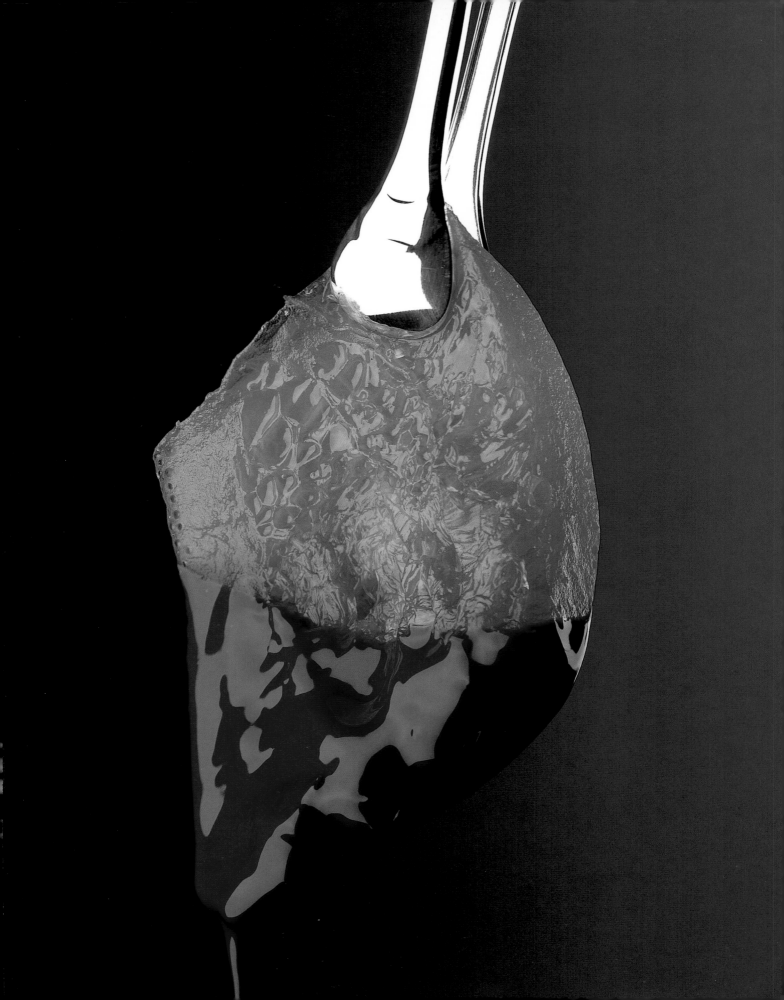

CHOCOLATE-COATED CANDIED CITRUS PEEL

Like Chocolate-Coated Caramelized Almonds (page 171), these are the kind of candy you find in the best chocolate shops, tucked into small clear cellophane sachets, tied with ribbon or sealed with a sticker displaying the shop's logo. Use fine bittersweet chocolate, and your candies will rival those of the best chocolatiers. It is most traditional to cut the candied peel into thin strips for chocolate coating, but nothing says you must hold to tradition — these are exceptional when the peel is cut into pieces you can measure in inches rather than fractions thereof. Similarly, the most usual peel for chocolate-dipping is orange, but you can candy-and-coat lemon and grapefruit peel as well.

A note on quantity: It's best to candy a large batch of orange peel, because it keeps for 3 weeks under refrigeration, but once the peel is coated with chocolate, it should be eaten — so you may want to coat only as much peel as you need.

■ Because the candied peel is sweet, tangy, and spicy, you'll get the best results if you choose a chocolate that is not too bitter. My recommendation for the coating is a fruity chocolate, such as Valrhona Manjari. ■ PH

- **Candied Citrus Peel (page 257)**
- **1 pound (450 grams) bittersweet chocolate, preferably Valrhona Manjari, tempered (see page 260)**

1. Drain the peel and pat each piece dry between paper towels. Lay the peel out on cooling racks in a single layer and allow the peel to dry overnight at room temperature.

2. Line a baking sheet with parchment and set it close to the tempered chocolate. One by one, dip the peels into the chocolate, allow the excess chocolate to drip back into the chocolate pot, and place on the parchment-lined pan. Chill the peel in the refrigerator for 15 minutes to set and dry the chocolate.

Makes about 2 pounds (900 grams) of candy (or more than 20 servings)

KEEPING: Chocolate-coated peel is best eaten the day it is made.

Mendiant means beggar in French, but in candy-land, a mendiant is a round of chocolate topped with dried fruits and nuts, often a mixture of golden raisins, hazelnuts, almonds, and pistachio nuts — but, like Pierre, you can add and subtract fruits at whim. You can use just one fruit or nut as the topping or stud the top with a cornucopia of six or seven types, and you can choose to make the rounds in dark, milk, or white chocolate.

This recipe can be halved or multiplied, depending on your needs.

- **1 pound (450 grams) chocolate, dark, milk, or white, or some of each, tempered (see page 260)**
- **1 cup (about 140 grams) dried fruits and nuts, such as golden raisins, slices of dried apricots, diced dried figs, pieces of dried cherries, whole hazelnuts, halved cashews, julienned almonds, and/or pecan, walnut, or pistachio pieces**

1. Line two baking sheets with parchment paper, sheets of acetate, or silicone baking mats. Make the chocolate rounds by spooning out about 1½ tea-spoons of chocolate for each round: Hold the spoon about 3 inches (7.5 cm) above the parchment and allow the chocolate to drip off the tip of the spoon onto the paper. There's no need to wiggle the spoon around, the chocolate will pour off the spoon and spread into a perfect round.

2. Dot each mendiant with an equal amount of fruits and nuts, then slide the baking sheets into the refrigerator to allow the chocolate to set, about 15 minutes.

Makes about 50 candies

KEEPING: Layered between sheets of parchment or waxed paper and packed in an airtight tin, the mendiants will keep at cool room temperature for 3 days.

CHOCOLATE-DIPPED
CANDIED MINT LEAVES

Mint is such a lively, versatile, pretty herb, yet it's often a Johnny-one-note in the dessert domain, frequently used as a last-minute decoration or tossed on a plate to add a dash of color — a practice Pierre abhors, since the mint usually has no relation to the dessert it's adorning. But here, fashioned into a candy, mint gets star treatment. For this confection, individual mint leaves are coated with sugar, then dipped in tempered chocolate to make vibrant bite-sized sweets.

This may seem an odd recipe in that there are no specific amounts, but the ingredients are few and the techniques simple and the same whether you're candying and dipping a handful of mint or an armload. And there's no waste — if you've poured out too much sugar or tempered too much chocolate, you can reuse either one.

■ You can use the same technique to dip verbena leaves; their light lemony flavor makes an interesting counterpoint to the chocolate coating. ■ PH

- **Fresh mint leaves**
- **Egg white(s)**
- **Sugar**
- **Bittersweet or milk chocolate, preferably Valrhona Caraïbe or Jivara, tempered (see page 260)**

1. Remove the mint leaves from their stems; if you'd like, you can leave the small stems that connect the leaves to the main stem — in fact, it might make it easier for you to handle the leaves if you do. Wash the leaves, shake off the excess water, and pat the leaves completely dry between a double thickness of paper towels.

2. Put the egg white in a small bowl and whisk it lightly, just to break it up and make it foamy. Pour some sugar onto a small plate; you want a layer that's

less than ¼ inch (7 mm) thick. (If you need more, you can add it at any time.) Place a piece of parchment paper close to your work surface.

3. Working with 1 mint leaf at a time, dip the leaf in the beaten egg white just to coat it, then allow the excess egg white to drip back into the bowl. Pass the egg white–coated leaf over the sugar, turning the leaf so that both sides are lightly covered in sugar. Place the leaf on the parchment and continue until you've candied as many leaves as you want. Leave the leaves on the paper to dry overnight at room temperature.

4. When you are ready to dip the leaves in chocolate, place a clean sheet of parchment paper on the counter, near the tempered chocolate. Holding a mint leaf at its stem end, dip it into the chocolate until the chocolate reaches the leaf's midpoint. Lift out the leaf, allow the excess chocolate to drip back into the container, run the edge of the leaf against the rim of the container to cut off any drips, and put the leaf on the paper.

5. When you have dipped as many leaves as you want, slide the parchment onto a baking sheet and slip it into the refrigerator to set the chocolate, about 15 minutes. The leaves are ready to serve.

KEEPING: The sugar-coated leaves can be kept at room temperature — provided your room is cool and dry — for 1 day. The chocolate-dipped leaves can be refrigerated in a closed container for 1 day.

ICE CREAM SCOOPS, COUPES,

SUNDAES, SPLITS, AND OTHER

FROZEN CHOCOLATE DESSERTS

BITTERSWEET
CHOCOLATE SORBET

Because this sorbet is made from premium-quality bittersweet chocolate, not cocoa powder, it has a compelling depth of flavor and an intensity usually associated with ice cream. That the sorbet is made with just chocolate, sugar, and water makes its flavor even more remarkable.

■ To have great chocolate flavor in this sorbet, you've got to use great chocolate. There's no skimping in this recipe, because, with only three ingredients, there's nothing to change the chocolate's taste. ■ PH

- 7 ounces (200 grams) bittersweet chocolate, preferably Valrhona Guanaja, finely chopped
- 1 (scant) cup (200 grams) sugar
- 2 cups (500 grams) water

1. So that you can quickly chill the sorbet mixture before you churn it, set up an ice-water bath by filling a large bowl with ice cubes and water. Set aside a smaller bowl that can hold all the ingredients.

2. Put all the ingredients in a heavy-bottomed medium saucepan over low heat. Cook, stirring frequently, until the mixture reaches the boil — this can take 10 minutes or more. Then stir without stop and pay attention: This will bubble furiously. Boil for 2 minutes, then pour the mixture into the smaller bowl. Set the bowl into the ice-water bath. Allow the mixture to chill, stirring now and then.

3. Freeze the sorbet in an ice-cream maker following the manufacturer's instructions. You can serve the sorbet directly from the ice-cream maker or pack it into an airtight container and freeze until needed.

Makes a generous pint (about ½ liter)

KEEPING: While best eaten within a few hours of churning, if packed airtight, the sorbet will keep its smooth texture for about 1 week in the freezer.

CHOCOLATE ICE CREAM, PLAIN AND VARIED

This is as pure a chocolate ice cream as it is possible to make. Unlike Pierre's allspice or caramel ice creams (pages 131 and 194), which are made with an egg-yolk-and-heavy-cream base, the perfect base for spices and strong flavorings, this ice cream is what Americans know as a Philadelphia ice cream — it's eggless, and creamless too. What you taste with each spoonful is chocolate, pure and simple, since there are no other full-bodied or full-flavored ingredients to stand in its way.

After you've made a batch of straight chocolate ice cream, you might want to vary it. If so, consider infusing the ice cream's milk with lavender or, when the ice cream is just about churned, tossing in chunks of brownies or caramelized macadamia nuts (see the variations below).

■ I have very definite opinions about chocolate ice cream: I don't think it should ever be made with eggs. Eggs make the ice cream too heavy and yolks change the taste of the chocolate. And I think that chocolate ice cream should always be made with chocolate — you should not even consider using cocoa powder. ■ PH

- ⅓ cup (30 grams) powdered milk
- 3 cups (750 grams) whole milk
- ⅓ cup (70 grams) sugar
- 8 ounces (230 grams) bittersweet chocolate, preferably Valrhona Caraïbe, finely chopped

1. So that you can quickly cool the chocolate mixture before you churn it, set up an ice-water bath by filling a large bowl with ice cubes and water. Set aside a smaller bowl that can hold all of the ingredients.

2. Place the powdered milk in a heavy-bottomed medium saucepan and gradually whisk in the whole milk. When the powdered milk is dissolved, whisk in the sugar. Bring the mixture to the boil, then stir in the chopped chocolate

and bring it to the boil again. Pull the pan from the heat and pour the hot chocolate mixture into the reserved small bowl. Set the bowl into the ice-water bath. Keep the chocolate over ice, stirring frequently, until it reaches room temperature or a bit cooler.

3. Churn the ice cream in an ice-cream maker following the manufacturer's directions. Pack the ice cream into a freezer container and store in the freezer for at least 2 hours, time enough for it to firm and ripen.

To make Chocolate-Lavender Ice Cream: Add 2 small pinches of dried lavender flowers to the hot milk-and-sugar mixture. Remove the pan from the heat, cover, and allow the mixture to infuse for 10 to 15 minutes. Strain the milk, discard the lavender, and bring the mixture to the boil again before adding the chocolate and continuing with the recipe.

To make Chocolate-Brownie Ice Cream: Just before the ice cream is frozen, add about 2 cups (¼ pound; 115 grams) of finely chunked Brownies (page 61).

To make Chocolate-Macadamia Ice Cream: Just before the ice cream is frozen, add about 1 cup (4 ounces; 115 grams) of coarsely chopped or halved caramelized macadamia nuts (see page 195).

Makes about 1½ pints (about ¾ liter)

KEEPING: Packed in an airtight container and stored in the freezer, the ice cream can be kept for about 1 week.

CHOCOLATE SEMIFREDDO
WITH COCONUT DACQUOISE

Semifreddo is a dessert that lives in a linguistic Never-Never Land, caught between what its Italian name says it is, something half-frozen, and what it is in reality, a mousse-like confection that can be served frozen, half-frozen, or chilled. This semifreddo, meant to be served fully frozen, may do nothing to clear up the confusion, but it could go a long way to becoming a model of the genre. Its base, decidedly chocolate, is a mousse–ice cream combination, and it produces a dessert that blends the best of both: It is as seductively silken as the finest ice cream and as light as the most splendid mousse. And it packs a surprise: Interleaved within the dessert are three disks of crackly coconut dacquoise, just enough to add here-and-there crunch.

The dessert is constructed in a soufflé mold and, indeed, if you use a 6-cup mold, you'll be able to mound the semifreddo above the rim so that it will have the look of a classic frozen soufflé. If you use a larger mold, the dacquoise disks will probably not touch the sides of the mold and, in all likelihood, you'll lose the rise — not to worry. In fact, if you must lose the above-the-collar height, you'll gain the opportunity to unmold the dessert. It's perfect either way.

■ I like the mousse in this dessert to be on the slightly dense side, but if you prefer a lighter mousse, you can add 1 more egg white to the mixture. ■ PH

- Three 6½-inch (16-cm) Coconut Dacquoise disks (page 231)
- 1 cup (250 grams) whole milk
- 8 large egg yolks
- 1¼ cups (250 grams) sugar
- 1¾ cups (435 grams) heavy cream
- 2 large egg whites
- 12½ ounces (350 grams) bittersweet chocolate, preferably Valrhona Caraïbe, coarsely chopped

1. The semifreddo should be constructed in a soufflé mold with a capacity of about 6 cups (1.5 liters). Before you get started, make certain the disks of coconut dacquoise will fit into the mold. If they're a little too large, shave them into shape using a serrated knife and a gentle sawing motion; keep the disks close at hand. (Don't panic if the disks crack — you'll still be able to fit the pieces into the soufflé mold, and the semifreddo will glue them together.) Also, prepare a foil strip that can be used as a collar for the soufflé mold by cutting a piece of aluminum foil about 25 inches (65 cm) long and folding it lengthwise in thirds; set it aside. If you are using a larger mold, cut the dacquoise disks to fit if necessary, but don't worry if they're too small. Omit the collar — it will not be needed, because once you layer the ingredients in the larger mold, you will probably not have anything left to spoon above the lip of the mold.

2. So that you can quickly cool the crème anglaise, the semifreddo's custard base, fill a large bowl with ice cubes and water. Set aside a smaller bowl that can hold all of the ingredients. Set aside a fine-meshed strainer too.

3. To make the crème anglaise, bring the milk to the boil in a heavy-bottomed medium saucepan. Meanwhile, whisk together the egg yolks and ¾ cup (150 grams) of the sugar in a large bowl, beating until the mixture is thick and pale.

4. Whisking without stop, drizzle a few tablespoons of the boiling milk into the yolk mixture. When the yolks are acclimated to the heat, add the remaining milk in a steadier stream. Pour the mixture into the saucepan, set it over medium heat, and, stirring constantly with a wooden spoon or spatula, cook the crème anglaise until it thickens slightly, lightens in color, and, most important, reaches 180°F (80°C), as measured on an instant-read thermometer — all of which will take less than 5 minutes. (Alternatively, you can stir the custard and then draw your finger down the spatula or the bowl of the wooden spoon — if the custard doesn't run into the track you've created, it's done.) Immediately pull the pan from the heat. Rinse and dry the smaller bowl, strain the custard into it, and place the bowl in the ice-water bath. Keep the custard on ice, stirring occasionally, until it has cooled completely. When it is cold, remove it from the ice bath.

5. Whip the heavy cream until it holds soft peaks; keep the cream aside on the counter.

6. In a mixer fitted with the whisk attachment (or working with a hand-held mixer), whip the egg whites on medium speed until they hold soft peaks. Gradually add the remaining ½ cup (100 grams) sugar and continue to beat until the peaks are firm but still very glossy.

7. Melt the chocolate in a bowl set over — not touching — simmering water or in a microwave oven. As soon as the chocolate is melted, remove it from the heat and set it on the counter. You want the chocolate to be very warm when you mix it with the other ingredients. If it is hot to the touch, give it 3 to 5 minutes to cool.

8. Working with a large flexible rubber spatula and a light touch, stir about one-third of the whipped cream into the chocolate, then gently fold in the rest of the cream. Turn the chocolate whipped cream into the bowl with the custard and fold the two mixtures together lightly — there's no need to be thorough now. Stir a spoonful of the beaten egg whites into the chocolate mixture, then add the remaining whites and fold everything together so that it is homogenous. The mousse mixture is ready and, in fact, should be used immediately.

9. To assemble the dessert, spoon enough chocolate mousse into the bottom of the soufflé mold to come ½ inch (1.5 cm) up the sides. Place 1 of the trimmed coconut dacquoise disks over the mousse. Spoon in one-third of the remaining mousse and smooth the top, then jiggle the second dacquoise disk into place over it. Spoon in half of the remaining chocolate mixture, to come almost to the top of the mold. Cover with the third dacquoise disk and jiggle that one into place as well.

10. Wrap the foil band you constructed around the soufflé mold to form a collar that extends about 3 inches (7.5 cm) above the mold. Secure the collar at the overlap with freezer tape, a straight pin, or a paper clip, then tie it tightly with kitchen twine so that it doesn't slip down. Spoon in the remainder of the mousse — it probably won't come to the top of the collar — and smooth the top with a spatula. (If you're using a larger soufflé mold, just fill it as directed and smooth the top.)

11. Slide the soufflé into the freezer — this is the "freddo" part — and freeze for at least 6 hours. (*Once frozen, the dessert can be wrapped airtight and kept in the freezer for up to 1 month.*)

12. To serve, remove the foil collar and cut the semifreddo into wedges. If your semifreddo doesn't have a collar, you can either cut it into wedges in the soufflé mold or unmold it after giving the mold a quick dunk in hot water. If the parfait was frozen for a long time, you might want to let it soften at room temperature for 5 to 10 minutes before serving.

Makes 10 to 12 servings

KEEPING: The coconut dacquoise disks can be made up to 1 month ahead and kept wrapped airtight in the freezer, but the chocolate mixture must be put into the soufflé mold as soon as it is prepared. Once assembled, the dessert must be frozen and then can remain frozen for up to 1 month.

T his is a banana split for the chocolate lover. The ice cream is chocolate — no ifs, ands, buts, or scoops of vanilla and strawberry, the flavors that tradition- ally appeared on either side of the one little ball of chocolate ice cream soda fountains used to serve with their splits. And there are no sauces except the best sauce — chocolate. There is, however, one nonchocolate addition: Pierre tops each split with some rum-soaked golden raisins. It's certainly not an addition you're likely to see gaining popularity at soda fountains around the country, but it's a very French touch and it's *"la différence"* between our eat-it-at-the- counter split and his polished sit-at-a-table, *salon de thé* split.

■ For an even more flavorful split, try sautéing the bananas in butter and sugar over high heat until they are caramelized. Do this at the last minute, so you'll have a nice play between the warm bananas and chocolate sauce and the cold ice cream and whipped cream. ■ PH

THE RAISINS

- ½ cup (60 grams) golden raisins
- 3 tablespoons dark rum
- 3 tablespoons water

Place all the ingredients in a small saucepan over low heat and cook, stirring, just until the raisins are soft and plump, about 2 minutes. Remove the pan from the heat and allow the raisins to macerate for at least 2 hours, and up to a day.

TO ASSEMBLE

- 4 ripe but firm bananas, peeled and cut lengthwise in half
- Chocolate Ice Cream (page 184)

Makes 4 servings

- **1 cup (250 grams) heavy cream, lightly sweetened and whipped**
- **Chocolate Sauce (page 253), warmed**

KEEPING: You can make the chocolate ice cream and the chocolate sauce up to a week ahead, the raisins up to a day ahead, and the bananas a few hours in advance, but, as with all ice cream treats, once you get these splits together, you've got to get them out to your guests.

For each split, arrange 2 banana halves toward the edges of a banana split glass or a bowl. Spoon 3 scoops of chocolate ice cream and some raisins along the length of the bananas. Top with whipped cream, either spooned over the ice cream or piped out in large rosettes from a pastry bag fitted with a fluted tip. Drizzle over some chocolate sauce and serve immediately.

CHOCOLATE, CARAMEL, AND PEAR BELLE HÉLÈNE

Here is a *poire* (pear) *belle hélène* for the true chocolate lover. In the classic version, a poached pear is perched on a couple of scoops of vanilla ice cream and the sundae is given a drizzle of chocolate sauce. This rendition preserves the pear, embellishing it by poaching it in a vanilla-bean syrup, ups the chocolate content by making it the flavor of choice for the ice cream, and replaces the chocolate sauce with a cream-smoothed caramel sauce, a winning companion to pears and chocolate ice cream. Like the original, this is a tri-part sundae, but there's nothing to say you can't gild the lily. When you're feeling extravagant, you can top it all with a swirl of lightly whipped cream, or you can drizzle a bit of Chocolate Sauce (page 253) alongside the caramel, or you can even add both the cream and the chocolate sauce — sometimes too much is just enough.

THE PEARS

- One 29-ounce (825-gram) can pear halves packed in syrup
- 1 cup (250 grams) water
- ½ cup (100 grams) sugar
- 1 tablespoon freshly squeezed lemon juice
- Pulp from ½ moist, plump vanilla bean (see page 279)

1. Drain the pears and place them in a large bowl (a deep bowl is best); set them aside for the moment.

2. Bring the water, sugar, lemon juice, and vanilla bean pulp to a boil in a medium saucepan or the microwave. Remove this syrup from the heat and pour it over the pears. Press a piece of waxed paper against the pears and, if the paper alone isn't enough to submerge the pears in the syrup, place a plate on top of it. Cover the setup with plastic wrap and refrigerate overnight. (*The pears can be made up to 3 days ahead and kept covered in the refrigerator.*)

THE CARAMEL SAUCE

- ½ cup (125 grams) heavy cream
- ½ cup (100 grams) sugar
- 3 tablespoons (1½ ounces; 45 grams) salted butter (or use unsalted butter plus a tiny pinch of salt)

1. Bring the cream to a boil in a saucepan or the microwave oven; set aside.
2. Set a heavy-bottomed medium saucepan over medium-high heat, sprinkle 2 tablespoons of the sugar over the bottom of the pan. As soon as the sugar starts to melt and color, stir it with a wooden spoon until it caramelizes. Sprinkle over half of the remaining sugar and, as soon as it starts to melt, stir it into the caramelized sugar in the pan; repeat with the last of the sugar and cook until the sugar is a deep brown color. (Test the color on a white plate.) Stand away from the pan and, still stirring, add the butter and then, when the butter is incorporated, the heavy cream. Continue to cook the sauce just until it starts to boil again, then pull the pan from the heat, pour the sauce into a bowl, and cool to room temperature. (*The sauce can be made up to 2 weeks ahead and kept in a tightly closed jar in the refrigerator. Bring it to room temperature or warm it gently before using.*)

TO ASSEMBLE

- **Chocolate Ice Cream (page 184)**

For each sundae, put 2 scoops of chocolate ice cream in the bottom of a long-stemmed ballon-shaped wineglass. Top with a few pear halves and drizzle over some caramel sauce.

Makes 4 servings

KEEPING: Each of the sundae's components should be made ahead: The ice cream needs to be made at least 2 hours in advance, but it can be kept for up to a week in the freezer; the caramel sauce can be made up to 2 weeks ahead; and the pears need to be made at least 1 day ahead. But as soon as the Pear Belle Hélène is assembled, it should be served.

COUPE MALSHERBES

That this ice cream sundae is named for a long elegant avenue in the 8th arrondisement of Paris really tells you nothing about how lavish — and luscious — it is. The sundae is meant to be served in long-stemmed balloon wineglasses so that all of its elements are temptingly on display. From the bottom of the coupe to the top, here's what you'll see: a scoop of almost-black Chocolate Sorbet, a middle scoop of Deep Chocolate Cream, and a scoop of golden, powerfully flavor-packed caramel ice cream; then there's a topping of whipped cream and a smattering of caramelized macadamia nuts. Seeing each of the ingredients in the balloon is attractive, but tasting them all together is what counts — and you can count on its being great, in part because of the caramel, which is one of chocolate's best friends. Caramel both boosts the chocolate flavor in a chocolate dessert and mellows it. Although the chocolate cream and sorbet are sensational on their own, see if you don't appreciate them even more in tandem with the caramel ice cream and caramelized nuts.

■ For me, this is nothing less than pure pleasure for the gourmand. ■ PH

THE CARAMEL ICE CREAM

- **2 cups (500 grams) whole milk**
- **⅔ cup (165 grams) heavy cream**
- **5 large egg yolks**
- **1⅓ cups (270 grams) sugar**

1. Bring the milk to the boil in a heavy-bottomed medium saucepan. Turn off the heat. At the same time, bring the cream to the boil in a small saucepan, then set it aside until needed.

2. Beat the egg yolks with ½ cup (100 grams) of the sugar in a medium bowl until the sugar is dissolved, and set this aside too.

3. Set up an ice-water bath so you can cool the custard mixture quickly before churning it: Fill a large bowl with ice cubes and cold water. Set aside a

smaller bowl that can hold the finished ice cream base and be placed in this ice-water bath. Set aside a fine-meshed strainer too.

4. Place a large heavy-bottomed saucepan or casserole over medium-high heat and sprinkle about one-third of the remaining sugar over the bottom of the pan. As soon as the sugar starts to melt and color, stir it with a wooden spoon until it caramelizes. Sprinkle over half of the remaining sugar and, as soon as it starts to melt, stir it into the caramelized sugar in the pan; repeat with the last of the sugar and cook until the sugar is a rich mahogany color. (Test the color on a white plate.) Stand away from the pan and, still stirring, pour in the heavy cream. Don't worry if the caramel seizes and clumps: stirring and heating will even it out.

5. Once it is smooth, pour the caramel-cream into the saucepan with the milk and stir to blend. Give the egg yolk mixture a quick beating with a whisk, then, while whisking, drizzle in about one-quarter of the hot liquid. When the liquid is incorporated, whisk in another cup or so more, then whisk the egg mixture into the saucepan with the remaining liquid. Set the pan over medium heat and, stirring constantly with a wooden spatula or spoon, cook this crème anglaise until it thickens slightly and reaches 180°F (80°C), as measured on an instant-read thermometer — which will take less than 5 minutes. (Alternatively, you can stir the crème anglaise and then draw your finger down the spatula or the bowl of the wooden spoon — if the custard doesn't run into the track you've created, it's done.) Immediately pull the pan from the heat. Rinse and dry the smaller bowl, strain the crème anglaise into it, and set the bowl into the ice-water bath to cool; stir the custard occasionally as it cools. (*The crème anglaise can be made ahead and kept, tightly covered, in the refrigerator for up to 3 days.*)

6. When the crème anglaise is cool, pour it into an ice-cream maker and churn according to the manufacturer's directions. Spoon the ice cream into a freezer container and freeze for at least 2 hours before using. (*The ice cream can be packed airtight and kept in the refrigerator for up to 1 week, but its flavor is at its peak the day it is made.*)

THE NUTS

- ½ cup (100 grams) sugar
- 3 tablespoons water
- Pulp from ¼ moist, plump vanilla bean (see page 279)
- 1½ cups (7 ounces; 200 grams) macadamia nuts, toasted (see page 275) and still warm or at room temperature

1. Line a baking sheet with a Silpat or other silicone baking mat or with parchment paper; keep it on the counter near the range. Bring the sugar, water, and vanilla bean pulp to a boil in a heavy-bottomed medium saucepan. Swirl the ingredients around to dissolve the sugar, then allow the mixture to boil, without stirring, until it reaches 248°F (119°C), as measured on a candy or instant-read thermometer. (If any sugar sticks to the sides of the pan, as might happen at the start of the cooking, wash it down with a pastry brush dipped in cold water.)

2. Add the macadamia nuts all at once and, working with a wooden spoon or spatula, stir the nuts into the sugar and continue to cook and stir over medium heat. As you stir the nuts, which will clump together at the start, they will separate and their sugar coating will become white and sandy. Continue to heat and, above all, stir and the coating will start to caramelize. When the sugar is a pale caramel color, turn the macadamia nuts out onto the lined baking sheet. Spread the nuts out on the sheet and allow them to cool to room temperature. When the nuts are cool, you can either break them into pieces, chop them into morsels, or crush them. (*The nuts can be caramelized up to 2 days ahead and kept at room temperature, away from heat and humidity, in a tightly sealed container.*)

TO ASSEMBLE

- **Bittersweet Chocolate Sorbet (page 183)**
- **Deep Chocolate Cream (page 224)**
- **1 cup (250 grams) heavy cream, whipped and lightly sweetened**

Makes 6 servings

KEEPING: Everything can be made ahead, but, once assembled, the coupe, like all ice cream confections, must be served immediately.

For each sundae, place a scoop each of sorbet, chocolate cream, and caramel ice cream in the bottom of a long-stemmed balloon-shaped wineglass. Top with a generous dollop of whipped cream — you can spoon the cream onto the ice cream or you can pipe it through a pastry bag fitted with a fluted tip — and finish by scattering over some caramelized macadamia nuts.

TRIPLE CHOCOLATE
MERINGUE AND
ICE CREAM PUFFS

As sophisticated as this dessert looks — and as sophisticated as it is — this triple chocolate confection is as much fun to eat as a kid's ice cream sandwich. In fact, a case could be made for calling it an ice cream sandwich, since the chocolate meringue puffs do, indeed, sandwich chocolate ice cream (or, if you'd like, chocolate sorbet). As for the swirl of chocolate whipped cream that crowns each dessert, it has no counterpart in the ice cream–sandwich world, but, in addition to being a delightful indulgence, it adds another texture and another degree of chocolatyness to the dessert. Serve the puffs centered on a large plate, the meringues anchoring the left and right sides, the sorbet in the center, and the cream on top, and make sure each person gets both a fork and a large spoon — they're the most efficient deconstruction tools.

■ This is a play on the very old-fashioned meringue chantilly (meringues filled and topped with whipped cream) and meringue glacée (meringues filled with ice cream and topped with whipped cream). What makes mine different is the chocolate — each element of my dessert is chocolate, a combination that was unheard of with the classic. If you want to really change this classic, sandwich the meringues with Allspice Ice Cream (page 131). ■ PH

THE MERINGUES

- 1 cup (100 grams) confectioners' sugar
- 3 tablespoons Dutch-processed cocoa powder, preferably Valrhona
- 4 large egg whites, at room temperature (see step 3)
- ½ cup minus 1 tablespoon (90 grams) sugar
- Confectioners' sugar and cocoa powder for dusting

1. Center a rack in the oven and preheat the oven to 250°F (120°C). Line two baking sheets with parchment paper and set them aside. Fit a large pastry bag with a plain ½- to ¾-inch (1.5- to 2-cm) tip — you want a large tip so that you can pipe generous meringue kisses. (If you don't have a large-enough tip, you can skip the pastry bag and use a zipper-lock plastic bag instead. Spoon the meringue into the plastic bag, seal the bag, and then snip off a corner so that it creates a "tip" that's just the right size.)

2. Sift together the confectioners' sugar and cocoa powder and keep close at hand.

3. For the egg whites to beat to their fullest volume, they need to be at room temperature. To get them to room temperature quickly, put them in a microwave-safe bowl and place them in a microwave oven set on lowest power; heat the whites for about 10 seconds. Stir the whites and continue to heat in 5-second spurts until they are about 75°F (23°C). If they're a little warmer, that's okay too.

4. In a clean, dry mixer bowl with a clean, dry whisk attachment in place, whip the egg whites on high speed until they turn opaque and form soft peaks. Still whipping on high, gradually add half the granulated sugar and continue to beat until the whites are glossy and hold firm peaks. Reduce the mixer speed to medium-low and gradually beat in the remaining granulated sugar.

5. Remove the bowl from the mixer and, working with a large rubber spatula, gradually fold in the sifted confectioners' sugar and cocoa mixture. Work quickly but delicately, and don't be discouraged when your beautifully airy meringue deflates a bit — it's inevitable.

6. Working with half the batter at a time, gently spoon the batter into the pastry bag and pipe out large, plump rounds about 2½ inches (6.5 cm) in diameter, finished with a peak in the center, onto the baking sheets (in other words, the puffs should look like giant chocolate kisses). Allow about 1 inch (2.5 cm) between each puff. You should have 20 meringue puffs. (If you have more, you'll have a great snack.) Dust the meringues with confectioners' sugar and let them sit on the counter for 10 minutes, then dust them with cocoa powder.

7. Place the baking sheets in the oven and insert the handle of a wooden spoon into the door to keep it slightly ajar. Bake the puffs for 2 hours.

8. Turn off the oven and continue to dry the meringues for another 2 hours, or as long as overnight, with the door closed. Transfer the meringues, parchment and all, to racks to cool to room temperature. Run a thin metal spatula under the puffs to release them from the paper. (*The meringues can be made up to 1 week in advance and kept in a cool, dry place, such as an airtight box.*)

TO ASSEMBLE

Makes 10 servings

KEEPING: The ice cream
or sorbet can be made up to
1 week ahead, as can the
meringues, as long as they're
kept in a cool, dry place. The
whipped cream can also be
made ahead — indeed, it
needs to be made ahead. Even
the meringue-and-ice-cream
sandwiches can be made
ahead and kept in the freezer
for 1 week. (Just remember to
soften the frozen meringues in
the refrigerator for 10 to 15
minutes before serving.)
But once the dessert is
assembled, you should
serve it immediately.

- **Chocolate Whipped Cream (page 223)**
- **Chocolate Ice Cream (page 184) or Bittersweet Chocolate Sorbet (page 183)**
- **Chocolate shavings (see page 258) (optional)**

1. So that the first dessert you assemble won't melt before the last one is put together, line a baking sheet with parchment paper and put the lined sheet in the freezer. If you want to be extra-safe in the chill department, you can freeze your dessert plates too. Fit a pastry bag with a ½-inch (1.5 cm) fluted tip, fill it with the whipped cream, and place the filled bag in the refrigerator.

2. For each dessert, scoop one large or two smaller balls of ice cream or sorbet onto the flat side of a meringue puff. Form a sandwich by pressing the flat side of another meringue against the ice cream, and stand the sandwich on edge on the baking sheet in the freezer. (*Once the meringues are frozen, they can be wrapped airtight and kept frozen for up to 1 week. Allow meringues that have frozen solid to soften in the refrigerator for about 10 to 15 minutes before serving.*)

3. At serving time, place one sandwich in the center of each dessert plate and top each sandwich with a swirl of chocolate whipped cream. If you're using the chocolate shavings, scatter them over the whipped cream, and take the plates to the table.

HOT AND COLD
CHOCOLATE DRINKS

These days, when most of us think of hot chocolate, we think of a rich chocolate drink made with milk. But the original hot chocolate was made with water, and, as you'll see when you make this recipe, it was rich nonetheless. In fact, in many ways this is the most chocolaty of hot chocolates, because the bittersweet chocolate that contributes most of the flavor to this drink is boosted with a little cocoa powder, and because the drink is made with water, so there's nothing to stand in the way of the full chocolate flavor.

■ This hot chocolate gives you the pure flavor of chocolate. ■ PH

- 2 cups (500 grams) water
- ¼ cup (50 grams) sugar
- 4¼ ounces (130 grams) bittersweet chocolate, preferably Valrhona Noir Gastronomie, melted
- ¼ cup (25 grams) Dutch-processed cocoa powder, preferably Valrhona

Bring the water and sugar to the boil in a medium saucepan, stirring until the sugar dissolves. Add the chocolate and cocoa and, stirring with a whisk, heat the mixture until one bubble pops on the surface. Pull the saucepan from the heat and whip the hot chocolate for about 1 minute with an immersion blender or in a regular blender. Serve immediately in large cups, or pour into a container to cool. (*The hot chocolate can be made up to 2 days ahead and kept tightly covered in the refrigerator.*)

To reheat the chilled chocolate, pour it into a medium saucepan, set the pan over low heat, and cook, whisking gently, just until the first bubble pops. Remove the pan from the heat, whip the chocolate for a minute with the immersion blender (or in a blender), and serve.

Makes 2 servings

CLASSIC
HOT CHOCOLATE

Hot chocolate may originally have been made with water (see page 203), but this hot chocolate, composed of milk, a little water, chocolate, and sugar, is what we've come to think of as the classic and perfect drink of its kind. It's the type of thick, rich hot chocolate that makes it such a pleasure to stop for a cup in one of Paris's many tea salons.

The chocolate can be served as soon as it's made, or you can cool and chill it, then reheat it gently. In addition, with just a little more water added to the mix, you can make a luscious Cold Hot Chocolate (see variation below), one that's so thick and true to its chocolate roots that it tastes as though you're drinking melted chocolate ice cream.

■ You can use this recipe to make Viennese Hot Chocolate. Just top each cup of hot chocolate with a spoonful of *schlag* (the German name for sweetened whipped cream). ■ PH

- **2 cups (500 grams) whole milk**
- **¼ cup (60 grams) water**
- **¼ cup (50 grams) sugar**
- **4 ounces (115 grams) bittersweet chocolate, preferably Valrhona Noir Gastronomie, melted**

Bring the milk, water, and sugar to the boil in a medium saucepan, stirring until the sugar dissolves. Add the chocolate and, stirring with a whisk, heat the mixture until one bubble pops on the surface. Pull the saucepan from the heat and whip the hot chocolate for about 1 minute with an immersion blender or in a regular blender. Serve immediately in large cups, or pour into a container to cool. (*The hot chocolate can be made up to 2 days ahead and kept tightly covered in the refrigerator.*)

To reheat the chilled chocolate, pour it into a medium saucepan, set the pan over low heat, and cook, whisking gently, just until the first bubble pops. Remove the pan from the heat, whip the chocolate for a minute with the immersion blender (or in a blender), and serve.

To make Cold Hot Chocolate: Cool the hot chocolate, then chill it. When the chocolate is cold, stir in ¼ cup (60 grams) cold water, then whip the cold chocolate for a minute with an immersion blender or in a blender. For each serving, put 1 to 2 ice cubes in a tall glass and pour over the chocolate. Serve with straws.

Makes 2 servings

CARAMELIZED
CINNAMON
HOT CHOCOLATE

You could serve this drink as dessert and no one would feel deprived, the flavors are that enticing. The components of this hot chocolate are very much like the ones for the Classic (page 205), with the important exception that in this recipe the sugar is caramelized, and it's caramelized along with a stick of fragrant cinnamon. It's a small difference, but it changes everything about the chocolate, quickly making it very unusual and, for those who love the combination of caramel, cinnamon, and fine chocolate, completely irresistible.

■ For an adults-only hot chocolate, one that would be wonderful after a winter's afternoon outdoors, add a spoonful of dark rum or some Grand Marnier to each cup. ■ PH

- **2¼ cups (560 grams) whole milk**
- **¼ cup (60 grams) water**
- **⅓ cup (70 grams) sugar**
- **1 cinnamon stick**
- **4 ounces (115 grams) bittersweet chocolate, preferably Valrhona Noir Gastronomie, melted**

1. Bring the milk and water to the boil in a saucepan. Turn off the heat.
2. Meanwhile, working in a heavy-bottomed medium saucepan over medium heat, caramelize the sugar with the cinnamon by allowing the sugar and cinnamon to rest undisturbed in the saucepan until the sugar starts to melt and color. As soon as you see the sugar coloring, start stirring it with a wooden spoon. Continue to cook and stir, making sure that the cinnamon is cooking along with the sugar, until the sugar is a deep amber color.
3. Still stirring, pour the hot milk and water mixture over the sugar and cinnamon. Don't be concerned if the caramel seizes and clumps — keep heating

and stirring it, and it will liquefy again. When the mixture is smooth, whisk in the chocolate. Continue to whisk and heat the mixture until one bubble pops on the surface. Pull the saucepan from the heat, remove the cinnamon stick, and whip the hot chocolate for about 1 minute with an immersion blender or in a regular blender. Serve immediately in large cups, or pour into a container to cool. (*The hot chocolate can be made up to 2 days ahead and kept tightly covered in the refrigerator.*)

To reheat the chilled chocolate, pour it into a medium saucepan, set the pan over low heat, and cook, whisking gently, just until the first bubble pops. Remove the pan from the heat, whip the chocolate for a minute with the immersion blender (or in a blender), and serve.

Makes 2 servings

F orget mulled cider and eggnog, this hot chocolate is bound to become your Christmas *spécialité de la maison*. It is a water-based hot chocolate made with chocolate and cocoa, and it is flavored boldly and exotically with cinnamon, vanilla, honey, lemon zest, and crushed black pepper. The recipe can be multiplied if you're serving a crowd and, no matter the quantity, it can be made ahead and reheated when needed.

■ When you're having a party, top this hot chocolate with buttery cubes of gingerbread. Just cut the gingerbread into bite-sized pieces and sauté them in butter until they're crispy on the outside. Serve a spoon with each cup. ■ PH

- 3 cups (750 grams) water
- ¼ cup (50 grams) sugar
- 1 tablespoon honey
- ½ cinnamon stick
- ½ moist, plump vanilla bean, split lengthwise and scraped (see page 279)
- 12 black Sarawak peppercorns (see page 266), crushed
- Zest of ½ lemon (removed with a vegetable peeler)
- 6½ ounces (185 grams) bittersweet chocolate, preferably Valrhona Noir Gastronomie, melted
- 6 tablespoons (40 grams) Dutch-processed cocoa powder, preferably Valrhona

Bring the water, sugar, honey, cinnamon, vanilla bean, peppercorns, and lemon zest to the boil in a medium saucepan. Add the chocolate and cocoa and, stirring with a whisk, heat the mixture until one bubble pops on the surface. Pull the saucepan from the heat and strain the hot chocolate; discard the solids. Pour the hot chocolate back into the saucepan and whip it for about 1 minute with an immersion blender, or whip it in a regular blender. Serve immediately in large cups, or pour into a container to cool. (*The hot chocolate can be made up to 2 days ahead and kept tightly covered in the refrigerator.*)

To reheat the chilled chocolate, pour it into a medium saucepan, set the pan over low heat, and cook, whisking gently, just until the first bubble pops. Remove the pan from the heat, whip the chocolate for a minute with the immersion blender (or in a blender), and serve.

Makes 4 servings

HOT CHOCOLATE
WITH COFFEE

There's just enough coffee in this mix to make it a real mocha drink, and just enough excellent bittersweet chocolate to guarantee that it will be a true hot chocolate. If it were the specialty at any of the American coffee-bar chains, it might be called a mochachococcino.

■ Even if you don't usually take milk in your coffee — and I never do — you'll enjoy this drink with a big spoonful of whipped cream. Mild, almost neutral cream provides a liaison between the intense flavors of espresso and chocolate. ■ PH

- 2⅔ cups (665 grams) whole milk
- ¼ cup (60 grams) water
- 5 tablespoons (10 grams) freshly ground coffee, preferably espresso ground medium-fine
- ¼ cup (50 grams) sugar
- 4 ounces (115 grams) bittersweet chocolate, preferably Valrhona Noir Gastronomie, melted

1. Bring the milk and water to the boil in a medium saucepan. Add the ground coffee, stir it around for a second or two, and then immediately pour the mixture through a strainer lined with a double thickness of dampened cheesecloth.

2. Return the coffee-milk to the saucepan and, taking care not to allow it to boil again, warm it over medium heat. Whisk in the sugar, followed by the chocolate; when the mixture is smooth, pull the saucepan from the heat. Whip the hot chocolate for about 1 minute with an immersion blender or in a regular blender and serve immediately in large cups, or pour into a container to cool. (*The hot chocolate can be made up to 2 days ahead and kept tightly covered in the refrigerator.*)

   To reheat the chilled chocolate, pour it into a medium saucepan, set the pan over low heat, and cook, whisking gently, just until the chocolate is hot. Remove the pan from the heat, whip the chocolate for a minute with the immersion blender (or in a blender), and serve.

Makes 2 servings

COLD PASSION FRUIT
HOT CHOCOLATE

This uncommon drink starts off as hot chocolate, but it is meant to be served cold over just an ice cube or maybe a little crushed ice, and it should definitely be served with a straw. Because Pierre mixes passion fruit juice (or nectar) into his classic hot chocolate mélange, the drink you get is at once light and refreshing — two sensations not usually associated with rich bittersweet chocolate and milk.

- **2 cups (500 grams) whole milk**
- **¾ cup (185 grams) passion fruit juice or nectar**
- **2 tablespoons sugar**
- **4 ounces (115 grams) bittersweet chocolate, preferably Valrhona Noir Gastronomie, melted**

1. Prepare an ice-water bath so that you can quickly cool the hot chocolate mixture by filling a large bowl with ice cubes and water. Set out a smaller bowl that will fit into the bath and hold all of the ingredients.

2. Bring the milk, passion fruit juice, and sugar to the boil in a medium saucepan. Don't be concerned if the mixture separates — it will come together when you zap it with the blender. Add the chocolate and, stirring with a whisk, heat the mixture until one bubble pops on the surface. Pull the saucepan from the heat and pour the hot chocolate into the small bowl. Place the bowl in the ice-water bath and, stirring often, let the mixture cool down and chill.

3. When the chocolate is cold, whip it for about 1 minute with an immersion blender or in a regular blender. Serve immediately in tall glasses over an ice cube (you don't want to use too much ice, because you don't want to dilute the flavor) or a little crushed ice. (*The hot chocolate can be made up to 2 days ahead and kept tightly covered in the refrigerator. Give the chilled chocolate another zap with the immersion blender, or whir it in a blender, before serving.*)

Makes 2 servings

BASE RECIPES

BITTERSWEET CHOCOLATE CREAM GANACHE

This is a quintessentially dark, rich, silken chocolate ganache. It melts slowly on the tongue and, like fine wine, has a long finish. The ganache is ideal as a filling for many types of tarts and splendid as a go-along for madeleines and chocolate cigarette cookies.

- **8 ounces (230 grams) bittersweet chocolate, preferably Valrhona Guanaja, finely chopped**
- **1 cup (250 grams) heavy cream**
- **4 tablespoons (2 ounces; 60 grams) unsalted butter, at room temperature**

1. Place the chocolate in a bowl that's large enough to hold the ingredients and keep it close at hand. Bring the cream to a full boil in a heavy-bottomed saucepan. While the cream is coming to the boil, work the butter with a rubber spatula until it is very soft and creamy. Keep the butter aside for the moment.

2. When the cream is at the boil, remove the pan from the heat and, working with the rubber spatula, gently stir the cream into the chocolate. Start stirring in the center of the mixture and work your way out in widening concentric circles. Continue to stir — without creating bubbles — until the chocolate is completely melted and the mixture is smooth. Leave the bowl on the counter for a minute or two to cool the mixture down a little before adding the butter.

3. Add the butter to the mixture in two additions, mixing with the spatula from the center of the mixture out in widening concentric circles. When the butter is fully incorporated, the ganache should be smooth and glossy. Depending on what you're making with the ganache, you can use it now, leave it on the counter to set to a spreadable or pipeable consistency (a process that could take over an hour, depending on your room's temperature) or chill it in the refrigerator, stirring now and then. (If the ganache chills too much and becomes too firm, you can give it a very quick zap in the microwave to bring it back to the desired consistency, or let it stand at room temperature.)

Makes about 2 cups (550 grams)

KEEPING: The ganache can be kept in the refrigerator for up to 2 days or frozen for up to 1 month. If the ganache has been refrigerated, leave it at room temperature or warm it quickly in the microwave oven to make it spreadable. (To be on the safe side, warm it in 5-second spurts, checking after each zap.) If the ganache has been frozen, defrost it overnight in the refrigerator and then bring it back to a spreadable consistency as above.

BITTERSWEET CHOCOLATE MILK GANACHE

This ganache is unusual in that it contains whole milk rather than cream. The milk makes a ganache that is lighter in texture and taste, and, because it's more delicate, one that needs a lighter hand in the mixing.

- **9 ounces (260 grams) bittersweet chocolate, preferably Valrhona Guanaja, finely chopped**
- **1 cup (250 grams) whole milk**
- **1 stick plus 1 tablespoon (4½ ounces; 130 grams) unsalted butter, at room temperature**

Makes about 2 cups
(550 grams)

KEEPING: The ganache can be kept in the refrigerator for up to 2 days or frozen for up to 1 month. If the ganache has been refrigerated, leave it at room temperature or warm it quickly in the microwave oven to make it spreadable. (To be on the safe side, warm it in 5-second spurts, checking after each zap.) If the ganache has been frozen, defrost it overnight in the refrigerator and then bring it back to a spreadable consistency as above.

1. Place the chocolate in a bowl that's large enough to hold the ingredients and keep it close at hand. Bring the milk to a full boil in a small heavy-bottomed saucepan. While the milk is coming to the boil, work the butter with a rubber spatula until it is very soft and creamy. Keep the butter aside for the moment.

2. When the milk is at the boil, remove the pan from the heat and, working with the rubber spatula, gently stir the milk into the chocolate. Start stirring in the center of the mixture and work your way out in widening concentric circles. Continue to stir — without creating bubbles — until the chocolate is completely melted and the mixture is smooth. Leave the bowl on the counter for a minute or two to cool the mixture a little before adding the butter.

3. Add the butter to the chocolate mixture in three additions, mixing with the spatula from the center of the mixture out in widening concentric circles. When the butter is fully incorporated, the ganache should be smooth and glossy. Depending on what you're making with the ganache, you can use it now, leave it on the counter to set to a spreadable or pipeable consistency (a process that could take over an hour, depending on your room's temperature), or chill it in the refrigerator, stirring now and then. (If the ganache chills too much and becomes too firm, you can give it a very quick zap in the microwave to bring it back to the desired consistency, or let it stand at room temperature.)

VANILLA CRÈME ANGLAISE

Crème anglaise — it translates from the French as English cream — can serve as the base of a recipe, as it does with ice cream, or it can be an accompaniment, as it is so often to cakes, tarts, and various fruit desserts. It is simply a mixture of egg yolks, cream, and whole milk flavored with vanilla bean pulp, but, when made properly, it is sublime. To attain sublimity, do not cool the crème anglaise immediately after it reaches the desired temperature and texture — allow it to "poach" for a minute or two in the pan, then cool it: You'll get a smoother cream. In addition, if you refrigerate the crème anglaise for a day before using it, you'll "ripen" it, giving the eggs and the lactates in the milk the time they need to create a perfect osmosis.

- **1 cup (250 grams) whole milk**
- **1 cup (250 grams) heavy cream**
- **2 moist, plump vanilla beans, split lengthwise and scraped (see page 279)**
- **6 large egg yolks**
- **½ cup (100 grams) sugar**

1. In a small saucepan, bring the milk, cream, and vanilla beans (pulp and pods) to a boil over medium heat (or do this in the microwave oven). Cover the pan, turn off the heat, and allow the mixture to rest for 10 minutes, time enough for the liquids to be infused with the warm flavor of vanilla.

2. Fill a large bowl with ice cubes and water. Set aside a smaller bowl that can hold the finished cream and be placed in this ice bath. Set aside a fine-meshed strainer too.

3. Put the yolks and sugar in a heavy-bottomed medium saucepan and whisk them together, off the heat, until they are thick and pale, about 3 minutes. Whisking without stop, gradually drizzle in the hot milk and cream; after about a third of the liquid has been added and the yolks are acclimated to the heat, you can add the remaining liquid in a steadier stream. When all the liquid has been whisked into the yolks, remove and discard the vanilla bean pods (or save them for another use; see page 279). Put the saucepan over medium heat and, stirring constantly with a wooden spatula or spoon, cook the cream until it thickens slightly, lightens in color, and, most important, reaches 180°F (80°C), as measured on an instant-read thermometer — all of

Makes about 2½ cups
(725 grams)

KEEPING: Covered tightly
with plastic wrap pressed
against its surface, crème
anglaise can be kept in the
refrigerator for up to 3 days.
Do not freeze this sauce.

which will take less than 5 minutes. (Alternatively, you can stir the cream and then draw your finger down the spatula or the bowl of the wooden spoon — if the cream doesn't run into the track you've created, it's done.)

4. Immediately remove the saucepan from the heat and allow the cream to rest, or "poach," for a few minutes until the temperature reaches 182°F (83°C) — again, just a matter of minutes. Place the smaller bowl into the ice-water bath and immediately strain the crème anglaise into it. Keep the cream over ice, stirring occasionally, until it has cooled completely.

5. When it is cold, cover the cream with plastic wrap, pressing the plastic against the cream's surface to create a seal, and refrigerate for 24 hours before using.

VANILLA
PASTRY CREAM

Pastry cream, a traditional and elegant filling for mille-feuille, éclairs, cream puffs, and tarts, is a crème anglaise (page 217) thickened with cornstarch and smoothed with butter.

■ If you let the pastry cream cool before you add the butter, the pastry cream won't separate and the butter won't lose its characteristic texture. ■ PH

- **2 cups (500 grams) whole milk**
- **1 moist, plump vanilla bean, split lengthwise and scraped (see page 279)**
- **6 large egg yolks**
- **½ cup (100 grams) sugar**
- **⅓ cup (45 grams) cornstarch, sifted**
- **3½ tablespoons (1¾ ounces; 50 grams) unsalted butter, at room temperature**

1. In a small saucepan, bring the milk and vanilla bean (pulp and pod) to a boil over medium heat (or do this in the microwave oven). Cover the pan, turn off the heat, and allow the mixture to rest for 10 minutes, time enough for the liquids to be infused with the warm flavor of vanilla.

2. Fill a large bowl with ice cubes and water. Set aside a smaller bowl that can hold the finished cream and be placed in this ice bath. Set aside a fine-meshed strainer too.

3. Whisk the yolks, sugar, and cornstarch together in a heavy-bottomed medium saucepan. Whisking all the while, very slowly drizzle a quarter of the hot milk into the yolks. Still whisking, pour the rest of the liquid in a steady stream into the tempered yolks. Remove and discard the vanilla bean pod (or save it for another use; see page 279). Place the pan over medium heat and, whisking vigorously and without stop, bring the mixture to the boil. Keep the mixture at the boil — whisking energetically — for 1 to 2 minutes, then remove the pan from the heat and scrape the pastry cream into the small bowl.

Makes about 2 cups
(800 grams)

KEEPING: Covered tightly
with plastic wrap (press the
plastic against the cream's
surface to create an airtight
seal), pastry cream can be
refrigerated for 2 days.

4. Set the bowl into the ice-water bath and, stirring frequently so that the mixture remains smooth, cool the pastry cream to 140°F (60°C), as measured on an instant-read thermometer. Remove the cream from the ice-water bath and stir in the butter in three or four additions. Return the cream to the ice-water bath and keep it there, stirring occasionally, until it is completely cool. The cream can be used now or packed for storage.

CHOCOLATE PASTRY CREAM

This cream has all the versatility of vanilla pastry cream with all the sex appeal of chocolate. It's thick, velvety, luscious, and, in many recipes, deliciously interchangeable with vanilla pastry cream.

- **2 cups (500 grams) whole milk**
- **4 large egg yolks**
- **6 tablespoons (75 grams) sugar**
- **3 tablespoons cornstarch, sifted**
- **7 ounces (200 grams) bittersweet chocolate, preferably Valrhona Guanaja, melted**
- **2½ tablespoons (1¼ ounces; 40 grams) unsalted butter, at room temperature**

1. Fill a large bowl with ice cubes and water. Set aside a smaller bowl that can hold the finished cream and be placed in this ice bath. Set aside a fine-meshed strainer too.

2. In a small saucepan, bring the milk to the boil. Meanwhile, whisk the yolks, sugar, and cornstarch together in a heavy-bottomed medium saucepan. Whisking all the while, very slowly drizzle a quarter of the hot milk into the yolks. Still whisking, pour the rest of the liquid in a steady stream into the tempered yolks.

3. Strain the mixture into the saucepan, place the pan over medium heat, and, whisking vigorously and without stop, bring the mixture to the boil. Keep the mixture at the boil — whisking energetically — for 1 to 2 minutes. Still over heat, stir in the chocolate, then remove the pan from the heat and scrape the pastry cream into the small bowl.

4. Set the bowl into the ice-water bath and, stirring frequently so that the mixture remains smooth, cool the pastry cream to 140°F (60°C), as measured on an instant-read thermometer. Remove the cream from the ice-water bath and stir in the butter in three or four additions. Return the cream to the ice-water bath and keep it there, stirring occasionally, until it is completely cool. The cream can be used now or packed for storage.

Makes 2½ cups (900 grams)

KEEPING: Covered tightly with plastic wrap (press the plastic against the cream's surface to create an airtight seal), pastry cream can be refrigerated for 2 days.

WHIPPED CREAM

Whipped cream is ubiquitous and often taken for granted, but properly beaten and slightly sweetened, it can be one of the simplest yet most sensuous preparations in the pastry chef's repertoire. The firmness to which you beat the cream will depend on the use to which you will put it. When whipped cream is to be used as a topping for a dessert or a slice of cake or tart, it's best to whip the cream only until it holds very soft peaks. When you need the whipped cream to add both lightness and some body to a filling, as is often the case when you mix whipped cream with pastry cream or when you fold it into a mousse, it's best to stop whipping the cream just this side of firm.

This recipe is for 1 cup (250 grams) of heavy cream. If you need more cream, whip more — the proportion of cream to sugar remains constant.

■ Cream whips best when it is cold, ideally, 40°F (4°C). If you are whipping the cream with a whisk, you might want to put the bowl of cream in a larger bowl filled with ice cubes and cold water. If you are whipping the cream with an electric mixer, keep the mixer at medium speed — you'll have more control over the process and you won't risk overbeating the cream. ■ PH

Makes about 2 cups
(250 grams)

- **1 cup (250 grams) chilled heavy cream**
- **1 tablespoon sugar**

KEEPING: Whipped cream can be kept covered in the refrigerator for up to 3 hours; just make certain to keep it away from foods with strong odors — whipped cream, like butter and chocolate, is a magnet for odors.

Working with a whisk, hand-held beater, or mixer fitted with the whisk attachment, beat the cream (at medium speed, if applicable) just until it is foamy and starts to thicken. Add the sugar in a light steady stream and continue to beat until the cream forms the peaks you need — soft, medium, or firm.

CHOCOLATE
WHIPPED CREAM

This cream is meant to be used as a filling or topping for ice cream desserts, cakes, and small pastries, but it is so beautifully smooth — voluptuous, really — and so downright delicious no one would blame you for thinking of it as a dessert in its own right.

■ The secret to making chocolate whipped cream is temperature — it must be very cold before you whip it. In fact, after the cream and chocolate are blended and chilled, the best thing to do is to whip the cream in an ice-water bath. Do this, and you'll find you'll have perfect cream every time. ■ PH

- **3½ ounces (100 grams) bittersweet chocolate, preferably Valrhona Caraïbe, finely chopped**
- **2 cups (500 grams) heavy cream**
- **2 tablespoons sugar**

1. Put the chocolate in a mixing bowl that's large enough to be used for whipping the cream. Bring the cream and sugar to a full boil in a heavy-bottomed medium saucepan. Pull the pan from the heat and pour the cream over the chocolate, mixing energetically with a whisk so that the chocolate is completely blended into the cream. Chill the chocolate cream for at least 5 hours or, better yet, overnight. (The cream should be chilled to about 40°F [4°C], as measured on an instant-read thermometer.)

2. Just before you are ready to whip the cream, place the bowl of cream in a larger bowl filled with ice cubes and cold water. Whip the cream with a whisk until it is almost firm. Go easy — because of the chocolate and the ice-water bath, the cream will thicken quickly. The consistency you're looking for is one that is firm enough to spread but soft enough to still feel light and creamy in your mouth.

Makes about 3 cups
(600 grams)

KEEPING: The unwhipped mixture can be refrigerated, covered and away from foods with strong odors, overnight. Once whipped, the cream is best used immediately, but it can be kept covered in the refrigerator for up to 3 hours.

DEEP CHOCOLATE
CREAM

Really a dense, smooth, bittersweet chocolate pudding, this cream is based on a crème anglaise, and, while it can be served on its own as a dessert, Pierre often uses it in combination with other creams and sweets. It forms the base of Chocolate, Coffee, and Whiskey Cappuccino (page 146) and keeps company with caramel ice cream and chocolate sorbet in the deliciously over-the-top Coupe Malsherbes (page 194).

THE CREAM

- **9½ ounces (270 grams) bittersweet chocolate, preferably Valrhona Manjari, finely chopped**
- **1⅔ cups (415 grams) whole milk**
- **1½ cups (375 grams) heavy cream**
- **5 large egg yolks**
- **⅔ cup (140 grams) sugar**

1. Put the chocolate in a bowl large enough to hold all of the ingredients and set it aside. (If you have a bowl with a spout, it would be perfect for this.) Bring the milk and heavy cream to a boil in a saucepan over medium heat or in a microwave oven.

2. While the liquids are coming to a boil, whisk the yolks and sugar together in a heavy-bottomed medium saucepan until they are thick and slightly pale. Whisking without stop, slowly drizzle about one-quarter of the hot liquid into the yolk mixture. When the yolks are acclimatized to the heat, add the remainder of the liquid in a steadier stream.

3. Place the saucepan over medium-high heat and, stirring energetically and constantly with a wooden spoon or spatula, cook the cream until it thickens slightly, lightens in color, and, most important, reaches 180°F (80°C), as measured on an instant-read thermometer — all of which will take less than 5 minutes. (Alternatively, you can stir the crème anglaise and then draw your finger down the spatula or the bowl of the wooden spoon — if the cream doesn't run into the track you've created, it's done.) Remove the saucepan from the heat.

4. Strain half of the crème anglaise over the chocolate and, working with a small spatula, slowly stir the cream into the chocolate: Start by stirring in a small circle in the center of the bowl, then slowly work in larger concentric circles. Add half of the remaining cream through the strainer, stirring in the same fashion, and then the remainder of the cream. The cream is now ready to be used according to the specific recipe's directions, or it can be poured into a container and chilled. Once the cream is cold, it should be covered. To avoid having a skin form on the cream, press a piece of plastic wrap against the top of the cream as soon as you pour it into a container.

Makes about 3 cups
(950 grams)

KEEPING: The cream can be made up to 2 days ahead and kept covered in the refrigerator.

LADYFINGER BATTER

This is the batter that's used to make the dainty, light, and airy French biscuits that are so popular with tea. You'll need this batter to make the disks for the White Chocolate and Rhubarb Charlotte (page 43), but you'll have enough left over to pipe out some ladyfingers — they're a bonus and a reward.

- **6 large egg whites, at room temperature**
- **⅔ cup plus 2 tablespoons (160 grams) sugar**
- **5 large egg yolks, at room temperature**
- **¾ cup plus 2½ tablespoons (270 grams) all-purpose flour**

1. Before you start mixing the batter, check the specific recipe for which you'll be using the ladyfingers, or read the baking instructions below for information on preheating the oven and preparing the pan.

2. In a clean, dry mixer bowl with a clean, dry whisk attachment in place, whip the egg whites on high speed until they turn opaque and form soft peaks. Still whipping on high, gradually add ⅔ cup (140 grams) of the sugar. Continue beating until the whites are glossy and hold very firm peaks. It's important that the whites develop into a really firm meringue — this is what will allow the piped-out batter to rest on the counter for 15 minutes and still maintain its shape. Set aside for the moment.

3. In another bowl, whisk the yolks and the remaining 2 tablespoons sugar together until they are well blended, about 1 to 2 minutes. Working with a rubber spatula, gently fold the yolk mixture into the beaten whites. Then fold in the flour, sifting the flour over the mixture in a few additions and incorporating it gingerly. The batter is now ready to be piped and baked according to your recipe's particular instructions or the instructions below.

TO PIPE AND BAKE

The following are general directions for piping and baking ladyfinger batter. If anything more specific is needed, you'll find it in the individual recipes that use a ladyfinger base.

- **Confectioners' sugar for dusting**

1. Position the racks to divide the oven into thirds and preheat the oven to 450°F (230°C). Fit a large pastry bag with a plain ½-inch (1.5-cm) tip, then set it aside until needed. Cut two pieces of parchment paper to fit two large baking sheets. On each sheet of paper, with a pencil, draw a 9-inch (24-cm) circle and, along the short sides of each sheet, draw a band that's 8 inches (20 cm) long and 4 inches (10 cm) wide. (The circles are for the cake disks, the bands for ladyfingers.) Turn the paper over. (If you can't see the outlines clearly now that the paper is flipped over, darken the pencil lines.) Place each piece of parchment on a baking sheet.

2. Gently spoon a little more than half the batter into the pastry bag. Position a baking sheet so that the outline for the 8-inch- (20-cm-) long band runs from your left to your right, and make a ladyfinger band by piping plump logs of batter from top to bottom within the pencil lines: Pipe each ladyfinger log right next to the preceding one — they'll touch, and they're supposed to. When you've piped the full 8-inch band, dust it lightly with confectioners' sugar. Pipe the second band in the same fashion; dust it with confectioners' sugar too. Refill the bag when you run out of batter; the bands will probably take about two-thirds of the batter. Next pipe the disks, keeping in mind that the disks shouldn't be as high as the plump ladyfinger bands (if you'd like, you can switch to a smaller piping tip for the disks): For each disk, begin piping the batter at the center of the circle. Work your way in a spiral to the penciled edge, trying to have each coil of batter touch the preceding coil. If you have any holes, you can run an offset spatula very lightly over the disks to fill in the spaces. Let the piped batter rest on the counter for 15 minutes, during which time the confectioners' sugar will pearl, or form beads.

3. Give the ladyfinger bands a second light dusting of confectioners' sugar (there's no need to sugar the disks) and slip the baking sheets into the oven. Insert the handle of a wooden spoon into the door to keep it slightly ajar. Bake for 8 to 10 minutes, just until the disks and bands are very lightly golden — you don't want the cakes to take on much color. Slide the parchment off the baking sheets and transfer the cakes, on their parchment sheets, to racks to cool to room temperature.

4. When the cakes are cool, run an offset spatula under the disks and bands to loosen them from the paper. If you want individual biscuits, separate the cookies with a sharp knife or pizza cutter. If you want a decorative ladyfinger band that can be wrapped around cakes or charlottes, keep the cookies intact, but cut the band lengthwise in half, or according to the instructions given in the specific recipe.

Makes enough batter for two 9-inch (24-cm) disks and two 8-inch- (20-cm-) long bands of biscuits

KEEPING: Once mixed, the batter should be used immediately. Once baked, the cakes can be wrapped well in plastic, or packed in an airtight tin, and kept at room temperature for 2 days or frozen for a month.

COCOA CAKE

Airy, light, and cocoa-dark, this recipe turns out a cake that serves as the base for both the loaf-shaped Faubourg Pavé (page 17) and the round Black Forest Cake (page 11). The cake gets its delicate crumb from a mixture of cake flour and potato starch, and its lightness from whipped egg whites. On its own, the cake may strike you as nothing more than a simple tea cake — but that's just as it should be, since it is never meant to go it alone. This is a cake designed to play a supporting role. Brush it with syrup, layer it with ganache or whipped cream, and then take another look at it: It makes the stars of any creation shine.

The recipe will make one round layer for a Black Forest Cake or two loaf cakes for two Faubourg Pavés. If you don't need two cakes, just wrap the extra cake and stow it in the freezer — it will be fine for a month.

- ⅓ cup plus 1 tablespoon (40 grams) Dutch-processed cocoa powder, preferably Valrhona
- ¼ cup (35 grams) cake flour
- 3½ tablespoons potato starch
- 5½ tablespoons (2¾ ounces; 75 grams) unsalted butter
- 9 large egg yolks, at room temperature
- 1¼ cups (150 grams) sugar
- 5 large egg whites, at room temperature

1. Center a rack in the oven and preheat the oven to 350°F (180°C). If you are making the Faubourg Pavé, butter two 7½ x 3½-inch (18 x 9-cm) loaf pans, then line the pans with parchment paper. If you are making the Black Forest Cake, place a buttered 8¾-inch (22-cm) cake ring on a parchment-lined baking sheet.

2. Sift together the cocoa powder, cake flour, and potato starch and keep close at hand. Melt the butter and set it aside to cool until it is barely warm to the touch.

3. Working in a mixer fitted with the whisk attachment, beat the egg yolks and ½ cup plus 2 tablespoons (75 grams) of the sugar on medium-high speed, scraping down the sides of the bowl as needed, until the mixture is thick and pale, about 5 minutes. If you do not have a second mixer bowl, scrape the thickened egg yolks into a large bowl and wash and dry your mixer bowl; wash and dry the whisk attachment in any case.

4. Fit the mixer with the clean, dry bowl and whisk and whip the egg whites at

medium speed just until they form soft peaks. Gradually add the remaining ½ cup plus 2 tablespoons (75 grams) sugar and beat until the peaks are firm and shiny.

5. Working with a large rubber spatula and a light hand, fold the sifted dry ingredients and one-quarter of the beaten whites into the yolk mixture. Stir a few tablespoons of this mixture into the cooled melted butter, stirring to incorporate the butter as much as possible, then add the butter and the remaining whites to the yolks. Working quickly and gently, fold everything together.

6. Pour the batter into the prepared pan(s) — it should come three-quarters of the way up the sides — then slide the pan(s) into the oven. Bake the loaves for 25 to 30 minutes, the round for 20 to 25 minutes. The test for doneness is the same for both shapes: A slender knife inserted into the center of the cake should come out clean.

7. To cool the loaves, allow them to rest for 3 minutes in their pans, then gently unmold them onto cooling racks, delicately lift off the parchment paper, and turn the cakes right side up to cool to room temperature. For the round, transfer the baking sheet to a cooling rack, run a knife around the inside of the cake ring, and allow the cake to cool to room temperature in its ring.

Makes two 7½ x 3½-inch (18-cm) loaf cakes or one 8¾-inch (22-cm) round cake

KEEPING: The cake(s) can be wrapped airtight in plastic and stored at room temperature for 2 days or frozen for a month.

COCONUT DACQUOISE

Dacquoise is the name for both a cake and the meringue disks in that cake. Traditionally, a dacquoise is a nut meringue (see the hazelnut dacquoise on page 39), and, indeed, this dacquoise has nuts, but it has coconut too. In fact, there is almost as much coconut in this dacquoise as almonds, and the combination gives the meringue an unusual texture and an exotic, not-easy-to-place flavor.

- ½ cup (40 grams) **finely grated unsweetened dried coconut**
- ⅓ cup (45 grams) **blanched almonds**
- ¾ cup (75 grams) **confectioners' sugar**
- **3 large egg whites, at room temperature**
- ⅓ cup (70 grams) **sugar**

1. Preheat the oven to 325°F (165°C). If you are making three 6½-inch (16-cm) disks to use in the Chocolate Semifreddo (page 186), center a rack in the oven and line a large baking sheet with parchment paper. If you are making two 9-inch (24-cm) disks to use in the Criollo (page 34), position the racks to divide the oven into thirds and line two baking sheets with parchment paper. Pencil the outline of the 6½-inch (16-cm) or 9-inch (24-cm) circles on the parchment. Turn the paper over; if you can't see the outline of the circles clearly now that the paper is flipped over, darken the pencil lines. Fit a medium pastry bag with a plain ⅓-inch (1-cm) tip.

2. For this recipe, the grated coconut should be as fine as powder (an unlikely possibility if you bought it in a health food store) and the almonds should be ground, so put the coconut, almonds, and confectioners' sugar in the work bowl of a food processor and process it in long pulses until the mixture is powdery. (It won't be light and fluffy, because of the oil in the nuts.) Turn the mixture into a not-too-fine mesh strainer, sift it onto a large piece of parchment or waxed paper, and keep it close at hand.

3. Put the egg whites in a clean, dry mixer bowl, fit the mixer with the whisk attachment, and beat on medium speed until the whites are opaque. Still beating, add the granulated sugar in a slow, steady stream, then continue to beat until the whites hold firm but still very glossy peaks. Remove the bowl from the mixer (if necessary) and, working with a large rubber spatula, fold the sifted dry ingredients gently into the whites in three or four additions.

Makes two 9-inch (24-cm) disks
or three 6½-inch (16-cm) disks

K E E P I N G : The meringues
can be made ahead and kept in
an airtight container safe from
humidity for up to 4 days or
wrapped airtight and frozen for
up to a month. The meringues
don't have to be defrosted if
you'll be layering them with
mousse (as you will in the
Criollo or the Chocolate Semifreddo) — they'll defrost while
you construct the dessert.

4. Spoon half the batter into the pastry bag. Begin piping the batter at the center of a circle. Work your way in a spiral to the penciled edge and try to have
   each coil of batter touch the preceding coil; pipe with light, consistent pressure. Refill the bag and pipe the remaining disks. (Any leftover meringue can
   be piped into little buttons — they'll make great cookies for espresso or tea.)
   If you see any spaces or uneven sections on the disks, give them a once-over-
   lightly with a metal spatula.

5. Slide the baking sheets into the oven and insert the handle of a wooden
   spoon into the door to keep it slightly ajar. Bake the disks for 30 to 35 minutes, until they are firm and very lightly caramel colored; if you're using two
   pans, rotate the pans front to back and top to bottom twice during the baking period. Transfer the meringues, parchment and all, to racks to cool to
   room temperature.

6. When the meringues are cool, run an offset spatula under the disks to loosen
   them from the paper.

Cream puff dough (*pâte à choux*) is pastry's Little Engine That Could. Put a spoonful of it in the oven and, as it's expanding, you can just about hear it chanting, "I think I can, I think I can." For sure, if you've got a window in your oven, you can watch it grow. Powered by the heat, the dough huffs and with each huff, it puffs, until it's about three times its original size. Puffed and golden, it's got a tender crust, a satiny sheen, and a hollow center whose inner shell is soft, moist, and custardy. This is the dough that makes eponymous cream puffs as well as éclairs (page 9), profiteroles (page 135), and the base of the Gâteau Saint-Honoré (page 21).

Once the dough is made, it must be shaped immediately. However, once it's shaped, it can be frozen. When you're ready to bake it, don't defrost it, just add another 3 to 5 minutes to the baking time.

- **½ cup (125 grams) whole milk**
- **½ cup (125 grams) water**
- **1 stick (4 ounces; 115 grams) unsalted butter, cut into 8 pieces**
- **¼ teaspoon sugar**
- **¼ teaspoon salt**
- **1 cup (140 grams) all-purpose flour**
- **5 large eggs, at room temperature**

1. Before you start mixing the batter, check the specific recipe in which you'll be using it for information on preheating the oven and preparing the pans and pastry bag.

2. Bring the milk, water, butter, sugar, and salt to the boil in a heavy-bottomed medium saucepan. When the mixture is boiling rapidly, add the flour all at once, reduce the heat to medium, and, without a second's hesitation, start stirring the mixture like mad with a wooden spoon. The dough will come together very quickly and a slight crust will form on the bottom of the pan, but you need to keep stirring — vigorously — for another 2 to 3 minutes to dry the dough. At the end of this time, the dough will be very smooth.

3. Turn the dough into the bowl of a mixer fitted with the paddle attachment,

Makes enough dough for about 30 large or 50 small cream puffs, 22 éclairs, or the base plus more than enough puffs for a Gâteau Saint-Honoré

KEEPING: You can pipe the dough and either bake it immediately or freeze it. To freeze, pipe the dough onto parchment-lined baking sheets and slide the sheets into the freezer. When the dough is completely frozen, remove the piped shapes from the baking sheets and wrap them airtight. They can be kept in the freezer for up to 1 month.

or, if you've still got some elbow grease left, continue by hand. One by one, add the eggs to the dough, beating until each egg is thoroughly incorporated. Don't be discouraged — as soon as you add the first egg, your lovely dough will separate. Keep working, and by the time you add the third egg, it will start coming together again. When all the eggs are incorporated, the dough will be thick and shiny and when you lift some of it up, it will fall back into the bowl in a ribbon. The dough will still be warm — it's supposed to be — and now is the time to use it. Shape the dough using a pastry bag and tip, following the directions in the specific recipe.

SWEET TART
DOUGH

This dough makes a cookie-like crust most commonly used for tarts and tartlets but superb as the base of Pierre's unusual Florentines (page 75). It has a fairly firm texture with some crunch and some buttery crumble and enough flavor to make it an important part of a recipe rather than merely a holder for a filling. To get the proper texture, work the dough as little as possible. If you've mixed the dough and still see a few large pieces of butter, leave them. It's better to have a few pieces of butter than an overworked dough.

■ You'll get the best texture if you make a large quantity of this dough; make only enough for one tart, and you'll run the risk of overworking the dough. Once made, the dough can be wrapped in individual tart-sized packages and frozen for up to a month. ■ PH

- 2½ sticks (10 ounces; 285 grams) unsalted butter, at room temperature
- 1½ cups (150 grams) confectioners' sugar, sifted
- ½ cup (lightly packed) (3¼ ounces; 100 grams) finely ground almond powder (see page 265) or finely ground blanched almonds (see page 265)
- ½ teaspoon salt
- ½ teaspoon vanilla bean pulp (see page 279) or pure vanilla extract
- 2 large eggs, at room temperature, lightly beaten
- 3½ cups (490 grams) all-purpose flour

To make the dough in a mixer:
Place the butter in the bowl of a mixer fitted with the paddle attachment and beat on low speed until creamy. Add the sugar, almond powder, salt, vanilla, and eggs and, still working on low speed, beat to blend the ingredients, scraping down the paddle and the sides of the bowl as needed. The dough may look curdled — that's all right. With the machine on low, add the flour in three or four additions and mix only until the mixture comes together to form a soft, moist dough — a matter of seconds. Don't overdo it.

To make the dough in a large-capacity food processor:
Place the butter in the work bowl of a food processor fitted with the metal blade and pulse and process, scraping down the sides of the bowl as needed, until creamy. Add the confectioners' sugar and process to blend well. Add the almond powder, salt, and vanilla and continue to process until smooth, scraping the bowl as necessary, then add the eggs and process to blend. Add the flour and pulse until the mixture just starts to come together. When the dough forms moist curds and clumps and then starts to gather into a ball, stop! — you don't want to overwork it. The dough will be very soft, pliable, and Play-Doh–ish, more like your favorite butter cookie dough than traditional pie dough — that's just the way it should be.

TO SHAPE AND CHILL

No matter the method you used to make the dough, gather it into a ball and divide it into 3 or 4 pieces: 3 pieces for 10-inch (26-cm) tarts, 4 for 9-inch (24-cm) tarts. (Of course, you can press the dough into one large disk and cut off as much as you need at the time that you need it.) Gently press each piece into a disk and wrap each disk in plastic. Allow the dough to rest in the refrigerator for at least 4 hours, or for up to 2 days, before rolling and baking. (*The dough can be wrapped airtight and frozen for up to a month.*)

TO ROLL AND BAKE

1. For each tart, place a buttered tart ring on a parchment-lined baking sheet and keep close at hand. Work with one piece of dough at a time; keep the remaining dough in the refrigerator.

2. Working on a lightly floured surface (marble is ideal), roll the dough to a thickness of between 1/16 and 1/8 inch (2 and 4 cm), lifting the dough often and making certain that the work surface and the dough are amply floured at all times. (Because this dough is so rich, it can be difficult to roll, but a well-floured surface makes the job easier. If you are a novice at rolling, you might find it easier to tape a large piece of plastic wrap to the counter and to roll the dough between that and another piece of plastic. If you do this, make sure to lift the top sheet of plastic wrap from time to time so that it doesn't crease and get rolled into the dough.) Roll the dough up around your rolling pin and unroll it onto the tart ring. Fit the dough into the bottom and up the sides of the ring, then run your rolling pin across the top of the ring to cut off the excess. If the dough cracks or splits as you work, don't worry — patch

the cracks with scraps (moisten the edges with water to "glue" them in place) and just make certain not to stretch the dough that's in the pan. (What you stretch now will shrink later.) Prick the dough all over with the tines of a fork (unless the tart will be filled with a runny custard or other loose filling) and chill it for at least 30 minutes in the refrigerator.

3. When you are ready to bake the crust(s), preheat the oven to 350°F (180°C). Fit a circle of parchment paper or foil into the crust and fill with dried beans or rice.

4. Bake the crust for 18 to 20 minutes, just until it is very lightly colored. If the crust needs to be fully baked, remove the parchment and beans and bake the crust for another 3 to 5 minutes, or until golden. Transfer the crust to a rack to cool.

Makes enough dough for three 10-inch (26-cm) or four 9-inch (24-cm) tart shells

K E E P I N G : The dough can be kept in the refrigerator for up to 2 days or wrapped airtight and frozen for a month. Frozen disks of dough take about 45 minutes to an hour at average room temperature to reach a good rolling-out consistency. Baked crusts can be kept uncovered at room temperature for about 8 hours.

CHOCOLATE-ALMOND
PÂTE SABLÉE

Sablée, or sandy, describes the appealing texture of this crust. The crust is buttery, soft (and rich) enough to melt in your mouth, but crumbly and just a little crunchy — that's the sandy part. It's definitely chocolate flavored, subtly almond flavored, and perfect with myriad fillings. It's also good all by itself — if you've got a few scraps of this dough left over, just roll them out and bake them like cookies. They're a nice reward for the baker.

This recipe makes enough for three large tarts, which may be more than you'll need at any one time, but, for the sake of texture, it's best to make more of this dough rather than less. The good news is that the dough freezes perfectly for a month and defrosts to rollability in about an hour.

- 2½ sticks plus 1 tablespoon (10½ ounces; 300 grams) unsalted butter, at room temperature
- ½ cup plus 1½ tablespoons (60 grams) confectioners' sugar, sifted
- ½ cup (slightly rounded) (3½ ounces; 105 grams) finely ground almond powder (see page 265) or finely ground blanched almonds (see page 265)
- ½ teaspoon salt
- 3 large eggs, at room temperature
- ½ cup (50 grams) Dutch-processed cocoa powder, preferably Valrhona, sifted
- 2¾ cups (385 grams) all-purpose flour

To make the dough in a mixer:
Place the butter in the bowl of a mixer fitted with the paddle attachment and beat on low speed until creamy. One by one, add the sugar, almond powder, salt, and eggs and, still working on low speed, beat to blend the ingredients, scraping down the paddle and the sides of the bowl as needed. The dough may look separated — that's all right. With the machine on low, add the cocoa, mixing until it is absorbed, then add the flour in three or four additions and mix only until the mixture comes together to form a soft, moist dough — a matter of seconds. Don't overdo it.

To make the dough in a large-capacity food processor:
Place the butter in the work bowl of a food processor fitted with the metal blade

and pulse and process, scraping down the sides of the bowl as needed, until creamy. Add the confectioners' sugar and process to blend well. Add the almond powder and salt and continue to process until smooth, scraping the bowl as necessary, then add the eggs and process to blend. Add the cocoa and pulse to blend, then add the flour and pulse until the mixture just starts to come together. When the dough forms moist curds and clumps and then starts to gather into a ball, stop! — you don't want to overwork it. The dough will be very soft, pliable, and Play-Doh–ish, more like your favorite butter cookie dough than traditional pie dough — and that's just the way it should be.

TO SHAPE AND CHILL

No matter the method you used to make the dough, gather it into a ball and divide it into 3 pieces. (Of course, you can press the dough into one large disk and cut off as much as you need at the time that you need it.) Gently press each piece into a disk and wrap each disk in plastic. Allow the dough to rest in the refrigerator for at least 4 hours, or for up to 2 days, before rolling and baking. (*The dough can be wrapped airtight and frozen for up to a month.*)

TO ROLL AND BAKE

1. For each tart, place a buttered tart ring on a parchment-lined baking sheet and keep close at hand. Work with one piece of dough at a time; keep the remaining dough in the refrigerator.

2. Working on a lightly floured surface (marble would be ideal), roll the dough to a thickness of between 1/16 and 1/8 inch (2 and 4 mm), lifting the dough often and making certain that the work surface and the dough are amply floured at all times. (Because this dough is so rich, it can be difficult to roll, but a well-floured surface makes the job easier. Alternatively, you might find it more convenient to tape a large piece of plastic wrap to the counter and to roll the dough between that and another piece of plastic. If you do this, make sure to lift the top sheet of plastic wrap from time to time so that it doesn't crease and get rolled into the dough.) Once the dough is rolled out, roll it up and around your rolling pin and unroll it onto the tart ring. Fit the dough into the bottom and up the sides of the ring, then run your rolling pin across the top of the ring to cut off the excess. If the dough cracks or splits as you work, don't worry — patch the cracks with scraps (moisten the edges with water to "glue" them in place) and just make certain not to stretch the dough that's in the pan. (What you stretch now will

Makes enough dough for three
9- or 10-inch (24- or 26-cm)
tart shells

KEEPING: The dough can
be kept in the refrigerator for
up to 2 days or wrapped
airtight and frozen for a
month. Frozen disks of dough
take 45 to 60 minutes at
average room temperature to
reach a good rolling-out
consistency. Baked crusts can
be kept uncovered at
room temperature for
about 8 hours.

shrink later.) Prick the dough all over with the tines of a fork (unless the tart will be filled with a runny custard or other loose filling) and chill it for at least 30 minutes in the refrigerator.

3. When you are ready to bake the crust(s), preheat the oven to 350°F (180°C). Fit a circle of parchment paper or foil into the crust and fill it with dried beans or rice.

4. Bake the crust for 23 to 25 minutes, just until it is very lightly colored. If the crust needs to be fully baked, remove the parchment and beans and bake the crust for another 3 to 5 minutes, or until it is firm and uniformly browned. Transfer the crust to a rack to cool.

There is no dough more elegant than puff pastry, no dough more sumptuous, and no dough more likely to make you feel like a million bucks after you've prepared it for the first time, in part because it's so dramatic — under heat, the hundreds of layers of cold butter in the dough melt, the water in the butter turns to steam, and the steam pushes the dough up to dizzying heights — and in part because you know you're making something legendary. For centuries, the reputations of pastry chefs and shops rose and fell on the quality of their mille-feuille, or what we call a napoleon, the classic cake that combines pastry cream with layers of puff pastry.

Pierre's puff pastry is an inversion of the classic recipe. In the classic, a flour-and-water dough encases a block of butter, then the package is rolled and folded six times until its *mille feuilles*, or 1,000 layers, are achieved. In this recipe, the dough is literally turned inside out. Most of the butter is on the outside; the inner block is a mix of flour, water, and melted butter; and the rolling and folding is accomplished in double rather than single turns, a neat trick that works because the dough is sturdy.

■ Because the butter is on the outside, this dough is actually easier to handle than classic puff pastry dough. Best of all, this dough produces a pastry that is both melting and crisp, tender and flaky. ■ PH

THE FIRST MIXTURE

- 3½ sticks (14 ounces; 400 grams) unsalted butter, at room temperature
- 1¼ cups (175 grams) all-purpose flour

Put the butter in a mixer fitted with the paddle attachment and work the butter until it is just smooth. Add the flour and mix just until the ingredients come together. There will always be a little flour left in the bottom of the bowl — just mix it into the butter with a spatula. Scrape the mixture out onto a large sheet of plastic wrap and, working with a dough scraper, flatten it into a square about 6 inches (15 cm) on a side. Wrap the mixture well and refrigerate it for at least 1½ hours.

THE SECOND MIXTURE

- ¾ cup (185 grams) water
- 2 teaspoons salt
- ¼ teaspoon white vinegar
- 3 cups (420 grams) all-purpose flour (or maybe a bit more)
- 1 stick (4 ounces; 115 grams) unsalted butter, melted and cooled

Mix the water, salt, and vinegar together and keep it at the ready. Put the flour into the mixer bowl and fit the mixer with the paddle attachment. With the mixer at medium-low speed, add the melted butter to the flour and mix until the flour is moistened. The dough will look lumpy and bumpy, like the topping for a fruit crisp. With the mixer still on medium-low speed, gradually add the vinegar-water by pouring it down the sides of the bowl a little at a time; add the water very slowly and keep a little of it in reserve — because the absorbency of flour differs, it's hard to know whether you'll need all of the water or not. Keep mixing, scraping down the bowl and adding water, until you have a dough that cleans the sides of the bowl. The dough will be soft, rather like an elastic tart dough, and that's fine. If the dough doesn't come together, it may need a tad more flour — add, up to about a tablespoon more, in sprinkles — or a tablespoon or two more water. Turn the soft dough out onto a sheet of plastic wrap and shape it into a square that's about an inch or two (2.5 to 5 cm) smaller than the butter-flour square. Wrap it well and chill it for at least 1½ hours.

TO ROLL AND TURN

1. Place the chilled first mixture on a very well floured work surface (marble is ideal) and dust the top of it with flour. If the dough is too hard to roll, press your rolling pin against it to create a series of parallel indentations that will soften the dough and help you get it going. Roll the dough out into a rectangle that's roughly 12 x 7 inches (30 x 18 cm), rolling in all directions, and on both sides, and making sure to lift and turn the dough as you roll; dust the work surface and the dough with flour as necessary. Position the chilled second mixture so that it covers the bottom half of the rolled-out dough. Fold the top half of the rolled-out dough over it and press the edges to form a neat sealed package. Make sure that the second mixture extends into each of the corners of this square. If you have to, smoosh the second mixture into the corners with your fingertips so that the package is an even thickness throughout. Tap your rolling pin against each of the sides of the dough to

square the bundle (which will probably be about 7 to 8 inches [18 to 20 cm] on a side). Wrap the dough well in plastic and refrigerate for at least an hour.

2. To make the first double turn, place the dough on a well-floured work surface and dust the top of it with flour. Again rolling the dough in all directions, and on both sides, taking care not to roll over the edges and keeping the work surface and the dough as well floured as needed, roll the dough until it is about three times longer than it is wide — about 7 to 8 inches (18 to 20 cm) wide and about 21 to 24 inches (52 to 60 cm) long. (Don't worry if your dough isn't exactly the specified measurements. Dough widens as you roll it — it's only natural. What's important is to roll the dough to three times its width, whatever its width — keep a ruler nearby.) If, as you're rolling, the dough cracks, just patch it as best you can and keep going. To create what's called the double turn, or the wallet turn, fold the bottom quarter of the dough up to the center of the dough, then fold the top quarter of the dough down to the center. Now fold the dough in half at the center. You'll have four layers of dough. Brush off any excess flour and wrap the dough well. Chill it again for at least 1 hour.

3. For the second double turn, position the dough so that the closed fold, the one that looks like the spine of a book, is to your left, and repeat the rolling and folding process as above. When you have folded the dough into its double turn, brush off the excess flour. Wrap the dough in plastic and chill it again for about an hour. (*The dough can be made to this point and kept refrigerated for up to 48 hours. In fact, at this point, it is good to give the dough a rest of more than 3 hours.*)

4. The morning of the day that you are going to use the dough, or a short while before you need the dough, give it its last turn, a single turn. To do this, position the dough with the closed fold to your left and roll the dough out as before. This time, fold the dough like a business letter: Fold the bottom third of the dough up so that it covers the middle third of the dough and then fold the top third over so that it meets the edge of the already folded dough. (If your dough was in fact three times longer than it was wide, this fold should result in a square; if not, it will still be fine.) Brush off any excess flour. Wrap the dough well and chill it for at least 30 minutes before rolling it out to use in any recipe. If you can, it's best to give the dough a longer chill now, and then, after you've rolled the dough out for your recipe (you'll probably divide this large piece and roll out only a portion of it), let the rolled-out dough chill for about 30 minutes before cutting and baking. The best plan is to roll the dough out, transfer it to a baking sheet, cover, and chill it on the baking sheet, then, with the chilled dough still on the sheet, do the actual cutting.

Makes about 2½ pounds
(1135 grams) dough

KEEPING: The refrigerator life of this dough is about 3 days from the time you make the two mixtures to the time you use the dough for a dessert. You can roll and turn the dough, then wrap it and let it stay in the refrigerator for several hours rather than the minimum 1½ hours — it can be rolled around your schedule. Once the dough is made, it can be divided into portions, wrapped airtight, and kept in the freezer for up to a month. Thaw, still wrapped, in the refrigerator overnight before rolling it out to cut and bake.

Like classic puff pastry — but not exactly like Pierre's Inside-Out Puff Pastry (page 241) — chocolate puff pastry is made of two doughs, one composed primarily of butter with a little cocoa, the other composed primarily of flour with a little butter. And, again like classic puff pastry but not like Pierre's Inside-Out Puff Pastry, the butter packet is encased in the flour dough and rolled out long and thin, folded into thirds like a business letter, and then given a quarter turn before the rolling and folding is repeated. Each roll, fold, and turn is called a turn, and this puff pastry, like most, needs six turns and a rest period in the refrigerator between turns to reach perfection. Once sufficiently rolled and turned, the dough needs at least six hours in the fridge before you bake it. Like much in pastry, the work is short but the process is long — and worth it.

You can use this dough in any recipe that calls for puff pastry — use it just as you would puff pastry; the chocolate doesn't change the way it rolls, shapes, or bakes.

THE DOUGH

- **3 cups (420 grams) all-purpose flour**
- **Approximately ¾ cup (185 grams) cold water**
- **2 teaspoons salt**
- **5 tablespoons (2½ ounces; 70 grams) unsalted butter, melted and cooled**

Put the flour in a large mixing bowl and hollow out a well in the center. Stir together ¾ cup (185 grams) water and the salt until the salt dissolves, and pour the water into the well. Using a rubber spatula or a fork, and starting at the inside of the wall of flour, stir the flour into the water. When most of the flour has been stirred into the water, pour the melted butter over the flour-water mixture and continue to stir. If the dough is dry — and it probably will be — stir in an additional 2 to 3 tablespoons of water, a little at a time. Don't expect perfection — the dough will be ropy, stringy, and not fully blended even after you've added additional water. Reach into the bowl and gently knead the dough for a minute or so to bring it together. Turn the dough out onto a lightly floured work surface and shape it into a 6-inch (15-cm) square. Wrap the dough in plastic and chill it for at least 2 hours.

THE BUTTER PACKET

- 3¾ sticks (15 ounces; 425 grams) unsalted butter, at room temperature
- ½ cup (50 grams) Dutch-processed cocoa powder, preferably Valrhona, sifted

Working in a mixer fitted with the paddle attachment or in a bowl with a large flexible rubber spatula, beat the butter until it is smooth but not airy. Add the cocoa powder and mix just until it blends into the butter. Scrape the soft butter out onto a lightly floured work surface, shape it into a square that's about an inch or two (2.5 to 5 cm) smaller than the dough package, and wrap it in plastic wrap. Chill the butter packet for at least 2 hours.

TO ROLL AND TURN

1. Place the chilled dough package on a very well floured work surface (marble is ideal) and dust the top of the dough with flour. If the dough is too hard to roll, press your rolling pin against it to create a series of parallel indentations that will soften the dough and help you get it going. Roll the dough out into a rectangle that's about ⅓ inch (1 cm) thick and roughly 12 x 7 inches (30 x 18 cm), rolling in all directions, and on both sides, and making sure to lift and turn the dough as you roll; dust the work surface and the dough with flour as necessary.

2. Remove the butter packet from the refrigerator. Ideally, the butter packet should be the same consistency as the dough packet — but it's bound to be harder when it comes out of the refrigerator — so either pound it lightly with your rolling pin or put it in the microwave oven for about 10 seconds. Position the now-slightly-softer (but still chilled) butter packet so that it covers the bottom half of the rolled-out dough. Fold the top half of the rolled-out dough over it and press the dough to form a neat sealed package. Make sure that the butter packet extends into each of the corners of this square. If you have to, smoosh the packet into the corners with your fingertips so that the entire package is an even thickness throughout. Tap your rolling pin against each side of the dough to square the bundle (which will probably be about 7 to 8 inches [18 to 20 cm] on a side). If the dough doesn't seem too soft, you can give it its first turn now. However, if it seems the least bit soft — or if you just want to play it safe — wrap the dough in plastic wrap and give it an hour's rest in the refrigerator.

3. To make the first single turn, place the dough on a well-floured work surface and dust the top of it with flour. Again rolling the dough in all directions, and

on both sides, taking care not to roll over the edges and keeping the work surface and the dough as well floured as needed, roll the dough until it is about three times longer than it is wide — about 7 to 8 inches (18 to 20 cm) wide and about 21 to 24 inches (52 to 60 cm) long. Don't worry if your dough isn't exactly the specified measurements. Dough widens as you roll it — it's only natural — what's important is to roll the dough to three times its width, whatever its width; keep a ruler nearby. (If, as you're rolling, the dough cracks, just patch it as best you can; if some butter seeps out, dab it with flour — these are minor problems and shouldn't hold up your progress. However, if the dough gets soft, then it's time to stop — slide the dough onto a cutting board, cover it with plastic, and give it a chill before continuing to roll it out.)

4. When the dough is three times as long as it is wide, fold it like a business letter: Fold the bottom third of the dough over the middle third, then fold the top third over so it meets the edge of the folded dough. You'll have created three layers of dough and finished your first turn. Brush any excess flour off the dough, wrap the dough in plastic wrap, make a note that you've completed one turn, and refrigerate the dough for at least 2 hours.

5. Working on a well-floured surface, place the dough in front of you so that the side of the dough that resembles the spine of a book is at your left, the "open pages" at your right. Keeping the fold to your left, repeat the rolling and folding procedure, rolling the dough to a length that's three times its width, then folding it like a business letter. When you've completed this second turn, brush off any excess flour, wrap the dough in plastic wrap, make a note that you've given it two turns, and refrigerate the dough for another 2 hours.

6. Always starting with the fold on your left, as though the dough were a book, give the dough another 4 turns, for a total of 6 turns. If you complete turn number 3 and find that the dough is still firm and rolling nicely, you can try doing turn number 4 — the turn during which the dough will start to look like chocolate dough — before chilling the dough for 2 hours. Similarly, after chilling, you might be able to do turns 5 and 6 without an interim chill. However, as soon as you feel the dough getting soft or see butter patches, or as soon as the dough is in any other way difficult to work — get it into the re-frigerator for a long chill. Remember, always mark the number of turns you've completed, and always chill the dough for about 2 hours between turns.

7. When you've completed all 6 turns, chill the dough for at least 6 hours. (*If it's more convenient, you can refrigerate the dough for up to 2 days or freeze it for up to 1 month.*) Once chilled, it is ready to be rolled out and used in any recipe.

Makes about 2¾ pounds (1250 grams) dough

KEEPING: The refrigerator life of this dough is about 3 days from the time you make the two mixtures until the time you use the dough for a dessert. You can roll and turn the dough, then wrap it and let it stay in the refrigerator for several hours rather than the minimum 2 hours — it can be rolled around your sched-ule. Once the dough is made, it can be divided into por-tions, wrapped airtight, and kept in the freezer for up to 1 month. Thaw the dough, still wrapped, overnight in the refrigerator before rolling it out to cut and bake.

CARAMELIZED PLAIN PUFF PASTRY

Here is a simple technique for doubling the characteristic crispness of puff pastry used to make mille-feuille, or napoleons — and it works well whether you're using homemade or store-bought puff pastry. The method involves nothing more than dusting the rolled-out puff pastry with sugar right before it goes into the oven and then, when the pastry's almost baked, turning it over and dusting it with confectioners' sugar. The double dusting produces a bottom layer of pastry with a slightly matte finish and a very crisp caramel-flavored coating and a top layer that is smooth, shiny, and inimitably puff-pastry flaky.

- **14 ounces (400 grams) plain puff pastry, homemade (slightly more than one third of the recipe on page 241) or store-bought, ready to use**
- **1½ tablespoons sugar**
- **2 tablespoons confectioners' sugar**

1. Cut a piece of parchment paper to cover a baking sheet or jelly-roll pan that is about 18 x 12 inches (45 x 30 cm). Lightly moisten the parchment with a pastry brush dipped in water. Have another baking sheet or jelly-roll pan the same size on hand, as well as another piece of parchment paper the same size, and a cooling rack that is also about the same size as the pan. Keep all this gear close by.

2. Working on a floured surface, roll the puff pastry into a rectangle about 10 x 14 inches (26 x 35 cm) and about ⅛ inch (4 mm) thick. Roll the dough up around your rolling pin, then unroll it onto the moistened parchment-covered baking sheet. Cover the dough with a piece of plastic wrap and chill it for 1 to 2 hours, the time needed for the flour's gluten to relax so the pastry will rise evenly and maintain its size and shape under heat.

3. Center a rack in the oven and preheat the oven to 450°F (230°C).

4. Remove the baking sheet from the refrigerator, lift off and discard the plastic wrap, and dust the top of the puff pastry evenly with the granulated sugar. Slide the baking sheet into the oven, close the oven door, and immediately lower the oven temperature to 375°F (190°C). Bake the pastry for 8 to 10

minutes, during which time it will rise and begin to brown. Gently place the cooling rack over the pastry — this will keep it from rising too exuberantly — and bake it for another 10 minutes. Pull the baking sheet from the oven and increase the oven temperature to 475°F (245°C).

5. Lift the cooling rack off the pastry and set the rack aside. Cover the pastry with the reserved sheet of parchment and then with the second baking sheet or jelly-roll pan. Carefully and gingerly turn the whole setup over and place it on a work surface. Pull away the first baking sheet and parchment; the plain, uncaramelized side of the puff pastry will be the side you see. Sift the confectioners' sugar evenly over this side.

6. Slide the baking sheet into the oven and bake it until the sugar is smooth, shiny, and caramelized, about 5 minutes — keep a close eye on this so you don't end up burning either the top or bottom of the pastry. Pull the pan from the oven, place it on a cooling rack, and allow the pastry to cool for at least 1 hour.

Makes enough puff pastry for 6 mille-feuilles

KEEPING: Like all puff pastry, caramelized puff pastry is best used shortly after it is baked; certainly it should be used the day it is made.

CARAMELIZED CHOCOLATE PUFF PASTRY

Like its sibling, plain puff pastry, chocolate puff pastry can get another layer of flavor and texture by being caramelized. But, unlike its sib, it's caramelized on only one side and only with granulated sugar, which gives the pastry a matte but lustrous finish, an even crisper texture, and a small dose of sweet caramel flavor, a perfect go-along with chocolate.

- **14 ounces (400 grams) Chocolate Puff Pastry (about one-third of the recipe on page 245), ready to use**
- **1½ tablespoons sugar**

1. Cut a piece of parchment paper to cover a baking sheet or jelly-roll pan that is about 18 x 12 inches (45 x 30 cm). Lightly moisten the parchment with a pastry brush dipped in water. Have another baking sheet or jelly-roll pan of the same size on hand, as well as another piece of parchment paper cut to the same size, and a cooling rack that is also about the same size as the pan. Keep all this gear close by.

2. Working on a floured surface, roll the puff pastry into a rectangle about 10 x 14 inches (26 x 35 cm) and about ⅛ inch (4 mm) thick. Roll the dough up around your rolling pin, then unroll it onto the moistened parchment-covered baking sheet. Cover the dough with a piece of plastic wrap and chill it for 1 to 2 hours, the time needed for the flour's gluten to relax so the pastry will rise evenly and maintain its size and shape under heat.

3. Center a rack in the oven and preheat the oven to 450°F (230°C).

4. Remove the baking sheet from the refrigerator, lift off and discard the plastic wrap, and dust the top of the puff pastry evenly with the sugar. Slide the baking sheet into the oven, close the oven door, and immediately lower the oven temperature to 375°F (190°C). Bake the pastry for 8 to 10 minutes, during which time it will rise and begin to brown. Gently place the cooling rack over the pastry — this will keep it from rising too exuberantly — and bake it for another 10 minutes.

5. Pull the baking sheet from the oven. Lift the cooling rack off the pastry and set the rack aside. Cover the pastry with the reserved sheet of parchment and then with the second baking sheet or jelly-roll pan. Carefully and gingerly turn the whole setup over and place it on a work surface. Pull away the first baking sheet and parchment; the plain, uncaramelized side of the puff pastry will be the side you see.

6. Slide the baking sheet back into the oven and bake for another 3 to 5 minutes, just until the caramelized layer on the bottom develops a smooth matte finish. Pull the pan from the oven, place it on a cooling rack, and allow the pastry to cool for at least 1 hour.

Makes enough puff pastry for 6 mille-feuilles

KEEPING: Like all puff pastry, caramelized puff pastry is best used shortly after it is baked; certainly it should be used the day it is made.

SIMPLE SYRUP

Makes about ½ cup
(150 grams)

KEEPING: The syrup can be used as soon as it cools, or it can be poured into a jar with a tight-fitting lid and stored in the refrigerator for several months.

A mix of sugar and water that's brought to the boil, then cooled, this syrup is the base for many sorbets and poaching liquids.

- **⅓ cup (70 grams) sugar**
- **6 tablespoons (70 grams) cold water**

Stir the sugar and water together in a heavy-bottomed saucepan, place over medium heat, and bring to the boil. As soon as the syrup comes to the boil, remove it from the heat. Cool to room temperature.

Properly bittersweet and just as properly shiny, this sauce is the ideal accompaniment to ice cream desserts, the topper of choice for profiteroles, a good drizzle for cakes and tarts, and a necessary ingredient in Chocolate Glaze (page 254).

- 4½ ounces (130 grams) bittersweet chocolate, preferably Valrhona Guanaja, finely chopped
- 1 cup (250 grams) water
- ½ cup (125 grams) crème fraîche, homemade (see page 270) or store-bought, or heavy cream
- ⅓ cup (70 grams) sugar

Place all the ingredients in a heavy-bottomed medium saucepan and bring to the boil over medium heat, stirring constantly. Reduce the heat to low and simmer, stirring frequently with a wooden spoon, until the sauce thickens very slightly and coats the back of the spoon. (It doesn't really thicken much, but it does really coat the spoon.) Alternatively, you can use the draw-a-line test: Dip the spoon into the sauce and draw your finger down the back of the spoon — if the sauce doesn't run into the track created by your finger, it's done. Be patient — this can take 10 to 15 minutes and shouldn't be rushed. Use the sauce immediately, or allow it to cool, then chill until needed. Reheat the sauce in a bowl set over a saucepan of simmering water or in a microwave oven.

Makes about 1½ cups
(525 grams)

KEEPING: The sauce will keep in a tightly sealed jar in the refrigerator for 2 weeks, or it can be packed airtight and frozen for 1 month. Reheat gently before using.

CHOCOLATE GLAZE

This is the ideal finish for individual pastries. It's a dark chocolate glaze that pours smoothly and sets quickly, which is just what you need when you have a large surface to cover.

■ This glaze, like most glazes, will lose its gloss under refrigeration. To bring back its shine, give it a few puffs of warm air from a hairdryer. ■ PH

Makes about 1 cup (300 grams)

- ⅓ cup (80 grams) heavy cream
- 3½ ounces (100 grams) bittersweet chocolate, preferably Valrhona Guanaja, very finely chopped
- 4 teaspoons (20 grams) unsalted butter, cut into 4 pieces, at room temperature
- 7 tablespoons (110 grams) Chocolate Sauce (page 253), warm or at room temperature

KEEPING: While it is best to use the glaze as soon as it is made, the glaze can be made up to 3 days ahead, kept in a tightly covered jar in the refrigerator, and brought up to the proper pouring temperature in a bowl over (not touching) simmering water or in a microwave oven at a low setting. If you reheat the glaze, resist the urge to stir it a lot — working the glaze can dull its beautiful sheen.

1. In a small saucepan, bring the heavy cream to a boil over medium heat. Remove the saucepan from the heat and, little by little, add the chocolate, stirring the mixture gently with a spatula: Start at the center of the pan and stir slowly in a small circle. As you add more chocolate, continue to stir gently in a circular fashion, gradually increasing the size of the circle. Measure the temperature of the mixture with an instant-read thermometer: it should be 140°F (60°C). If it is too cool — as will often be the case — warm it in a microwave oven or scrape the mixture into a metal bowl and warm it over (not touching) simmering water; remove from the heat as soon as it reaches the proper temperature. If the mixture is too hot, let it cool to 140°F (60°C).

2. Stirring gently, blend in the butter, piece by piece, and the chocolate sauce. Once again, take the temperature of the glaze: You're aiming for 95° to 104°F (35° to 40°C), the temperature at which the glaze attains prime pourability. If the glaze is too cold, it can be warmed in a hot-water bath or a microwave oven at a low setting. The glaze is now ready to use.

The word *coulis* has passed into our culinary vocabulary from the French and been applied to everything from a thin tomato sauce to a thick fruit puree. Here, the coulis is a medium-bodied sauce made from pureed sweetened fresh raspberries. It is lovely drizzled over a wedge of Warm Chocolate and Raspberry Tart (page 97) or a slice of Linzer Tart (page 106) and wonderful served over Deep Chocolate Cream (page 224).

- **1 pint (220 grams) raspberries**
- **3 tablespoons (45 grams) sugar, or more to taste**

Place the raspberries and sugar in a blender or the work bowl of a food processor and whir until pureed. Taste and blend in more sugar if you think it needs it. Press the coulis through a strainer.

Makes about 1 cup
(265 grams)

KEEPING: The coulis can be made a day ahead and kept covered in the refrigerator.

CARAMELIZED RICE KRISPIES

These crispy treats are used to top desserts, such as Simple Chocolate Mousse (page 123) or Chocolate Rice Pudding (page 125), or to press into the dacquoise layers of Pierre's milk-chocolate specialty, Plaisir Sucré (page 53). However, they can easily be eaten out of hand as a sweet snack and are terrific sprinkled over ice cream of any flavor. Once you've caramelized the Rice Krispies, they are spread out on a Silpat or piece of parchment to cool, then broken into pieces large or small. This recipe makes more caramelized treats than you'll need for any one dessert, so you can, if you'd like, cut the recipe down — but it's nice to have leftovers to nibble.

- ½ cup (100 grams) sugar
- 3 tablespoons water
- 2⅓ cups (35 grams) Rice Krispies

1. Bring the sugar and water to a boil in a heavy-bottomed medium saucepan. Swirl the ingredients around to dissolve the sugar and then allow the mixture to boil, without stirring, until it reaches 248°F (120°C), as measured on a candy or instant-read thermometer. (If any sugar sticks to the sides of the pan, as might happen at the start of the cooking, wash it down with a pastry brush dipped in cold water.)

2. Add the Rice Krispies and, working with a wooden spoon or spatula, stir the cereal into the sugar. Remove the pan from the heat and continue to stir until the cereal is coated with the sugar, about 2 to 3 minutes. The sugar will be white and sandy — don't expect an even coating at this stage. Turn the cereal out onto a plate.

3. Set a Silpat or a piece of parchment paper and a metal spatula or pancake turner aside on the counter. Wash and dry the saucepan and return it to the stove. Heat the pan and then add half of the sugar-coated cereal. Using the wooden spoon or spatula, stir the cereal without stopping until the sugar caramelizes — you're looking for the sugar to turn a light amber color; this could take about 4 minutes. Turn the caramelized Rice Krispies out onto the parchment paper — try not to turn them into a mound — and quickly flatten the cereal with the back of the metal spatula or pancake turner. Wash the pan and repeat with the remaining cereal.

4. When the Rice Krispies are cool enough to handle, break into uneven pieces.

Makes about 2½ cups
(150 grams)

KEEPING: The caramelized cereal can be made up to 1 day ahead if it's not humid. Store the broken pieces of candy in a tin in a cool, dry place.

Whether you use grapefruit, orange, or lemon peel, this recipe will give you thick peel that is thoroughly infused with a sweet and spicy syrup. Once candied, the peel can be kept in its syrup, ready to be chopped and used in Florentines (page 75), dried and tossed in sugar to be served alongside coffee or tea, or dried and dipped in tempered chocolate (page 260).

- **4 pink grapefruit, preferably Ruby Red, 5 oranges, or 6 lemons**
- **4 cups (1000 grams) water**
- **2⅓ cups (470 grams) sugar**
- **¼ cup (60 grams) freshly squeezed lemon juice**
- **10 black peppercorns, bruised**
- **1 piece star anise**
- **Pulp from 1 moist, plump vanilla bean (see page 279)**

1. Put a large pot of water on to boil and have a colander ready. Working with a sharp knife, cut off a thin slice from the top and bottom of each fruit, then, cutting from top to bottom, cut off wide bands of peel about 1 inch (2.5 cm) across, making certain that as you cut, you include a sliver of fruit as well. Toss the slices of peel into the boiling water and allow them to boil for 2 minutes. Remove the peel from the water with a slotted spoon (don't pour out the water — you'll need it in a minute) and put it in the colander. Rinse the peel under cold running water for 2 minutes, then repeat the boiling and cooling process twice. Set the peel aside for the moment.

2. Place all the remaining ingredients in a large casserole and bring them to the boil. Add the peel, cover the pot, and adjust the heat so that the syrup simmers gently. Allow the peel to simmer, stirring occasionally, for 1½ hours, after which time the peel should be soft and completely candied. Remove the casserole from the heat and, with the cover still in place, allow the peel to macerate overnight.

3. The next day, pour the peel and its syrup into a canning jar and store it in the refrigerator, or lay the peel out on a rack to dry. Once the peel is dry, you can toss it in sugar to coat.

Makes about 12 servings

KEEPING: The candied peel in its syrup can be kept in a tightly sealed jar in the refrigerator for 3 weeks. Dried peel tossed with sugar will keep in an airtight tin for 4 days.

CHOCOLATE SHAVINGS
AND CURLS

A shower of chocolate shavings or curls is a handsome, traditional, and professional-looking finish for cakes and tarts. You can make shavings and curls from any kind of chocolate — white, milk, or dark, semisweet, bittersweet, or sweet — the trick is to use a block of chocolate (you've got to have room to maneuver) and to choose a vegetable peeler, the preferred shaver and curler, with a blade that is both sturdy and sharp. For this job, a stationary rather than a swivel blade is best. If you want to make larger, broader, or more open shavings or curls, you'll need a dough scraper.

- **A block of chocolate**

1. Choose a block of chocolate that is large enough for you to hold it at an angle and long and broad enough (on at least one side) to allow you enough room to slide the vegetable peeler down its length and get a healthy curl of chocolate. So that you get shavings and curls, not chocolate flakes and chunks, the chocolate must be at warm room temperature — 75°F (23°C) is just right. If you can't set your chocolate out to warm in a 75°F (23°C) room, then you can take both chocolate and courage in hand and pass the block of chocolate very quickly (in fact, very, very quickly) over a gas or electric burner. Wait 2 minutes and then repeat this act of daring. At this point, the chocolate should be warm enough to shave.

2. Stand the block of chocolate on edge on a piece of parchment or waxed paper, holding it at an angle, and scrape down the side of it with the tip of the vegetable peeler to produce small shavings, or use more of the peeler's blade to produce curls. This is not hard, but it does take practice to find the right angles for the chocolate and the vegetable peeler, and the right pressure for the scraping. (For broader curls, use the same technique but substitute a dough scraper for the vegetable peeler.) Failures can be eaten or used in recipes that call for melted chocolate, and successes can either be lifted off the parchment with a dough scraper and used immediately or covered with another piece of parchment and set aside at cool room temperature or refrigerated (best for white and milk chocolate) until needed.

KEEPING: Shavings and curls can be kept in a cool place, or refrigerated, for a couple of hours.

TEMPERED CHOCOLATE

Tempered chocolate is chocolate that, through a process of melting, cooling, and reheating, is rendered firm, shiny, and snappable, meaning it breaks crisply and cleanly. Indeed, snap and shine are the hallmarks of fine tempered chocolate; they're what make bars of chocolate and dipped chocolate candies so appealing.

While you can make the vast majority of Pierre's recipes without tempered chocolate (chocolate that is mixed into a batter, dough, or cream never needs tempering), you'll want to know how to temper chocolate for his candies — for example, his fruit-and-nut studded Mendiants (page 177), Chocolate-Dipped Mint Leaves (page 179) and Candied Citrus Peel (page 257), and Chocolate-Coated Caramelized Almonds (page 171). And you'll certainly want to know how to temper milk chocolate so that you can produce the thin chocolate leaves that layer his milk chocolate showstopper, Plaisir Sucré (page 53).

Tempering is finicky but not difficult. It requires patience and precision but neither skill nor finesse. To temper chocolate, you start with fine white, milk, or dark chocolate that is "in temper" ("real" chocolate purchased in bars and blocks will be in temper) and melt it, causing the cocoa butter crystals to lose their temper and become unstable; cool it, causing the crystals to firm in a form different from their original; and then reheat it, causing the crystals to return to their original stable state. Once the chocolate is tempered and liquid, you can use it for dipping, coating or molding and it will set to a sheen, it will be smooth, and, if you've tempered it correctly, it will not have any streaks.

While you may temper your first batch of chocolate perfectly, it is just as likely that you'll have a streak here and there or some other kind of imperfection the first time out. But if this is the case, all you will have lost is some time — your chocolate can be remelted, tempered again, and used.

It is difficult to give quantities for tempering chocolate, but it is certain that it is easier to temper chocolate in larger rather than smaller quantities. We've suggested you temper a pound of chocolate, but you can, of course, temper more.

- **At least 1 pound (450 grams) premium-quality chocolate, preferably Valrhona Caraïbe (bittersweet), Jivara (milk chocolate), or Ivoire (white chocolate), finely chopped**

1. Have ready a chocolate or instant-read thermometer and, if you will be working with the tempered chocolate for a while and will need to keep it

warm and in temper, a heating pad (wrap a towel around it and tuck the wrapped pad into a plastic bag to keep it clean) or a heat lamp.

2. Melt the chocolate in a bowl over — not touching — simmering water, or do this in a microwave oven. (If you plan to "seed" the chocolate [see step 3 below], keep one-quarter to one-third of the chocolate aside, unmelted.) How you melt the chocolate is not very important; what is vital is that it reaches a temperature of about 120°F (49°C). It is important that the chocolate melts completely, so it must reach at least 115°F (45°C). If you are melting the chocolate in the microwave oven, it's best to heat it for a minute, stir it, heat it for 45 seconds, stir it, and then heat it in 30-second-or-less spurts, stirring after each one, until it is melted and its temperature is within the 115° to 120°F (45° to 49°C) range.

3. Remove the chocolate from the heat. The chocolate now has to cool to a temperature between 80° and 83°F (27° and 28°C). You can keep the chocolate at room temperature, stirring it occasionally, until it reaches the correct temperature, or you can add some chunks of chocolate (of the same type of chocolate you're using) to the melted chocolate. If you decide to add chunks of chocolate (this is called seeding), you should not add more than 30 percent of the weight of the melted chocolate. Whether you're allowing the chocolate to cool at room temperature or you're seeding it, keep an eye on its temperature. You'll know that the chocolate is nearing the right temperature when it begins to set around the edges.

4. The final step is to reheat the chocolate and restabilize the cocoa butter crystals. Again, you can do this by placing the chocolate over — not touching — simmering water or by putting it in the microwave. In either case, you want to expose the chocolate to heat for very short intervals and you want to keep a really close watch on the temperature, because you will not be increasing it by much. Here's what you're aiming for: Dark chocolate should be heated to between 87° and 89°F (30° and 32°C), and milk and white chocolate to between 85° and 88°F (29° and 31°C). (If the temperature goes above the highest temperature in the range, you'll have to start from the beginning, remelting the chocolate and bringing it to 120°F [49°C], cooling it, and then heating it.)

5. The chocolate is now in temper and ready to use. If you want to test that you've gotten it right, dip a knife in the chocolate and put the knife in the refrigerator for a couple of seconds — it should emerge coated with a shiny, nonstreaked layer of chocolate. To keep the chocolate warm and in temper, you can either place it on the wrapped heating pad, turning the pad to its lowest setting, or place it under the infrared heat lamp. If you use a heat lamp, keep it about a foot or so away from the bowl and keep an eye on the chocolate; you don't want to risk overheating it.

A DICTIONARY

OF TERMS, TECHNIQUES, EQUIPMENT,

AND INGREDIENTS

Acetate

The clear acetate sheets that you might use for report covers or to protect a pastel sketch from smearing provide the ideal surface for setting the bottom of tempered chocolate to a shine. Although you can put such chocolate confections as Mendiants or Florentines on a sheet of parchment paper (or even a silicone mat) to set and dry, the thin chocolate layers needed for Plaisir Sucré can only set to a sheen on acetate. When tempered chocolate comes in contact with acetate's perfectly smooth and naturally nonstick surface, it develops the sleek, shiny finish that is the hallmark of professionally made chocolates. You can buy acetate report covers in office supply stores and acetate sheets of varying sizes at art supply stores.

Almond paste

A mixture of ground almonds, confectioners' sugar, and corn syrup or glucose, almond paste is available in supermarkets, where it is sold in cans under the Solo label and in tubes under the name Odense, a Danish manufacturer. Both can be stored at room temperature until you're ready to use them, but any leftovers will dry out quickly unless you wrap them airtight in two or three layers of plastic. Well wrapped, almond paste can be kept in the refrigerator for about 6 months. While almond paste is firmer than marzipan, you can use either in these recipes.

Almond powder

Also called almond flour, almond powder is nothing more than blanched almonds ground as fine as powder. (Hazelnuts are given the same treatment.) You can buy almond powder commercially (see Source Guide, page 281) or make a worthy substitute at home. *To make almond powder (or hazelnut) at home*, put blanched almonds (they can be whole, sliced, or slivered) in the work bowl of a food processor fitted with the metal blade. (Or use skinned hazelnuts.) Add some of the recipe's sugar to the almonds — the sugar will help keep the nuts from turning to butter — and process until the mixture is as fine as flour, at least 3 minutes. Stop after every minute to check your progress and to scrape down the sides of the bowl. When the mixture is ground, using a wooden spoon, press it through a medium strainer.

Wrapped airtight, almond powder can be kept in the freezer for 2 months, so it pays to make more than you need for any one recipe.

Baking powder

Recipes using baking powder were tested with double-acting powder, a leavening agent that releases its first round of rising power when it's mixed with liquid and its second when it's heated in the oven. Baking powder, a supermarket staple, should be kept tightly covered in a cool, dry cupboard. Regardless of the use-before date stamped on the tin, replace opened tins every 6 months.

Baking sheets

As used in these recipes, a baking sheet is what home cooks often refer to as a cookie sheet, that is, a large flat metal sheet with one or both of the short ends slightly raised. The raised ends give you something to hold on to when you're slipping the sheet in and out of the oven, and the long rimless sides give you room to slide cookies and tarts onto and off the sheet. When buying baking sheets, buy the largest ones you can, making certain that there will be at least an inch, preferably two, of air space between the sheet and your oven's walls. And, because the sheets will often be used at high temperatures, you'll do well to buy the heaviest sheets available, so they won't warp. Finally, it makes sense to buy at least two baking sheets — four would be even better. Since nothing unbaked should ever go on a hot sheet, having two sets of sheets means that while one set is in the oven, you can be setting up another batch of cookies on the other.

It's a good idea to have at least one baking sheet with a nonstick finish. While in most cases you'll be lining the baking sheets with parchment paper, there are some cookies, tuiles, for example, that must be baked on nonstick sheets.

Finally, while insulated baking sheets, the kind with a built-in air cushion, are not recommended for baking cookies — most brands don't let enough heat hit the cookies' bottoms — they're great under loaf cakes that need only gentle bottom heat. You can always double up on regular baking sheets to get this kind of protection, but an all-in-one insulated sheet is a nice, if optional, addition to your batterie de cuisine.

Baking times

Baking times are usually given as a range (such as "bake for 30 to 35 minutes") because even the same cake won't bake in the same amount of time every time. To be on the safe side, you should always start testing your dessert for doneness at the lowest end of the range (or even a few minutes before, especially if the cake or tart has been in the oven for 30 minutes or more), and always pay attention to the visual clues, such as browning, rising, or shrinking — sometimes they're your best indicators of doneness.

Batterie de cuisine

All the tools, gadgets, and equipment, such as pots, pans, tins, and molds, used to prepare food.

Bench or dough scrapers

Used most often by bread bakers, a bench or dough scraper is a good tool for pastry chefs as well. The business end of a scraper is a square of metal. It's attached to a grip, either wood or plastic, and while it makes handling sticky bread doughs manageable, it's also very well suited to cleaning off a work surface after you've rolled out pastry dough. Once you get the hang of using a scraper, you'll think of it as an extension of your hand and find it's convenient to have close by for cutting doughs into portions or for transferring ingredients, like chopped fruits and nuts, from cutting board to work bowl.

Flexible dough scrapers, or bowl scrapers, are tear-shaped pieces of plastic that have enough bend to skim the sides of a bowl and pick up the last bits of batter and dough. These small tools are also ideal for lifting delicate cookies, like tuiles, off baking sheets. This is particularly true of flexible scrapers that have slightly beveled edges.

Black pepper

Pierre keeps his pepper mill at the ready in his pastry kitchen, using the pungent spice to give spark to fruit desserts, especially those that feature apricots, pineapple, and berries. Pepper should always be freshly ground — don't even think about buying ground pepper from the spice rack in the supermarket. Pierre's favorite pepper is Sarawak, a black pepper from Borneo, which he likes for its subtle heat and lovely fragrance. While it's not readily available everywhere, it is often on display in specialty shops, since Flavorbank, a spice company with national distribution, offers it in plastic tubes. (See Source Guide, page 281.)

Blender

In most cases, when a recipe says to put something in a blender, you can use a food processor or often an immersion blender (see page 273) in its stead. However, the opposite is not true. For example, the food processor is great for pastry dough, while the blender is hopelessly inappropriate.

Butter

Butter has no substitute, neither for flavor, nor for texture. Never use margarine or a "spread" — the results will fall short on every count. For most recipes, you'll use unsalted, sometimes called "sweet," butter. But there are some recipes, most notably those that include caramel, that call for salted butter. If you do not have salted butter, use unsalted and add a pinch of salt to the mix.

Butter should be kept in the refrigerator, well wrapped and away from foods with strong odors. Wrapped airtight, butter can be frozen for up to 6 months.

These recipes were tested with nationally available Land O'Lakes butter from the supermarket.

Measuring butter: Depending on quantities, you'll find the measurements for butter given in tablespoons or sticks (or parts thereof), ounces, and grams. It's helpful to know that 3 teaspoons equal 1 tablespoon (about 15 grams) and that there are 8 tablespoons of butter in a stick; these measurements are usually marked on the wrapper. Each stick weighs 4 ounces (115 grams) and there are four sticks to a pound (454 grams).

Softening butter: When a recipe calls for room-temperature butter, it means the butter should be malleable but not gooey or oily. You can leave butter at room temperature to get to the soft stage; you can give it a few good bashes with the heel of your hand or the end of a French-style (no-handles) rolling pin; or you can place the unwrapped sticks of butter on a paper towel and soften them for about 10 seconds in the microwave oven.

Buttering pans: Pans should be buttered with softened, not melted, butter. Apply a thin coating of butter to all the interior surfaces of the pan, paying particular attention to the oft-neglected and hard-to-get-to corners. The easiest way to get an even coating is to apply the softened butter with a pastry brush, although a scrunched-up paper towel works well too. Small molds, like madeleine or financier pans, can be given a light coating of vegetable oil spray (such as Pam) instead of being buttered — it's often easier.

When a recipe instructs you to butter and flour a pan, you should butter the inside of the pan as usual, then toss in a couple of spoonfuls of flour. Shake the pan to get the flour across the bottom, and tilt and tap the pan to get a light dusting of flour on the sides. Turn the pan upside down over a trash bin and tap out the excess flour.

The amount of butter and flour you need to prepare pans is never included in a recipe's ingredient list — it's always extra.

Cake pans

For the recipes in this book, you'll need conventional round cake pans and loaf cake pans, cake or dessert rings (see below), and tart or flan rings (see page 278). Most of the cakes that form the foundations for Pierre's gâteaux are baked in cake or tart rings. The exception is Suzy's Cake, which is baked in a 9-inch (24-cm) round cake pan with sides that are at least 2 inches (5 cm) high.

Translating the loaf cakes from their French forms to their American equivalents was particularly difficult because of the great differences between French loaf pans, called *moules à cake*, and American pans. The French pans are long thin affairs with sides that often slant out, while American pans are, for the most part, shorter, stouter, and straighter. However, you'll have no problem producing Pierre's simple French loaf cakes with American loaf pans. You'll need: two 7½ x 3½ x 2½-inch pans (or 18-cm *moules à cake*) and one 9 x 5 x 3-inch pan (or a 28-cm *moule à cake*). For loaf cakes, avoid dark metal pans — the cakes bake for a long time, and dark pans, which attract and maintain heat, will make their crusts too dark. Whether or not you purchase a pan with a non-stick finish is a matter of personal preference; however, if a recipe instructs you to line a loaf pan with parchment paper, you should prepare this lining regardless of the pan's finish.

Cake (or dessert) rings

The majority of Pierre's cakes are baked and/or constructed in cake rings, known as *cercles d'entremets*, bottomless stainless steel rings that are 1½ inches (4 cm) high. Most cakes use 8¾-inch (22-cm) rings or 10¼-inch (26-cm) rings.

Using a cake ring as the "mold" in which you build a cake means you'll get a straight-sided, polished, professional-looking cake every time. If you've never used one, the first time you lift it off (see Hairdryer, page 273) and get a look at your layers of cake and cream, mousse, or fruit, stacked up with military precision, you'll be thrilled — and using a cake ring is easier (and neater) than filling and stacking layers freehand.

Cake rings (and tart or flan rings; see page 278) are essentially European and/or professional equipment, so in many stores you'll find only the metric measurements listed. Cake rings are available in professional baking and restaurant supply stores and in well-equipped housewares stores (see Source Guide, page 281). Rings cost about $10 to $15, and it's worth having one or two each of the 8¾-inch (22-cm) rings and the 10¼-inch (26-cm) rings on hand, especially if you're planning to serve more than one cake at a time. Don't be seduced by those adjustable rings that can be sized from very small to larger-than-you'll-probably-ever-need. The band that makes these rings adjustable also makes a dent in the side of your cake. Also, don't buy a ring in black metal — it can turn whipped creams and fillings an unpleasant color and give an off taste to anything acidic.

If you do not have a cake ring, you can substitute the ring of an appropriately sized springform pan, but you'll never get the perfectly smooth edge that's a hallmark of the cake ring.

Candy thermometer

Also called a sugar thermometer, a candy thermometer reads temperatures up to 400°F (200°C). While an instant-read thermometer (see page 273) can be used for most of the recipes in this book, a candy thermometer is designed specifically for handling sugar and is most useful when you are making syrups and caramels. With a candy thermometer, the mercury reservoir is lifted above the base of the thermometer. This means you can plunge it into a pot, hit bottom, and not worry that the reading might reflect the heat at the bottom of the pot rather than the mixture in the pot. Also, most candy thermometers have clips so you can attach them to the side of a pot and get a continuous hands-free reading. If you plan to do some serious candy making, this is a tool to have in your batterie, but keep in mind that a candy thermometer is not appropriate for tempering chocolate, since it does not register temperatures below 100°F (38°C).

Cardboard cake rounds

There are lots of small jobs in the pastry kitchen that are made easier with a stack of cardboard cake rounds at your disposal. The rounds, available at baking supply houses, specialty shops, and by mail-order (see Source Guide, page 281), are made of corrugated cardboard, have one smooth white paper side, and come in various sizes, the 10-inch (25-cm) round being the most convenient since it's big enough for everything, including cutting it down to size. All of the recipes that are constructed in cake and tart rings are best built on a cardboard cake round. If you do not want to purchase rounds, you can use the removable bottom of a fluted metal tart pan or the base of a springform pan.

Chocolate

Although chocolate comes in varieties from so-bitter-one-taste-makes-you-shiver to so-sweet-it's-cloying and colors that range from mahogany to ivory, every chocolate starts with chocolate liquor, the ground nib of the cacao bean. Chocolate liquor is pure chocolate — it's about half cocoa butter and half cocoa — and it's all there is in unsweetened chocolate, sometimes called baking chocolate in America. To make the gamut of chocolates from unsweetened to bittersweet to semisweet to sweet, sugar is added and usually more cocoa butter (especially if the chocolate is meant for melting or dipping); sometimes cocoa powder is added too. Since it is the chocolate liquor that gives chocolate its depth of flavor — its chocolatyness — the higher the percentage of chocolate liquor, the more chocolaty and the less sweet the chocolate will be.

In the United States, the minimum amount of chocolate liquor in specific types of chocolate is regulated by the Food and Drug Administration — but the percentage is not required to be on the label. Thus, while one manufacturer's bittersweet may taste like another's semisweet (the FDA makes no distinction between the two names), both must contain at least 35 percent chocolate liquor. Sweet chocolate, a designation that can be used by producers in America, indicates at least 15 percent chocolate liquor; milk chocolate must have at least 10 percent.

For the most part, American chocolate, especially the popular brands found at supermarkets, is much sweeter and less deeply chocolaty than premium-quality imported chocolate. How much sweeter and less chocolaty by the numbers? Who knows? Manufacturers are not required to list the percentage of chocolate liquor in their products. In fact, percentages are listed only on the packages of selected very high quality imported chocolates, such as Valrhona, the first company to go public with their chocolate liquor, cocoa butter, and cocoa percentages.

Valrhona chocolate, made in France, is Pierre's chocolate of choice for these desserts and, all of the chocolate recipes were tested with Valrhona and carry a recommendation for which of Valrhona's several chocolates you should use. The following are the Valrhona chocolates used in the recipes:

Guanaja: 70.5 percent cocoa

Caraïbe: 66.5 percent cocoa

Manjari: 64.5 percent cocoa

Noir Gastronomie: 61 percent cocoa

Jivara Milk Chocolate: 40 percent cocoa

Ivoire White Chocolate: 35 percent cocoa

These chocolates are available at specialty stores and directly from Valrhona (see Source Guide, page 281).

Storing chocolate: It's best to keep chocolate in a cool, dry cupboard away from light. In fact, chocolate benefits from being wrapped in aluminum foil, which will not only block the light, but will keep odors away from the chocolate. Like butter, chocolate picks up odors from neighboring foods. Don't store chocolate in the refrigerator or freezer — you risk having it come in contact with its archenemy, humidity — and don't be discouraged if your chocolate develops "bloom," a cloudy or grayish look. Bloom isn't admirable, or attractive — it's a sign that the chocolate was stored in a warm place and an indication that the cocoa butter has separated — but it doesn't affect the chocolate's flavor or its melting properties. In fact, when the chocolate is melted, the cocoa butter reincorporates itself and the bloom disappears. Stored properly, unsweetened, bittersweet, and semisweet chocolate can be kept for a year or more; milk and white chocolate are more perishable.

Melting chocolate: Chocolate melts evenly and safely over hot water or in the microwave oven. No matter which method you use to melt chocolate, you should always start with chocolate that has been chopped into small, evenly sized pieces — even pieces mean even melting.

To melt chocolate over water, place the chocolate in a heatproof bowl and set the bowl over a saucepan of simmering, not boiling, water; the bowl should not touch the water. (Alternatively, you can put the chocolate in the top of a double boiler over simmering water.) Keep the heat very low and stir the chocolate often. As soon as the chocolate is melted, remove it from the heat and stir to smooth it.

To melt chocolate in the microwave oven, place it in a microwave-safe container. Heat on medium power for a minute, stir the chocolate, and then continue to heat in 30-second spurts until melted. (If you're melting 4 ounces [115 grams] or more of chocolate at a time, you can start with 2 minutes in the oven and then go to shorter spurts.) It's important to keep checking the chocolate, because the microwave oven has a way of allowing the chocolate to keep its shape even though it's thoroughly melted — a deception that can cost you the batch. To avoid mishaps, press on the chocolate to check that it's melted.

Whether you melt over water or in the microwave, remember that water is chocolate's enemy. Even one drop of water splashed onto the chocolate while it's melting is enough to cause it to seize and go dull. However, if a recipe specifies melting chocolate with a liquid (butter for example), don't worry — it's only moisture added midmelt that will give you problems.

For information on tempering chocolate, see page 260.

Cinnamon

Pierre is unusual among French pastry chefs in that his affection for cinnamon rivals that of Americans. Not particularly admired by the French, cinnamon is a spice Pierre finds appealing and uses often in stick and powdered forms. Pierre's preference is for cinnamon from Ceylon, not readily found on your supermarket shelves, but available through the Penzey's Spices catalog (see Source Guide, page 282). According to Pierre, "People who say they don't like cinnamon taste Ceylon cinnamon and change their minds." He attributes this to Ceylon cinnamon's mild flavor.

Most cinnamon on the market comes from China and is actually not true cinnamon but its cousin, cassia. Cassia is darker, sweeter, and stronger than real cinnamon. You can use either kind of cinnamon for any of these recipes, but if you can get your hands on cinnamon from Ceylon, do a comparative taste test — you'll find it interesting.

Cinnamon sticks, also called quills, can be stored at room temperature indefinitely; cinnamon powder, like all ground spices, loses its flavor and fragrance in the tin or jar. It's best to replace opened jars of ground cinnamon every 6 months.

Cocoa powder

These recipes were tested with Valrhona Dutch-processed cocoa powder, which is unsweetened cocoa powder treated with an alkali. "Dutched" powder is darker and less acidic than cocoa powder that has not been treated. When a recipe calls for cocoa powder, it always means unsweetened cocoa powder.

Coconut

All the recipes that use coconut call for finely grated or shredded unsweetened dried coconut. Available in some supermarkets, unsweetened coconut is easily found in health food and natural food stores. In France, unsweetened coconut is grated so fine it is powdery. To get the best results with American coconut, use a food processor or blender to pulverize the coconut with a small amount of sugar (use a spoonful of the sugar called for in the recipe).

Coconut milk

Rich, thick, and white, coconut milk is available, canned, in most supermarkets and Asian food stores. Always use unsweetened coconut milk — don't confuse it with coconut cream (seen most often under the Coco Lopez label), which is fine for piña coladas, not for pastry.

Cooling racks

Cooling racks with closely spaced metal wires are a must in the pastry kitchen. Whatever size racks you buy, make certain that they are sturdy and have feet that put them at least ½ inch (1.5 cm) above the counter — you need room for air to circulate around the cake or pastry that's cooling on the rack. It's nice to have three round racks for cakes and tarts and at least one large rectangular rack for cookies and for the caramelized puff pastry.

Coulis

A French term, pronounced "coo-lee" (the s is silent), that refers to sauces made from pureed fruits or vegetables; think raspberry coulis.

Cream

Cream is what gives desserts richness, smoothness, and, when whipped, lightness. All of the recipes that use cream specify heavy cream, but if your market stocks only whipping cream (as is true in some parts of the country), buy it and it will be fine. The difference between the two creams is in their butterfat content. Heavy cream contains between 36 and 40 percent butterfat while whipping cream weighs in at between 30 and 36 percent. Their differences are less important than their major similarity: Both can be whipped.

Whipping cream: Cream whips best when it is cold. It's even easier to whip cream when the bowl and beater are cold too. If you're using an electric mixer, start whipping the cream on low speed and then increase the speed when the cream begins to thicken a bit. Because the line between perfectly whipped cream and overwhipped cream (the kind that's on the verge of turning into butter) is thin, it's always best to whip the cream to a softer-than-it-should-be stage and then finish it by hand, giving it a few turns with a whisk. Although whipped cream is best whipped right before it's needed, it can wait a few hours if necessary — just keep it refrigerated

and make sure that it's well sealed with plastic wrap, since whipped cream is a magnet for refrigerator odors.

Crème fraîche: Crème fraîche is sour cream's French cousin. It has sour cream's smooth, thick texture and tangy taste, but, unlike sour cream, it can be heated without separating and whipped just like heavy cream. Commercially made crème fraîche is more and more easily found in the States, although it is expensive.

To make crème fraîche simply and inexpensively at home, pour 1 cup (250 grams) heavy cream into a clean jar, add 1 tablespoon buttermilk, cover the jar tightly, and shake it for about a minute. Leave the jar on the counter for between 12 and 24 hours, or until the crème fraîche thickens slightly. How quickly the mixture thickens will depend on the temperature of your room — the warmer the room, the quicker the thickening action. When it has thickened, put the crème fraîche in the refrigerator and let it chill thoroughly before you use it. Crème fraîche can be kept covered in the refrigerator for about 2 weeks, and it will get tangier and tangier day after day.

Decorating combs

The simplest way to decorate the sides or top of a cake that is covered with ganache or frosting is to run the tines of a fork across its surface. But if you want the tine-effect to be perfect, then you want to trade in the fork for a decorating comb, a piece of metal or plastic, often triangular but sometimes square, with at least one serrated side. Combs come with different designs — on some the serrations are very fine and spaced very close to one another, on some the zigs and zags are farther apart, and on some there might be a flat area, a serration, another flat area, and so on. Whatever the design, the combs have it over the forks in the precision department because their designs are well cut and defined. Keep the comb clean, wiping off the excess frosting after each pass, and you'll get a clear design every time with just about no effort. A decorating comb is recommended for finishing the sides of the Faubourg Pavé.

Decorating turntable or cake decorating stand

This is the kind of tool you think you can do without until you have it — use it once, and you'll decide it's indispensable. A good cake decorating turntable (Ateco makes a very good one) is constructed like a potter's wheel. It has a heavy cast-iron base topped with a thick 12-inch (30-cm) round aluminum plate that rotates smoothly and evenly, allowing you to apply a perfect layer of ganache or frosting to a cake, smooth a glaze over and around a cake, or pat a few toasted almonds onto the sides of a cake.

Dried fruits

No matter the variety of dried fruit used in a recipe, it should always be soft and moist. If you start out with hard fruit, it won't get soft and moist after you mix it into a batter, dough, or cream; instead, it will spoil your creation. If your fruit is not soft and moist, you can "plump" it by placing it in a strainer over boiling water. Steam the fruit for a short time — sometimes a minute is all it takes — until it is soft. Remove it from the heat, pat it dry between sheets of paper towels, and proceed with your recipe.

Eggs

The recipes in this book were tested with U.S. Grade A large eggs, which come as close as possible to the size of the eggs Pierre uses in Paris, eggs that weigh about 60 grams: 30 grams for the white, 20 grams for the yolk, and 10 grams for the shell.

Eggs should be bought from a reliable market, kept properly, and handled well. Here are some points to keep in mind:

- Always buy your eggs from a market that keeps them refrigerated at all times.
- Always keep eggs under refrigeration at home. If a recipe calls for eggs at room temperature — and most do — take the eggs from the fridge 20 minutes ahead of time. Never leave eggs at room temperature for more than 2 hours.
- Never use an egg that has a cracked shell.
- Wash your hands before and after you handle eggs, and make sure to scrub your work surface and utensils after working with eggs.

Separating and whipping egg whites: Eggs separate most easily when they are cold, but egg whites whip to their fullest volume when they are at room temperature or warmer, so it's best to separate eggs as soon as they come from the refrigerator and whip the whites after

they've had time to lose their chill. To bring whites to a good whipping temperature quickly, put them in a microwave-safe bowl and place them in a microwave oven set on lowest power; heat the whites for about 10 seconds, stir, then continue to heat the whites in 5-second spurts until they are about 75°F (24°C). If they are a little warmer, that's okay too.

Whites must always be whipped in an impeccably clean, dry bowl — even a speck of fat of any kind, including a drop of yolk, is enough to stand in the way of whipping whites to maximum capacity. While many people insist on whipping their whites in a copper bowl — there's an interaction between the copper and the whites that pushes the whites to extreme fullness — whites can be whipped beautifully and easily in a mixer fitted with the whisk attachment. The key to whipping whites is not to overwhip them. Pay attention to the changes in texture and sheen as the whites whip. Your ideal whipped-to-firm-peaks white is, indeed, white, smooth, and glossy. When the whites go dull, it means you've gone too far. Ditto for whites that break up into puffs and clouds. When you lift some whites on a whisk, the whites should, in fact, peak, and the peak, while it might bend over a little — a very little — should stay, as though it's been lacquered.

As firm and proud as the peaks may be, it's only a show: Whipped egg whites are wimps — they'll collapse under the slightest pressure. Keep this in mind when you're folding the whites into another, heavier mixture — use a flexible rubber spatula and a very light hand and stop as soon as the whites are incorporated.

Combining yolks and sugar: There'll be many times when you'll have to whisk yolks and sugar together, often until they turn pale and thicken. Keep in mind that as soon as you add sugar to egg yolks, you've got to start stirring immediately — otherwise, the yolks will "burn," a term bakers use to describe the lumps that develop when sugar is added to, but not mixed into, yolks.

Flour

The recipes in this book were tested with all-purpose flour, that is, bleached and enriched flour, the kind found in the supermarket under national brand labels such as Gold Medal or Pillsbury. The Cocoa Cake, the base of the Faubourg Pavé and the Black Forest Cake, is made with cake flour, a flour particularly low in protein. (While all-purpose flours have between 10 and 12 grams of protein per cup, cake flour has only about 8 grams.)

Regardless of the type of flour you're using, you should store it in an airtight tin in a cool, dry cupboard. Stored properly, white flours should keep for about 6 months.

In most cases, there's no need to sift all-purpose flour. Not so with cake flour, which is always lumpy and always needs to be sifted before it is added to a batter. In Pierre's recipes, flour is measured before it is sifted.

Always use the scoop-and-sweep method to measure flour (see page 275).

Folding

When you're instructed to fold one ingredient into another — usually a light, airy ingredient, such as meringue or whipped cream, into a heavier mixture, such as a batter or a crème anglaise — you're meant to do so very gently. It's a delicate maneuver, one most easily achieved by using a flexible rubber spatula, a roomy bowl, and a soft touch.

If a batter is particularly thick and heavy, it's a good idea to stir a little of the lighter ingredient into it before folding in the rest. No matter what you're folding into what, the motion is always the same. Put some of whatever you're folding in on top of the mixture in the bowl, placing it in the center, and then use the side of your spatula to cut down through both ingredients. As you hit the bottom of the bowl, do three things: Give the bowl a quarter turn, simultaneously turn your wrist slightly (to angle the spatula), and draw the spatula against the bottom of the bowl and then up the side, finishing with the edge of the spatula breaking the surface first. Continue until the two mixtures are combined — no further. If you're new to folding, you might be so happy to get it right that you might overdo it — resist the temptation.

Food processor

Having a food processor on your counter is like having an assistant. It's the tool you should use when you need to grind nuts or pulverize coconut, and it's terrific for making pastry dough. If you're buying a food processor for the first time, buy the best one you can afford (they last for years) and the one with the largest capacity. When you're making pastry, having a large work bowl is key.

Freezing

Many of Pierre's cakes, tarts, and cookies can be frozen, either at some point in their production or as finished desserts. You'll find information on a specific recipe's freezability in the recipe (as appropriate) or in the "Keeping" notes at the end of the recipe. At whatever stage you freeze something, you must always make certain to freeze it airtight. Double-wrapping in plastic bags or plastic film and finishing the package off with an aluminum foil wrap is not overkill. Use your judgment when freezing decorated cakes; often it's best to put the cake in the freezer uncovered until it's firm, then wrap it airtight. If you have the time, the best way to defrost a cake is the slowest: Keep it in its wrapper and give it a leisurely overnight rest in the refrigerator. This is a particularly good way to defrost mousse and cream cakes — they're not shocked into defrosting, as they are when you leave them at room temperature, and you don't risk the unpleasant surprise of biting into a seemingly soft and luscious cake only to find that the center is colder and harder than the sides.

Ganache

Always chocolate and always rich, a traditional, simple ganache is a mixture of melted chocolate and heavy cream. (There are ganaches that have butter and some that include eggs.) Depending on the proportion of chocolate to cream, ganache can be thick enough to use as a cake filling or thin enough to pour over a cake as a glaze. Because it is essentially an emulsion, like mayonnaise, Pierre advises that you mix it the same way you would mayonnaise, slowly and gently. When you add the hot cream to the chocolate to make a classic ganache, add a little of the cream to the center of the bowl of chocolate and blend it in by stirring in small circles, then, as you add more cream, continue to stir gently in increasingly wider concentric circles.

Gelatin

In the French pastry kitchen, gelatin is used as a stabilizer in much the same ways as meringue and whipped cream. Used in very small amounts (so small that they're almost unnoticeable in the texture and totally undetectable in the taste), gelatin is the secret weapon that gives a featherlight mousse the strength to work as a layer in a fancy gâteau and a crème anglaise the muscle to make it as a filling. While Pierre and most other professional pastry chefs use sheet gelatin (leaves of gelatin that look like glassine), these recipes were tested with the more commonly available powdered gelatin (Knox gelatin was used).

Dissolving gelatin: The easiest way to prepare gelatin for incorporation into a dessert is to sprinkle it over the specified amount of cold water, allow it to rest until it is softened and spongy (a minute or so), and then pop it into the microwave oven for 15 seconds to dissolve it. It can also be dissolved over very low heat.

If you are using sheet gelatin, soften it in cold water, squeeze the excess water from the sheet, and either stir the sheet into the hot mixture that needs to be gelled or, if the mixture is cold, melt the soaked gelatin in a small amount of water in the microwave, then incorporate it.

Hairdryer

To remove cake rings quickly and neatly, nothing is as effective as a hairdryer. Many of Pierre's cakes and desserts are constructed in cake rings and then chilled or frozen, processes that cause the dessert to stick to the ring. Running a knife around the edge of the ring is one way to release the ring, but it's not the best way, because you'll damage your dessert's sleek, smooth sides — the reason you used a ring in the first place. By blowing a little hot air around the outside of the ring with a hairdryer, you'll warm the ring and the edges of the dessert just enough to allow you to lift the ring off cleanly. It's the perfect tool for the job.

But a hairdryer's not a one-job Johnny. You'll be glad to have it at hand when you want to press chocolate curls, cake cubes, or toasted nuts onto the sides of a chilled cake. Hit the cake with a little heat and the unyielding mousse, cream, or glaze on the sides will become a model of stickability. And if your ganache or glaze looks a little dull, give it a quick (and gentle) puff of heat and watch it shine. All this work can be done with a travel-sized hairdryer small enough to tuck into a kitchen drawer.

Hazelnuts

Hazelnuts, often called filberts, particularly in the Northwest, where they are grown, can be purchased whole or chopped, usually with their skins intact. Already peeled hazelnuts and hazelnut powder can be purchased from specialty suppliers (see Source Guide, page 281).

Skinning hazelnuts: Hazelnuts have a dark skin that takes a little elbow grease to remove. The traditional method of skinning, or peeling, hazelnuts is to toast them in a jelly-roll pan in a 350°F (180°C) oven for 10 to 12 minutes (see page 275), until they are well toasted, then turn them onto a kitchen towel and fold the towel over them. Wait a couple of minutes, and, while the nuts are still hot, rub the towel against them to scrape off their skins. (You might want to wear kitchen mitts for this operation.) Be advised: No matter how hard you rub, you'll never get every bit of skin off — perfection is impossible with these nuts.

Alternatively, you can put the nuts in 1 quart (1 liter) of boiling water to which you've added 6 tablespoons (about 40 grams) baking soda. Boil for 4 to 5 minutes — the water will be black — then test a nut. If the skin slips off easily, the nuts are ready. Turn them into a colander, run them under cold water, and slip off the skins. Dry the nuts with a towel and toast them on a jelly-roll pan.

For information on making hazelnut powder, see Almond Powder, page 265.

Immersion blender

You can manage in the pastry kitchen without this nifty tool, but once you've got one, you'll find lots of uses for it. The immersion blender does the work of a traditional blender, but it's portable — the blending blade is at the end of a grippable rod (the French call this machine a "giraffe" because it's all neck), which means you can blend, crush, puree, or liquefy a mixture in its mixing bowl or pot. (Think of the cleanup you save!) The immersion blender is good for doing a final mixing of chocolate drinks, making coulis and other sauces, and smoothing out anything that doesn't go exactly according to plan. Outside of the pastry kitchen, you'll find it's a wizard with soups — you can puree them in their stockpots.

Instant-read thermometer

You should always have a thermometer close to your work area. As you work, you'll need to measure the temperature of melted chocolate, crème anglaise, sugar syrup, an egg mixture, or any number of preparations. All of these operations, as well as tempering — which is totally about temperature — can be performed with an instant-read thermometer. The simplest instant-read has a standard 5-inch- (12.5-cm-) long metal probe that finishes in an analog readout. This thermometer is fine for crème anglaise and chocolate for ganache, but since it only goes up to 220°F (104°C), it is not right for sugar syrups and caramels. Also, it's a little pokey, making it inappropriate for tempering. The second version is constructed exactly like the first, but its display is digital and it measures ingredients up to 302°F (150°C). Finally, there's the digital thermometer made by Polder (available at Williams-Sonoma and New York Cake & Baking Distributors; see Source Guide, page 281), which is not technically an instant-read thermometer, but more a continuous-read one. Its probe is attached to a long, flexible metal wire that, in turn, is attached to the magnetized digital display, a large-enough-to-read-easily affair. The separation of probe and display and the design of the probe — it is gently curved at the point at which it meets the thread — mean you can do a hands-free readout: The probe can rest in the saucepan while you stir the custard. In addition, you can set this ingenious instrument to beep after a certain amount of time or, more important, to beep when your mixture has reached its desired temperature — a boon when you've got chocolate cooling and you're doing other things.

Jelly-roll pans

Referred to as sheet pans by professional bakers, these pans are rectangular and, unlike baking sheets, have raised sides. They're good for making sheet and jelly-roll cakes (hence their name), transferring doughs from counter to refrigerator, toasting nuts, and similar jobs. However, they're not very good for cookies or for baking tart crusts in tart rings — their sides make sliding things onto and off them tough. (Of course, if all you've got are jelly-roll pans, you can make do. Line the pans with parchment paper and, when you're finished baking, just remove the cookies with a spatula. If you've got a crust, transfer the crust, still on the paper, from the pan to a cooling rack.) Jelly-roll pans can be either 10½ x 15½ x 1 inch (26 x 37 x 2 cm) or 12½ x 17½ x 1 inch

(30 x 42 x 2 cm) and can be purchased with nonstick finishes.

Marble

Rich, buttery pastry doughs — the best kind — can be finicky when it comes to rolling, but you can keep some of their finickiness in check if you roll them out on a smooth, cool surface; marble is among the smoothest and coolest surfaces you can find. (Stainless steel, polished onyx, and granite are great too.) Ideally, you should have a large marble slab that you can slide in and out of the refrigerator so that if, while you're rolling, the dough gets a little soft or otherwise unwieldy, you can give it a quick chill (the secret to bringing it under control). If you can, have a marble slab custom-cut so that it is the exact size of one of your refrigerator shelves. Of course, any surface can be cooled down before you start by filling a pan with ice cubes and running the bottom of the pan over the area on which you'll be rolling.

Marzipan

Marzipan is a little softer and a little sweeter than almond paste, but the two ingredients can be used interchangeably. Wrapped airtight, marzipan can be kept in the refrigerator for up to 6 months.

Measuring

Accurate measuring is the cornerstone of success with these or any other pastry recipes — baking is not a little-bit-of-this-little-bit-of-that craft. Pierre's recipes, originally written for metric measures, have been converted and tested using the American measuring system, which is based on volume, not weight. It is for this reason that you'll come across unorthodox measurements, such as ¾ cup plus 2 tablespoons, or 1 cup minus 1 tablespoon. Metric measures are indicated in parentheses following the volume measures. Ingredients best measured in spoonfuls have been left in spoonfuls. An American tablespoon is the equivalent of a French *cuillère à soupe*; an American teaspoon is the equivalent of a French *cuillère à café*; and 3 American teaspoons equal 1 French *cuillère à soupe*.

To measure volumes accurately, you need accurate measuring cups and spoons for liquid and dry ingredients.

Liquids should be measured in clearly calibrated glass

measuring cups. The best way to get an accurate liquid measure is to place the measuring cup on a flat surface, bend down so that the calibrations are at eye level, and pour in the liquid. Don't lift the cup up to eye level, it will throw off the measurements — get down there and look. If you're measuring less than ¼ cup of liquid, you'd do better to measure the liquid in measuring spoons.

Dry ingredients should be measured in metal measuring cups and spoons. Your batterie de cuisine should include cups to measure ¼, ⅓, ½, and 1 cup; ⅛-cup and 2-cup measures are optional but nice. As for measuring spoons, your set should include ¼-, ½-, and 1-teaspoon measures as well as a 1-tablespoon measure. It's good to have two sets of both measuring cups and spoons.

Whatever you're measuring, it's important that, unless specified that the measure be "full," as in "1 (full) cup," the ingredients be level with the rim of the (dry) measuring cup or spoon. For instance, if the recipe calls for ½ cup sugar, you should dip the ½-cup measure into the sugar bin, scoop up a rounded measure of sugar, and then sweep it level with a straightedge (the back of a knife or a ruler works well). Most important, never use a "dry" measuring cup that's larger than the amount you need — you won't be able to level it.

When measuring flour, it's best to aerate the flour in the bin by fluffing it with a fork before you measure it. For flour, as for all dry ingredients, you should use the scoop-and-sweep method — scoop up enough flour to overflow the cup and, with a straightedge, sweep the flour level with the rim of the measuring cup, taking special care not to tamp down the flour (which would really throw off the measurements). In these recipes, if flour needs to be sifted, it is sifted after it is measured.

Granulated sugar is measured like flour; brown sugar, the exception to the rule, should be packed snugly into its measuring cup. Confectioners' sugar needs to be sifted after it's measured because it's always lumpy.

Milk

All of these recipes were tested with whole milk.

Mixers

A heavy-duty standing mixer is an invaluable kitchen tool, particularly when you're making cakes that de-pend on beaten eggs for their lift and structure, meringues that are heated with syrup and then need to be whipped until cool, or desserts that have several components or steps that must be accomplished simultaneously or in quick succession — although, of course, all of these recipes can be made with a strong hand-held mixer. Standing mixers are expensive, but good ones last for years and make light work of heavy jobs. (These recipes were tested with a twenty-plus-year-old never-fail KitchenAid mixer with a 5-quart [5-liter] bowl.) In the best of all possible worlds, you would have two bowls for your standing mixer (extra bowls are usually available from the manufacturer and are an inexpensive but very useful addition to your batterie de cuisine) and a high-quality hand-held mixer at the ready for quick, light jobs and those times when you have to beat two things at once.

Mixing bowls

Equip yourself with a set (or two) of nesting stainless steel mixing bowls — available in all housewares stores and even many supermarkets — and you'll have what you need to mix up these recipes. While you can use plastic or glass bowls, it's important to have at least one metal bowl that can be set comfortably over a saucepan (preferably a 2-quart [2-liter] pan) to serve as the top of a double boiler.

Nuts

Nuts add incomparable flavor and texture to desserts, but they must be treated with care. The oils that make nuts delicious can also make them rancid, so taste before you buy (if that's possible) and then taste again before you bake. To keep fresh nuts fresh, it's best to wrap them airtight and store them in the freezer, where they'll keep for a few months. There's no need to thaw frozen nuts before you use them.

To toast nuts, place them in a single layer on a baking sheet or in a jelly-roll pan and either bake them in a 350°F (180°C) oven for about 10 to 12 minutes or do as Pierre does — toast them in a 300° to 325°F (150° to 165°C) oven for 18 to 20 minutes. Toasting them at a lower temperature for a longer time ensures that the nuts will be toasted evenly all the way through.

Oven thermometers

Even if you've just bought a brand-new oven that cost the earth and is the darling of world-class chefs, check its temperature with a reliable oven thermometer before you bake. In fact, you'd do well to make the thermometer a permanent fixture in your oven — a few degrees higher or lower and your cake could be burnt, your crust tough.

Parchment paper

Professional pastry chefs never use waxed paper — they depend instead on parchment paper, usually silicone-coated and often sold in precut large sheets. (The sheets are available from specialty shops and through the King Arthur Flour Baker's Catalogue; see Source Guide, page 281.) Parchment paper is just right for lining baking sheets, especially when you're baking in bottomless cake or tart rings, and it's the perfect catch sheet for anything that you're sifting or grating. After you've sifted flour or grated zest, for instance, you have only to lift the parchment paper and turn up the sides a bit, and you've got a funnel that makes easy work of transporting ingredients from counter to mixing bowl.

Pastry bags and tips

Making professional-looking ladyfinger biscuits and disks, meringues, and decorations requires a pastry bag and tip. The bags, cone-shaped and available in a variety of sizes, are made of plastic-coated canvas, nylon, or plastic (special disposable plastic bags are available from baking supply houses; see Source Guide, page 281), and can be fitted with metal or plastic tips that can be plain or decorative. At a minimum, you should have two pastry bags, one about 18 inches (45 cm) long and the other about 10 inches (25 cm), a ¼-inch (7-mm) plain tip, a ½-inch (1.5-cm) plain tip, and a star tip, but if you're interested in cake decorating, you'll want a collection of tips. Unless they're disposable, pastry bags should be turned inside out and washed well in soapy water, then hung up to dry after each use.

Pastry brush or feather

Bristle brushes, whether from a baking supply shop or the hardware store, are good to have on hand in narrow widths (about ½ inch [1.5 cm] across) for applying an egg wash or glaze, and in wider widths (about 1 inch [2.5 cm] across) for brushing excess flour off pastry dough or softened butter onto the insides of baking rings and pans. For really delicate jobs, such as glazing a dainty petit four, it's nice to have a feather brush — one or two white plumes bound together at their quills. Whether brushes or feathers, it's important to wash them well after each use and allow them to air-dry.

Pie or pastry weights

Pie or pastry weights are used when you are baking a crust blind — that is, without filling. Line the crust with parchment paper or foil and then fill the bottom with weights to keep the crust from puffing during baking. When it comes to weighting a pie, a little is good and a little more is not. Pierre is firm in his disapproval of commercially available pie weights, pellets made from metal or ceramic: "They're too heavy. They leave pockmarks in the crust. They destroy the texture of the pastry. And," he adds, just in case his statements need clarification, "they're bad." Rather than pie weights, Pierre suggests you use good old (inexpensive) rice or dried beans. Set aside a jar of rice or beans for the exclusive use of weighting down pastry; when you remove the parchment or foil liner from the tart shell, let the rice or beans cool and then pack them into the jar (or other container), ready to be used again and again. But don't use the rice or beans for dinner — once they're baked, they're good for nothing else but baking.

Piping

Piping is the term used to describe the act of pushing something — often a batter or a frosting — out of a pastry bag.

Rolling dough

The key to rolling dough is cold, cold, and more cold. Always make certain that your dough, whether it's tart dough, cinnamon, cookie, or puff, is well chilled before you start rolling, and, if it gets warm while you're rolling it, stop and put it back in the refrigerator to chill again (and again, if necessary).

You'll have an easier time rolling a dough out to an even thickness (important for tarts and other pastries) if the dough is the right consistency before you start rolling. You want the dough to be firm enough so that it doesn't stick to the rolling surface, yet soft enough so that it starts moving easily under the rolling pin. (Dough that cracks around the edges as soon as you start rolling is too cold and therefore too hard.) Let the dough sit at room temperature before you start rolling and then, if when you start, the dough doesn't get moving, you can help it along by pressing your rolling pin into it gently; just press a series of parallel indentations into the dough and it will soften up enough to roll. If the dough softens too much during the rolling process, pop it into the refrigerator for a quick chill before continuing.

Because Pierre's doughs are particularly short, the term used to describe doughs with a high proportion of butter, they sometimes need a little extra TLC. Always roll dough on a lightly floured surface with a rolling pin that's been rubbed with a little flour. Dust the top of the dough lightly with flour before you start rolling and, as you're rolling, lift the dough off the work surface and toss a little flour under it from time to time. While you've got the dough up from the counter, you should rotate it too — giving the dough an eighth of a turn will keep it round, as will always rolling the dough from the center out. Be sure to brush the excess flour off pastry before fitting it into a tart ring or pan or baking it. If you've got the time, it's a good idea to chill the dough slightly after you've rolled it and before you fit it into the tart ring.

To fit the dough into a ring, roll the dough up and around your rolling pin and then unroll the dough over the ring. Gently fit the dough into the bottom and up the sides of the ring, always taking care not to stretch it. Remember: What you stretch on the work surface will shrink in the oven. Chill the dough in its ring before baking it.

Rolling pin

The rolling pin of choice in the pastry kitchen is the one known as the French-style pin. It's 2 inches (5 cm) across (right down its length; it doesn't taper at the ends), weighs 1¼ pounds (681 grams), and has no handles. The fact that it has no handles makes it easy to control, and its weight is ideal — not so light that it forces you to use pressure and not so heavy that it deflates rather than rolls the dough. Bring out the big pins when you're rolling out puffy yeast doughs.

Rotating pans

If you have pans on two oven racks, or even two pans on the same oven rack, it's usually best to rotate the pans halfway through the baking period in order to compensate for any hot spots or other inconsistencies in your oven. Do a double rotation: Turn the pans front to back (so that the side of the pan that was facing the oven door now faces the back of the oven) and switch their position in the oven by putting the pan that was on the upper rack on the lower and vice versa. Or, if you have two tarts or cakes on one rack (which is fine as long as there's plenty of air space between the pans), turn the pans front to back and switch them left and right. Of course, if something will be in the oven for just 10 minutes, it's better to leave it in peace than to open the oven door and have the oven's precious heat escape.

Salt

Salt may not be the first ingredient that springs to mind when asked what's most important in a pastry chef's pantry, but it's an ingredient that Pierre takes very seriously. Pierre's salt of choice is fleur de sel de Guerande. *Fleur de sel* means, literally, "flower of the salt," and *de Guerande* means it comes from Guerande, a town, famous for its salt, along Brittany's rugged coast. Referred to and used as a condiment, fleur de sel is moister, larger-grained, and less salty than common salt. It is not washed, iodized, or treated with antihumidity chemicals; it is a natural sea salt that is rich in minerals and not easy to harvest. Fleur de sel is the finest salt that floats to the surface of salt ponds. It is harvested by hand and not always available — whether or not fleur de sel appears in the ponds depends on the season, the sun, the winds, the humidity, and, one has to believe, the whim of the salt gods. Its taste is distinctive and deliciously addictive — once you've tried it, you may take to doing what some Frenchmen do: carrying a cache at the ready to sprinkle on restaurant dishes that lack that certain je ne sais quoi. Not surprisingly, fleur de sel is expensive. Once difficult to find, it is now becoming more readily available in specialty stores and it can be purchased by mail (see Source Guide, page 281). Of course, table salt or fine sea salt can be used in any of these recipes.

Saucepans

It's important to have at least one heavy-bottomed medium — 2-quart (2-liter) — saucepan in your kitchen. You'll use it to make crème anglaise and pastry cream, caramel, and syrups. It will also come in handy when you want to make a *bain-marie*, or double boiler, for melting chocolate. However, you'll find it good to have a larger saucepan too — one you can use for caramelizing sugar and as the base of a *bain-marie* when you're working in larger quantities — and a tiny saucepan, preferably one with a spout, for boiling small quantities of sugar syrup to pour into meringues or custards.

Scale

While all of Pierre's recipes have been adapted for American volume measures, it's good to have a kitchen scale available for weighing bulky fare like chocolate and fruits. Whether you buy a balance scale or an electronic scale (more compact, and more versatile, since it can usually be switched easily between pound and metric measurements), look for one that, at minimum, will be accurate to within a quarter ounce (or 5 grams).

Silpat and other silicone baking mats

Made in France and marketed most commonly under the names Silpat and Exopat, these thin, flexible mats are made of rubberized silicone and are slightly nubby on one side and smooth on the other — the side you put your baked goods or chocolates on. The mats are available in a 16½ x 11½-inch (41 x 29-cm) size, perfect for lining baking sheets and jelly-roll pans, but they can be bought in larger sizes. Slip one of these mats onto a baking sheet or pan and you'll have a perfectly nonstick surface, one on which you can bake delicate cookies or sticky buns or pour out caramel. Since absolutely nothing sticks to the mats, cleanup is a cinch. The mats are expensive — a silicone mat can cost almost as much as the pan it will line — but, according to the manufacturer, a mat can be used at least two thousand times and can withstand oven temperatures of 500°F (260°C), so you'll certainly have a chance to get your money's worth from it.

Spatulas

You'll need both rubber and metal spatulas to work your way through these recipes. When buying rubber spatu-las, look for commercial-grade spatulas — they're more flexible, more durable, and usually have a larger working surface than supermarket-brand spatulas. Ideally, you should have two each of small, medium, and large rubber spatulas, and at least one of the medium and large spatulas should be heatproof.

You'll use metal spatulas to fill and finish cakes, smooth batter into cake or tart rings, and lift cookies from baking sheets and cooling racks. Look for short slim spatulas for small jobs, long straight ones for icing, wide ones for lifting, and offset spatulas in varying lengths and widths for smoothing. Specialty houseware and restaurant supply houses are the best sources for high-quality metal spatulas, especially offset spatulas, the ones with their blades angled slightly below their handles, like pancake flippers.

Sugar

If a recipe calls for "sugar," it's granulated sugar that you're meant to use. The only other sugars used in Pierre's recipes are light brown sugar and confectioners', (or 10-X) sugar. Granulated sugar should be measured using the scoop-and-sweep method (see page 275), brown sugar should always be packed into the measuring cup or spoon, and confectioners' sugar should always be sifted after measuring, since it's always lumpy.

Tart or flan rings

Unless otherwise noted, the tart recipes were tested in tart or flan rings rather than tart pans. A tart ring is a metal ring, which is placed on a parchment-lined baking sheet (which becomes its bottom); the ring serves as the mold or pan for the tart dough. A tart ring is straight-sided and only ¾ inch (2 cm) high, lower than a tart pan. To make these recipes, you'll need tart rings that are 8¾ inches (22 cm), 9½ inches (24 cm), and 10¼ inches (26-cm) in diameter.

When fitting tart dough into a ring, it's best to place the ring on a baking sheet rather than a jelly-roll pan so that, once the tart is baked, you can slide it off the sheet without lifting it — tart shells in general are fragile and shells that have no bottom support are more fragile still. In a pinch, you can use a fluted metal tart pan with a removable bottom instead of a ring, but because a tin is higher than a ring, your results will differ (the filling may be skimpy in some cases). That said, it's better to bake a tart whose proportions are a little off than not to bake a tart at all.

Temperature conversions

All of the temperatures you'll need for these recipes are given in Fahrenheit and Centigrade, or Celsius. If you should ever need to convert one system to the other, here are the methods: To convert a Centigrade temperature to Fahrenheit, multiply the temperature by 9, divide by 5, and add 32; if you need to convert Fahrenheit to Centigrade, subtract 32, multiply by 5, and divide by 9.

Vanilla

Vanilla is one of Pierre's favorite flavors and fragrances, and he uses it often, most frequently in bean form, in both starring and supporting roles. Until recently, Pierre's vanilla of choice was Tahitian, but currently the supply is extremely limited and the price extremely high, so this rare treat has become even rarer. In all likelihood, the beans you'll find most readily will be Madagascan or Bourbon, and they'll be fine for any of these or other recipes. However, if you can find Mexican beans (see Source Guide, page 281), do use them. Like Tahitian beans, Mexican beans are more expensive than Bourbon or Madagascan and they have a stronger and more distinctively floral fragrance. If you can, buy a variety of beans and choose your own favorite.

No matter which beans you choose, they should always be plump, moist, pliable, and, of course, fragrant. It's usually the soft, pulpy, aromatic seeds inside the pod that you're after, but the pod is a flavoring agent too and each recipe will tell you what part of the bean you're to use and how. If the recipe calls for a vanilla bean "split lengthwise and scraped," you're meant to split the bean in half from blossom to stem end with a small sharp paring knife. You will probably find it's easiest to do this if you lay the bean flat on a cutting board. Once the bean is split, use the point of the knife to scrape out the soft interior pulp. If you're infusing a liquid with vanilla, you'll put both the pod and the scraped pulp into the liquid and then, after the liquid has steeped, strain out the pod. Don't toss away these used pods. Wash and dry them well (in a slow oven or on a rack at room temperature) and use them to flavor sugar. You can either bury the pods in the sugar canister or pulverize them with sugar in the food processor.

Zest and zesters

Zest is the colorful outer rind of citrus fruit. Whether a recipe calls for broad strips of zest or thin shreds, you should always avoid the cottony, bitter white pith that's just under the zest's surface. When you need broad strips of zest, as you will if you're infusing a liquid with the zest's bright flavor, you can remove the zest with a swivel-blade vegetable peeler or a small sharp knife. But when you need thin ribbons of zest or finely chopped zest, the fastest, cleanest, and most elegant way to get these ribbons (which can then be chopped) is to use a zester, a simple tool composed of a handle, wooden or plastic, on which is mounted a thin metal blade with five holes at the top. Hold the tool so that the holes rest against the top of the fruit, and then scrape the zester down the side of the fruit, applying gentle pressure to the zester as you move it down the fruit. Continue until you've got the amount of zest you need. Do it right and the zested fruit, with its evenly spaced stripes, will be pretty enough to slice and use for a decoration on sweets or savories. Finally, when a recipe calls for grated zest, you can pull out your old-fashioned box grater or you can turn to the laser-sharp graters from Microplane. Available at kitchenware shops, Microplane graters are based on woodworkers' rasps, and it takes just one pass across the grating surface to deliver a shower of zest.

Bazzini
339 Greenwich Street
New York, NY 10013
212-334-1280
Nuts of every variety in every form, including powder.

Bridge Kitchenware
214 East 52nd Street
New York, NY 10022
800-274-3435
www.bridgekitchenware.com
Extensive stock of professional-quality baking, pastry, decorating, and cooking equipment and accessories, including tart and cake rings, parchment, and cake rounds. Catalog available.

Dean & DeLuca
560 Broadway
New York, NY 10012
212-226-6800
www.deananddeluca.com
General and specialty bakeware and cookware; specialty ingredients, including chocolate and an extensive supply of spices. Catalog available.

ECM, Inc./Valrhona
1901 Avenue of the Stars, Suite 1800
Los Angeles, CA 90067
310-277-0401
Valrhona chocolate. Catalog available.

Flavorbank
4710 Eisenhower Boulevard #E–8
Tampa, FL 33614
800-825-7603
Spices.

King Arthur Flour Company
The Baker's Catalogue
P.O. Box 876
Norwich, VT 05055
800-827-6836
www.kingarthurflour.com
Wide variety of ingredients and tools including nut powders, Mexican and other vanilla beans, fleur de sel, thermometers, and scales. Catalog available.

The Native Game Company
800-952-6321
This company is the retail distributor of the more than forty fruit purees available from the Perfect Purée of Napa Valley. Professionals can order directly from: The

Perfect Purée of Napa Valley, 975 Vintage Avenue, Suite B, St. Helena, CA 94574; 800-556-3707; www.perfect-puree.com.

New York Cake & Baking Distributors
56 West 22nd Street
New York, NY 10010
212-675-2253
General and specialized baking, pastry, and decorating equipment and tools, including tart and cake rings, parchment paper, and cake rounds; chocolate in bulk. Catalog available.

Penzeys Ltd.
P.O. Box 933
Muskego, WI 53150
414-574-0277
www.penzeys.com
Spices. Catalog available.

Sur la Table
1765 Sixth Avenue South
Seattle, WA 98134
800-243-0852
www.surlatable.com
General and specialty baking, pastry, and decorating equipment and tools, including tart and cake rings. Catalog available.

Williams-Sonoma
Mail Order Department
P.O. Box 7456
San Francisco, CA 94120
800-541-2233
www.williams-sonoma.com
General baking and pastry equipment and tools, including tart and cake rings as well as thermometers. Catalog available.

Wilton Industries
2240 West 75th Street
Woodridge, IL 60517
800-323-1717
Extensive selection of baking, pastry, and decorating equipment. Catalog available.

Zabar's
249 West 80th Street
New York, NY 10024
800-697-6301
www.zabars.com
General baking and pastry equipment and tools, including tart and cake rings, thermometers, scales, parchment, and cake rounds; specialty ingredients. Catalog available.

INDEX